Death Wasn't Painful

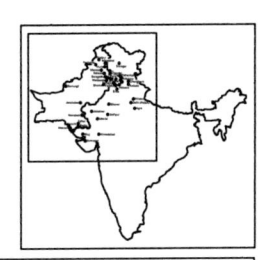

Sketch of India–Pakistan airfields and radar stations during 1971 War (not to scale).
Source: Author.

Death Wasn't Painful

Stories of Indian Fighter Pilots
from the 1971 War

Dhirendra S. Jafa

$SAGE www.sagepublications.com
Los Angeles • London • New Delhi • Singapore • Washington DC

Copyright © Dhirendra S. Jafa, 2014

All rights reserved. No part of this book may be reproduced or utilized in any form or by any means, electronic or mechanical, including photocopying, recording or by any information storage or retrieval system, without permission in writing from the publisher.

All photographs courtesy: Dhirendra S. Jafa

First published in 2014 by

SAGE Publications India Pvt Ltd
B1/I-1 Mohan Cooperative Industrial Area
Mathura Road, New Delhi 110 044, India
www.sagepub.in

SAGE Publications Inc
2455 Teller Road
Thousand Oaks, California 91320, USA

SAGE Publications Ltd
1 Oliver's Yard, 55 City Road
London EC1Y 1SP, United Kingdom

SAGE Publications Asia-Pacific Pte Ltd
3 Church Street
#10-04 Samsung Hub
Singapore 049483

Published by Vivek Mehra for SAGE Publications India Pvt Ltd, typeset in 11/13 Adobe Garamond Pro by RECTO Graphics, Delhi and printed at Sai Print-O-Pack Pvt Ltd, New Delhi.

Library of Congress Cataloging-in-Publication Data

Jafa, Dhirendra Singh.
  Death wasn't painful : stories of Indian fighter pilots from the 1971 war / Dhirendra S. Jafa.
    pages cm
  1. India–Pakistan Conflict, 1971—Personal narratives, East Indian. 2. India–Pakistan Conflict, 1971—Aerial operations, East Indian. 3. India–Pakistan Conflict, 1971—Prisoners and prisons, Pakistani. 4. Prisoners of war—India—Biography. 5. Prisoners of war—Pakistan—Biography. I. Title.
  DS388.J325   954.9205'148092254—dc23   2014   2014013677

ISBN: 978-81-321-1789-6 (PB)

The SAGE Team: Shambhu Sahu, Neha Sharma, Nand Kumar Jha and Rajinder Kaur

To
Chitra
For the dreams, the daring and the deeds

Thank you for choosing a SAGE product! If you have any comment, observation or feedback, I would like to personally hear from you. Please write to me at contactceo@sagepub.in

—Vivek Mehra, Managing Director and CEO,
SAGE Publications India Pvt Ltd, New Delhi

Bulk Sales

SAGE India offers special discounts for purchase of books in bulk. We also make available special imprints and excerpts from our books on demand.

For orders and enquiries, write to us at

Marketing Department
SAGE Publications India Pvt Ltd
B1/I-1, Mohan Cooperative Industrial Area
Mathura Road, Post Bag 7
New Delhi 110044, India
E-mail us at marketing@sagepub.in

Get to know more about SAGE, be invited to SAGE events, get on our mailing list. Write today to marketing@sagepub.in

This book is also available as an e-book.

Contents

Author's Note	xi
1. Death Wasn't Painful	1
2. Compassion and Cruelty	6
3. Secrets and Sleuths	13
4. The Hospital Interlude	19
5. Myths and Misconceptions	25
6. Compatriots and Colleagues	36
7. A Yankee Comes Calling	44
8. Some Fun, Some Frolic	49
9. Courage and Cowardice	55
10. Daring and Devilry	64
11. Kala Sandhu	71
12. The Times, They Were Bad	84
13. Tigers in the Cage	106
14. Freedom Beckons	110
15. Preparations and Doubts	128
16. The Breakout	139
17. The Aftermath	166
18. Wages of Sin	182
19. Ayesha	188
20. The Great Homecoming	211
Annexure: Pen Portraits	226
Acknowledgements	242
Glossary	244

Author's Note

I joined the staff of Air Chief Marshal P.C. Lal as an aide-de-camp (ADC) in January 1971 after graduating from the Royal Air Force Staff College, Bracknell, UK. The Chief gave me a variety of tasks and my duties developed more along the lines of an operational staff officer.

I was with the Chief in Jorhat, Assam, on the fateful day—25 March 1971—the day the Pakistan Army began its crackdown on East Pakistanis protesting for their democratic rights. An urgent summon from the Prime Minister brought us to Delhi the same evening.

As the crisis in East Pakistan deepened and refugees from there started pouring into India's West Bengal, the Indian armed forces alerted themselves to the fast deteriorating political and military scenario and began preparations to face the inevitable turmoil in the subcontinent. Working for the Chief of the Air Staff during such times became the most rewarding experience of my life. For, besides Air Chief Marshal P.C. Lal, the other stalwarts were General (later Field Marshal) Sam Manekshaw and Admiral S.M. Nanda, leading the Army and the Navy, a combination of top military leadership that is hard to come by at any one time, anywhere. Even a glimpse into their working was perhaps equal to a hundred lectures on military operations.

In early November 1971, it was clear that the war would be upon us before the end of the year. It was time for me to take the personal decision to give up my safe, secure and prestigious job at Air Headquarters and rejoin my operational Squadron. The crucial hour for testing courage and flying efficiency as well as discharging the moral duty of sharing risk and danger was fast approaching. I am happy to say that, on a personal level, my wife understood my dilemma and finally nudged me in the right direction without a thought to her own and the children's well-being in case I did not come back alive.

The second task was to obtain the Chief's permission. A person holding supreme responsibility comes to depend a great deal upon subordinates who provide him a welter of services that facilitate his work and decision-making. Allowing me to leave at this juncture would mean a diminution in the services that he most needed. So, when I broached the subject one day in the isolation of an elevator in Air Headquarters, I only got a cold stare from the Chief. Again on 26th November I made bold to say, 'Sir, will you permit me to rejoin my Squadron?'

'Isn't this job important enough for the war?' was the Chief's question.

'Sir, I feel I should be there when the shooting starts, otherwise I shall not be able to look the younger pilots in the eye again. I am of the right age and seniority and I must volunteer.' The Chief said nothing.

Half-an-hour later the intercom buzzed; the Chief was on the line. 'Which station am I visiting this afternoon?' he asked.

'Pathankot, Sir,' I replied.

'Well, change that to Adampur. Isn't that where your Squadron is ... and, by the way, you may pack your bags.' This was the Chief's crisp order.

I was stunned for a moment. So ... this was it, the war for me. I had about 20 minutes to collect my flying kit and bid farewell to my family.

I returned to a flying unit, No. 26 Squadron, after a gap of two years but was able to get my hand in on the SU-7 fighter-bomber aircraft in a few sorties with my old colleagues. The morale in the Squadron was very high. All operational pilots were raring to go into the war. And when the shooting began they acquitted themselves

Author's Note

with great bravery and courage. As a result, while they inflicted heavy damage upon the enemy, they also suffered heavy losses—three pilots lost their lives over the battlefield while attacking Pakistani Army positions, and two bailed out after being hit by anti-aircraft artillery and were captured as prisoners of war (POWs), myself being one of the two.

In the POW camp of the Pakistan air force at Rawalpindi, there were a total of 12 Indian pilots of whom one had been apprehended on the ground. All of them had passed through a difficult time and borne travails of capture, beatings, injuries, deprivation of food and medical assistance. But they were all in one piece and had been declared as POWs which, in itself, assured their return to the home country in the near future.

This, thus, is the tale of these twelve fighter pilots in enemy captivity—their deprivations, their longings for home and families, their interactions with Pakistani military officers and men as well as civilians, their pride in being Indians and representatives of a victorious nation always implicit in their actions and utterances, though with a persistent disquiet at having been left to the mercy of the enemy when they could have been retrieved gracefully almost immediately on cessation of hostilities; and three of them setting an example of daring and bravery by breaking out of prison and travelling across Pakistan and not bending before the enemy even after their capture just one hill short of the Afghanistan border.

This is a personal account in the sense that it reflects the perceptions of the author, the way he looked at individuals and events, even in the selection of just three episodes (*Courage and Cowardice*, *Daring and Devilry* and *Kala Sandhu*) out of the innumerable acts of gallantry, to highlight the mental make-up of fighter pilots in three different situations.

The Indian prisoners were objects of great curiosity in Pakistan; people from different walks of life came to meet them in the prison camps. The conversations during such meetings inevitably turned to the war and its causes, the great Hindu–Muslim divide, the partition of the country, dictatorship and democracy, politics and likely future relations between the two countries. Such discussions took place in bits and pieces over a whole year with different people and in different situations. For ease of narration, these have been collated and presented mainly in two episodes—*The Times, They Were Bad* and *The Great Homecoming*. In recounting the events and discussions, care has been taken to keep close to the actual happenings and expression of sentiments and views on different issues. Of course, certain juxtaposition of events and situations were considered necessary for narrative fluidity and comprehension of the total picture. For such minor trespasses the author craves the reader's understanding.

In the end, it has to be said that out of those who go the extra mile, who take greater risks in battle, some return and some are lost to enemy guns. And out of those who are shot in enemy territory, some survive and some don't. This is the tale of those gallants who survived.

Dhirendra S. Jafa

1

Death Wasn't Painful

December 1970

General elections in Pakistan throw up East Pakistan's Awami League as the majority party. Its leader, Mujib-ur-Rehman, with 167 members in the National Assembly, stakes his claim to the prime ministership of Pakistan. In West Pakistan the military–landlord–business nexus of Punjabi Mussalmans is unable to stomach the domination of the country by their Bengali brethren. Advised and instigated by Zulfiqar Ali Bhutto, leader of the Peoples Party with only 88 seats in the National Assembly, the military ruler of Pakistan, General Yahya Khan dithers and delays inviting Mujib, a Bengali from East Pakistan, to form the government. The Bengalis in the East grow restive and resort to protests and demonstrations in support of their democratic rights.

March 1971

As the Bengali disenchantment with the Punjabi-dominated central government of Pakistan mounts and erupts in violent defiance, General Yahya Khan orders a military crackdown. The hostilities escalate. The army adopts increasingly harsher methods to quell the rebellion in the eastern fiefdom. Faced with vindictive harassment, arrests, outright killings and the defilement of women, the hapless Bengalis begin an exodus to neighbouring India, quickly exceeding ten million in the hastily put up refugee camps in Indian Bengal.

Indira Gandhi, the prime minister of the largest, poorest and longest-lasting democracy in the developing world, appeals to the big powers and flits from capital to capital begging presidents and prime ministers to prevail upon Pakistan to take care of its own peoples and problems and save India from the financial and social chaos that the presence of ten million refugees was beginning to unleash upon her. She returns unheeded and unaided by the unmoved great countries and kings. She decides to support the Awami League of Sheikh Mujib-ur-Rehman and its guerrilla-type military organisation, the Mukti Vahini, to resist and contain the excesses of the Pakistan Army, to halt the flow of refugees into India and to seek, if they so wished, liberation of their land from the army of occupation.

December 1971

To punish India for her support to the Bengalis in East Pakistan, the ruling coterie in Pakistan launches an all-out attack upon India in the West. The Indian armed forces retaliate. The Indian Air Force launches every single flyable aircraft into the attack on West Pakistan. Among them, a few days into the war, a formation of four Sukhoi-7 fighters led by Jafa ('Jeff' to friends).

* * * * *

'Red One, you are on fire,' came the urgent voice of Fernandez (Ferdy), the No. 3 in the formation of four fighter aircraft, using the radio call-sign for the formation leader. They were attacking the heavy artillery guns in enemy territory.

'Bail Out, Red One, Bail Out,' shouted Mohan, the No. 4, into Jafa's earphones, urging him to get out of the burning aeroplane and use the parachute to descend to the safety of mother earth.

'Jeff, Sir, ... you ... are ... on ... fire. Get out, for God's sake, bail out.' This was Jaggu Saklani, desperately goading him to make the decisive move even as the radio reception in his aircraft was fading out.

An hour earlier Jafa had returned from an attack against enemy tanks, which had cornered an army battalion in the Hussainiwala area near Ferozepur and were mercilessly tightening the noose around them. He reported to the Base Commander that of the eight tanks reported in the area, he and Jaggu had been able to halt five, damaged or destroyed. Our troops on the ground were thus given the much needed respite to recoup, regroup, fight or withdraw.

'Well done, Jeff,' the Base Commander said. 'But the Army is on my back again, this time to stop the heavy guns, north of Lahore which are playing up hell in the Amritsar area pounding the Army round the clock. We made two attempts but our chaps were unable to locate the guns. I don't know what to do ... the army is getting desperate.'

Just then, Ferdy had walked into the operations room—the hub of all activity in the aerial war. Besides rendering the report on his last mission, he had some valuable information for the Commander.

'I was returning from my mission, Sir, when, north of Lahore, I was fired upon from the ground. On looking down I saw a big array of guns. I didn't have fuel or ammunition to attack them so I came back. It is some array of guns, Sir, believe me....'

Since these were the cannons that were on everyone's mind, the Commander immediately got on to the army's formation in the Amritsar area and assured them that help from the Air Force was on the way. Then turning to Jafa he said, 'Come on, Jafa, you better go yourself. Take anyone you want.'

In less than thirty minutes, four aeroplanes, suitably armed and readied, were airborne and heading towards the big cannons north of Lahore. In the next twelve minutes, Jafa pulled up for the first rocket attack with Jaggu, Ferdy and Mohan following. The enemy, being aware that their position and armament were no longer secret, launched every anti-aircraft weapon in their armoury at the attacking aircraft. Bullets beyond counting came from below, like reversed rain, the whole sky dotted with puffs of smoke as tracer bullets spent themselves to show where the more lethal ammunition was going. On the ground, among the cannons, fires were breaking out, showing that the targets were being hit.

Inside the aeroplanes there was an eerie silence, except for the soft whine of the engine penetrating through the pilots' earphones. Every two minutes or so came Jafa's gravelly voice on the radio, 'Going in again,' announcing yet another attack. In almost every dive, firing and pull-out, a mild pit-pat was felt on the underside of the aircraft as the enemy's bullets found their mark. But these were strikes against the less vulnerable parts of the aeroplanes and therefore not lethal.

Flashes of fire and smoke in the sky, fire and explosions in half a dozen places on the ground, the tenacity and ferocity matched on both sides, fighters in the air and on the ground, clenched teeth, fingers on triggers, the target as the only perception in the world, determined to kill or get killed.

Then suddenly Jafa's aeroplane rocked as if hit by a rain of stones from underneath. There was a muffled explosion behind his seat in the cockpit, the plane tilted to the right and began spinning horizontally, out of control, and losing height rapidly. With each roll and spin it was heading closer to a crash on the ground. Unable to control the machine whose parts had been shot up, Jafa knew the dire emergency he was in.

Then the voices on the radio ... 'get out, bail out ... you are on fire ... fire ... fire.' The flames were now coming up over the canopy of the cockpit, the plane a burning pyre. Unable to control the plane, he felt helpless and immobilised. Strangely, there was no fear, only a kind of numbness before the impending disaster. Then, the years of training and the repeated conditioning of the mind to recall the drill in emergency situations took over, the voices of his comrades on the radio now acting like commands. In quick reflex he grabbed the seat ejection handles and heaved. There was a swish of air as the canopy automatically lifted up and flew away, followed by the firing of the ejection seat rockets. Then, the sensation of being lifted up and away, out of the burning aeroplane. Just as suddenly it was all quiet, and dark ... no, neither dark nor light, only a silent weightlessness, he was everywhere and nowhere, no space, no time, in total release from the physical, as if suspended in bliss.... Only one fading thought, one feeling, one lingering perception ... death wasn't painful.

A mind often tormented by thoughts of death accompanied by much pain and suffering, now suddenly relieved, already across the *Vaitarani*, with one awareness, one gratefulness ... death wasn't painful.

2

Compassion and Cruelty

The euphoria of non-existence was broken by a gush of cool breeze across his face. As the chilly wind rushed at him faster and faster he realised that he wasn't where he thought he was. He was still very much in this world. His eyes opened, the vision returned, the restraining effect of the parachute harness became apparent as he saw the ground rushing up at him. Then the impact of the body with the ground, the parachute collapsing to one side, still attached to him with straps around his torso.

Remember the drill, he told himself. Disengage the parachute, roll it up for subsequent use, and look for a place to hide. Hide, in enemy land, hide and then think and plan the escape. But try as he might, his hands would not move. With a shock he realised that he was not able to move any limb at all. He remained in the squatting position in which the fall on the ground had first placed him. There was total awareness but no motor control. Then came the dreadful realisation that he had sustained serious injury to the spinal column. The momentary blackout and perception of death had been caused by the snapping of some vertebrae.

'*Allah-O-Akbar*' came the war cry of a horde of villagers rushing at him from all sides. Here it comes, he thought, first the looting, then the lynching, and, finally, possibly dying at their hands. Such was the vehemence of intolerance, anger, even hatred among the divided people of same lineage that war was not limited to battlefields and uniformed persons but had to be fought, in the name of patriotism, at every level, without compassion, even when a helpless individual happened to be in the grasp of a multitude.

Suddenly, scores of men were ripping apart his clothing, their hands deep into all pockets, taking away the watch, cigarettes, lighter, cash, the scarf, the gloves. They pulled and they pushed him every which way, he gritted his teeth to stop himself from crying out loud for the agony it was causing him. Two hands were now hurriedly unlacing his boots when suddenly everyone halted in his act. Jafa saw the mob being pulled and pushed away from him by men in olive green battle dress. Jafa heaved a sigh of relief; the Pakistani troops had arrived; he expected to be in safer hands now. The fighting men did their duty without let or hindrance, they fought with valour, but without cruelty. A downed man was to be treated according to the rules, but with kindness and respect due to a fighting man as one would expect for oneself.

The tall Pathan soldiers surrounded him. An authoritative voice enquired, 'Got any weapons?'

'I had a revolver. May have been taken away,' said Jafa referring to the just concluded loot by the villagers.

'Hurt?' asked the Pakistani officer.

'Looks like the spine is gone. Can't move any limbs,' he whispered.

The officer said something to his men in a language that Jafa assumed to be Pushto. He was frisked for weapons and then picked up from the ground by two burly soldiers who carried him like a rag doll across wheat fields to a camouflaged tent in the open countryside. There he was gently lowered onto a camp bed and covered with a blanket. The officer immediately went to a field telephone and Jafa heard him say at the end of the conversation, 'Okay, we'll bring him to you.'

Jafa understood that he would now be taken from this frontline position and delivered to some faceless, taciturn men in the rear;

men who may wear an uniform but may never have heard guns fired in anger, men who wielded enormous power from safe areas and looked disdainfully at the slogging, fighting foot-soldiers, men whose own inadequacies impelled them to heap humiliation and torture upon those who constantly shed their blood for the safety and integrity of the motherland. Jafa knew that the ordeal of becoming a prisoner of war (POW) was about to begin.

'Give him some tea,' said the officer gently to one of his men. Immediately, a *jawan* appeared with the steaming beverage, but Jafa was unable to move his limbs to take the proffered mug of tea. The soldier understood; he fetched a spoon and without uttering a word began to feed him tea, spoon by spoon. The hot liquid warmed his very heart and his eyes grew moist with gratefulness.

'Smoke?' asked the officer. Jafa nodded with his eyes. The officer lighted a cigarette and held it to his lips for a drag. Refreshed with tea and a smoke Jafa looked at the placid, handsome face of the officer and a thought flashed across his mind. Are we enemies? Or is there a mistake, a misunderstanding?

* * * * *

And as he lay on a camp cot in an enemy bunker, in enemy land, his energy replenished with enemy tea and cigarette, his mind drifted to a strange encounter he had a couple of months earlier. He was in an Air Force transport aeroplane somewhere between Bangalore and Delhi, at a height of about 30,000 feet, sitting comfortably in a cabin with just one senior officer across the aisle for company. Air Commodore Soundarajan was an aeronautical engineer of repute. In private life he was known to be a deeply religious man with extraordinary spiritual powers. He was a successful water diviner as well. Once, when several attempts to find water at a desert airfield had failed, he had gone around the entire area barefoot with a V-shaped twig to determine in his own mysterious way where the underground waters lay. He finally received the cosmic signals and indicated the exact spot where the drilling for water was likely to succeed. And he was proved absolutely right when the tube well bored at that very spot gushed with good, plentiful water and gave no signs of letting up.

Now sitting across the aisle Jafa became aware that Soundarajan's gaze was fixed on him. He felt uncomfortable as the spiritualist continued to fix him with a concentrated, unmoving stare. Perplexed, he tried to break the spell by saying, 'Would you like some coffee, Sir?' Soundarajan continued to stare, he had apparently not heard him.

'Two months. Yes, two months,' he finally uttered. Soundarajan's eyes shifted and he seemed to be coming out of some kind of a trance. Jafa, quite perplexed and in some agitation of his own, asked, 'Two months? What will happen in two months?'

Soundarajan was fully relaxed now though still in a serious frame of mind. Very gently he said, 'Sorry, Jeff, but there is some trouble in store for you. In about two months time. But you will live through it ... don't worry. God be with you.'

'Will it be an accident?' he asked. 'Yes.'

'Car, aircraft or what?'

'I can't say. I don't know.'

'Will I live through it?' Jafa sought reassurance on the most vital aspect of the matter.

'Yes, I think so. Rather I am positive about it. But you must understand that a mishap, an accident, means a measure of suffering, injuries, wounds, complications. But at the end of it I see life and hope.'

Jafa had always been sceptical, even disdainful, of soothsayers and fortune tellers. But Soundarajan was a different kettle of fish. His probity and prowess, both seen and talked about, had been known to him. Soundarajan's whole demeanour, the calm on his countenance, the concentrated power of his gaze, the few words that carried profound meaning, could not be disregarded lightly. So, like a mystified person but one who faces danger every day of his life and cannot allow it to affect his daily routine, he said, 'Alright, Sir. But if I am going to live through it, as you say, I wouldn't worry about a few broken bones.'

Lying on the cot now it occurred to him that Soundarajan's prophecy had been fulfilled. He had been brought up in a deeply religious household with prayers twice a day and all kinds of rituals every now and then, but in adult life he had drifted towards agnosticism and used God's name only for swearing when he was hopelessly exasperated. But, now what? Well, for the time being he was alive, and the very fact of being alive gave him the confidence that he would live through this ordeal as well, and the courage to face whatever was to come.

* * * * *

'Time to move,' said the officer as dusk began to give way to the enveloping darkness of the early winter night. He was lifted gently by two men and placed on the front seat of a jeep, his spine supported by the backrest. The driver took his position on one side and the officer on the other. Two armed men got in at the back.

'It's a rough road for some distance. Do let me know if you find the jolts very painful,' said the officer. A little later he said, 'You might as well relax now if you can. It won't be the same when I hand you over to others who are waiting for you. And, I am afraid, I will have to blindfold you now.' A long cotton cloth was wound several times around Jafa's eyes and knotted firmly at the back of his head.

They drove for about half an hour and then turned sharply to the left. A short distance and a few curves later the jeep was stopped. He heard voices that kept coming closer. The officer got down and exchanged greetings with some people and told them of his present charge – an Indian fighter pilot, his prisoner, his prize catch. Jafa sensed people rushing towards the jeep and surrounding it from all sides. They talked in excited whispers and pointed him out to the late comers. Even through the blindfold he could make out that a powerful flashlight was focussed on him for everyone to take a really good look. From their manner of talking he divined that he was among civilians, perhaps in the officer's home village where the proud captor simply had to display his prize captive. But there was kindness too. A glass of tea and biscuits were brought out and someone in the crowd came forward to feed him and help him to drink the tea.

'*Shukriya*,' said Jafa. 'Thank you very, very much.' He wished he could get down to meet these people, shake their hands, speak with them, acknowledge their compassion, show them that he was not an Indian monster as some of their leaders were telling them.

Just then a hush fell over the assembly and one voice came up clearly. It was the voice of an elderly person, measured, educated, authoritative.

'We are sorry to see that you are injured and in captivity. We hope our authorities will tend to you and look after you. Just as we hope that our people on your side will be treated with kindness and care. It is sad, but it is war. All I can say is that, *Insha Allah*, your ordeal may soon be over and you may be re-united with your near and dear ones. *Khuda Hafiz*!'

The old man patted his knee and held his hands in his own. Jafa was overwhelmed and speechless. '*Khuda Hafiz*,' he cried, as the jeep moved forward. 'God be with you.'

It was another hour's driving before the jeep slowed down. The challenge by a sentry, the use of torchlight, the whispered conversation between the officer and the guards indicated that they had reached their destination. As the jeep was cleared to move forward the officer clamped handcuffs on his wrists saying, 'Sorry about this but that's the form. I might as well hand you over in the regulation manner.'

A few moments later the jeep halted again. Jafa sensed people walking up to the vehicle, flashlights focussed on him.

'Bring him out,' boomed an order from someone outside. The escort party began helping him out of the jeep.

'Can't he bloody-well walk? Why are you pampering him?' rasped the same voice again.

'He's injured, Sir,' replied the escorting officer. 'He can't stand on his own.' By now Jafa was out of the jeep, being held up by two men with their shoulders under his armpits.

'Leave the bastard Indian alone,' shouted the new boss. 'Let me see what's wrong with him.' As the men eased their shoulders out, he began slumping to the ground. The two *jawans* almost involuntarily reached down and pulled him back up again.

'Injured or feigning? Let me see for myself.' With this the bully walked up behind Jafa, held him by the collar of the overall and shook him violently, viciously. A searing pain shot down his spine, spreading all over the body. Defiantly he tried to stifle the cry emanating from the unbearable anguish, but a dull moan could not be held back.

'Can't even stand up on your own feet, you bloody Indian chicken? Come to fight us, eh ...? We ... the martial people?' he rasped and went on for a while with a harangue even more insulting and abusive against everything Indian. Jafa mentally typed him as one of those who strut around in dress uniforms, exploiting the privileges, flaunting rank and authority, but keeping meticulously away from the battle lines. Having never faced or subjugated the enemy in combat, they become awesome in the safety of the rear echelons. They can quote all the rules and regulations and proffer all the reasons why an honest, deserving request from the simple-minded field troops and formations cannot be met. Their ego and martial pretensions feed and bloom upon what is known in common parlance as the throwing around of hapless junior cadres and formations. There is no getting away from such individuals, he sadly thought, till they have had their fill of self-aggrandisement or till higher authority intervenes.

Then a vicious slap on the back of his head sent him moving forward, along with the bark, 'Take the damn fellow inside.'

He was taken to a dimly lit room and lowered into a chair. He found himself sitting well away from a long table over which hung a low electric bulb, most of the light focussed on him. Gradually he became aware of men already sitting on chairs on the other side of the table, ten in number. They were barely discernible as vague forms, their faces in total darkness. The interrogation begins now, he thought, the most dreadful, distasteful facet of being a soldier, sometimes perhaps worse than dying. And this was only the beginning.

3

Secrets and Sleuths

'What's your name?' asked a gruff voice in Urdu.

'My name is Jafa, he replied in English.

'Jafa or Jaffer?' asked the inquisitor.

'Jafa ... Just Jafa,' replied the prisoner.

'Jafa? What kind of name is that? Are you some kind of a Shair or poet?'

'No.'

Then, 'what's your full name?'

'My full name is Dhirendra S. Jafa,' replied the prisoner, again in English.

There was silence for a few moments and then again the question, 'Where is your home town, I mean, which province you come from?'

'I come from Uttar Pradesh.'

'Ah!' sighed yet another hidden face. 'I thought as much. You bloody *hindiwallah* ...,' he uttered in contempt.

'You have been slaves, always. You will remain slaves, forever,' yet another pronounced in their kind of Urdu. 'The British left you a quarter of a century ago, but you continue to be slaves, now to their language. You can't help it, I suppose. It's in your blood. You were under our heel for centuries, and even after gaining independence you can't rid yourselves of your former masters, neither in language nor in awe.'

'Can't you speak your own language? Have you no pride in it? Or do you have so many damned tongues that nobody knows which one to use?' This was yet another voice, harsh, deprecating and insulting. Jafa kept silent.

'Come on, speak up, you *hindiwallah*! Or, is your boss a damned Anglo-Indian or a *Madrasi* that you are afraid to speak in your own lingo?' came yet another voice.

A quibbling over language could certainly not be the object of an interrogation of a POW, Jafa thought to himself. He was being browbeaten, shouted upon, put on the defensive, softened up for the actual, substantive questioning that must follow. On the spur of the moment he decided to play for a diversion.

'Excuse me, but what language are you gentlemen using?' he asked gently in English.

'Why, you U.P. *wallah*! You can't discern Urdu as being spoken by us? Didn't your forefathers use this language when grovelling at our feet? And you ask what language we are using?' again with unremitting belligerence.

'*Janab-e-ala*,' said Jafa, now in chaste Urdu. 'I come from a place near Aligarh and have lived most of my life in Lucknow. But I am afraid your Urdu does not quite sound like the Urdu I have known and spoken all my life. Neither in usage, nor in accent. May be it is a different kind of dialect, I thought, one with which I am not familiar. But if my present language is acceptable to you, I shall only speak in this.'

He had of course referred to the acknowledged fact that the Urdu as spoken in Lucknow is roughly the same to the Urdu spoken in far-flung corners of the subcontinent as the Oxford English is to the cockney. But this was as far as he dared to go and the ensuing silence assured him that psychologically perhaps he had levelled with them. This was going to be a game of wits and he was obviously arraigned before experts now as the coarse bully of the reception area was not to be seen there. He would have to be very alert, very quick in thinking through the questions, formulating the answers and delivering them with polite confidence. Above all, he must not appear to be obdurate and negative if he hoped to deflect them from their real purpose.

'Your unit?' came the crisp question.

* * * * *

Jafa's mind flashed back to a visit to his unit by a very senior officer of the Air Force. That was about ten years ago, in the aftermath of the brief war with China when the tensions and states of alertness were still high. After the official agenda, the Air Marshal came to sip a customary glass of tea with the squadron pilots. In an equally customary manner the dignitary enquired, 'Is there anything you boys want to ask or know? Ask me whatever you wish.'

Normally, for fear of making a fool of oneself no one asked an Air Marshal anything. Only polite enquiries could be made about his last foreign jaunt and his impressions of other Air Forces that he may have visited. But the Chinese war had unleashed all kinds of questions and uncertainties and induced endless debates over tactics, the best modes for attack and defence in the difficult mountain terrains. Equally, the special requirements of the aircrew had come to be discussed and crystallised. In air warfare, once the engineering and support problems have been sorted out the goods still remain to be delivered by those who fly the aeroplanes. They need clear-cut directives and some assurances, not about living or dying, but for contingencies like getting shot up in battle and having to bail out over frozen mountains or in remote jungles.

Finally, one middle-level officer summoned the courage to voice the concerns of many. 'Sir, in order to reach the enemy positions we shall be flying mostly over mountainous terrain. From Himachal onwards it is all frozen and covered with snow. In the event of having to bail out by parachute one would need specially warm clothing to survive for even a couple of hours. And one would need to be picked up by a helicopter. Since we have been discussing this among ourselves, I have taken the liberty to put it up to you, Sir.'

The Air Marshal blinked and pondered for a while and when he spoke it was of quite another matter, for the issue raised by the young officer had obviously not crossed his mind.

'First you tell me ... what would you do if you are taken prisoner by the Chinese? I mean, what would you tell them?'

There was silence all around, every one waiting for someone else to make a fool of himself.

'Come on, boys! You are the ones who are going to go out there and you should know what you can tell them and what you cannot,' persisted the Air Marshal.

One young Flying Officer began hesitatingly, 'Sir, I will tell them my name, number, unit....'

'No, no, no!' cut in the Air Marshal. 'You will tell them only your rank, name and service number. Nothing more. Remember, just the rank, name and number.'

Then, turning to the unit's commanding officer he spoke testily, 'Don't your boys know about the Geneva Convention? Make sure they are properly briefed on the Geneva Convention and should they fall into enemy hands they are not to give away anything more than that.'

'Yes, Sir,' said the Commanding Officer, wondering where in the world was he to find the damned Geneva Convention.

And with that the dignitary made his exit. There was no further reference to the matter of warm clothing or rescue arrangements, for such things hadn't until then occurred to the leaders in the armed forces of a country which had unilaterally decided to live in peace with all and sundry.

'Like hell you can tell them just your rank, name and number! And like hell they will let you get away with that!' remarked one officer.

'Geneva Convention, my foot!' said another. 'I would like to see who can hold out when the third degree begins.'

Yet another officer enquired in a measured, mature tone, 'In any case what can we give away? If one of our aircraft is shot down they would have access to all its secrets anyway. I mean they would merely verify physically all that is already mentioned in the Jane's Aircraft of the World. And what the hell do we know of policy or strategy?'

* * * * *

'Come on, don't sit like a dumb idiot! We asked you—which unit? Or do we have to get it out of you?' came the admonition and the threat.

'Just a moment, please,' said Jafa in a feeble voice as a spasm of pain seared through his back. He squirmed and shifted slightly in the chair to find better support for his aching back. 'It's my back ... so just a minute,' he repeated.

* * * * *

And his mind flashed back again, to the period shortly before the outbreak of the war. Sitting at his desk job at the headquarters he had come across a document giving the current locations, in other words the war stations, of all the fighter and bomber squadrons of the Indian Air Force. At the bottom of the document the originating officer had made a note, 'circulated to all the foreign air/military attaches posted in India by the Pakistan Air Advisor during a briefing this morning.' He knew that the details of units and their locations enumerated in the document were one hundred percent correct. The Pakistanis knew already what they were now asking him.

* * * * *

'No. 26 Squadron,' he blurted out. Also, when asked where it was based he gave the location as well. Where thousands of intelligence operatives prowled incessantly among the declared enemies, as well as those from the great powers in addition to all kinds of electronic probes and the developing satellite reconnaissance, precisely what secrets remained unknown he did not know. Certainly not the locations, nor the fighting machines nor their armaments as these were in any case bought from outsiders, sometimes both sides buying from the same source. Perhaps tactics, reaction timings, carefully planned surprise attacks, the level of training and state of preparedness were the only things that could be safeguarded for sometime in modern warfare. Elements like the first ever deployment of radar or the atomic bomb developed during a protracted war were of course another matter and not quite relevant in our context.

'Who is your Commanding Officer?'

'Who is the Station Commander?'

'What are the names of pilots in your Squadron?'

And what is in a name, wondered Jafa. H. Singh or Y. Singh or D. Kumar or A.U. Khan had no significance really other than appearing in the list of gallantry award winners or in obituaries. He rattled off names, some correct, some fictitious and took his own time in recollecting them. It went on like this for a few hours, as if some kind of groundwork was being laid. The long hours, the injury, the fatigue, hunger and sheer nervous exhaustion were taking their toll. His replies became slower, voice fainter, the interrogators shouting louder until he just slumped in the chair and passed out.

He had the sensation of being lifted up and carried away. He next woke up in the glare of powerful torchlights with half a dozen men in different uniforms standing around him. A short, stocky, gray-haired person in an officer's uniform walked with thumping boots all around him, as if taking a good look from all angles.

'It has been our precept to behead the enemy as he falls into our hands,' he screeched in tones of loathing and exasperation. 'I don't understand why we are not doing this!'

He continued to stomp around in rage, perhaps more against his own people for not following the precepts. 'And we are to look after him in custody, give him food and water and tend to his wounds? Oh, what have we come to! Anyway, let the bastard lie here,' he pronounced and stomped out of the prison cell.

The strong iron-rod door was swung shut and padlocked from the outside. He became aware that he was lying on the bare concrete floor and without any covering other than the flying overall and the undergarments he had arrived in. A chilly draught of mid-winter air came at him steadily through the door and he began to shiver uncontrollably. His last thought before passing out again was that he may not see the sun again.

4

The Hospital Interlude

But wake up he did, and in a glorious manner, with the bright rays of the morning sun streaming through the rods of the iron door and falling straight upon his face, lighting it and warming it with their benign touch. He saw the sun in its full morning glory and it appeared to be spurring him on to life and vigour.

A while later, the iron door opened and a sentry brought in a tin plate of food and a tin mug of tea. The food consisted of two cold, dried up *chapattis* with a spoonful of *daal*. He lifted himself up on one elbow and lunged at the *chapattis*. He was going to chew and swallow every bit of everything; his body needed it and he couldn't be sure when the next meal might come. After licking the plate clean and drinking up the cold stale tea, he lay back to soak in the sunlight, wriggling his body around to catch the maximum warmth. He lay there for a couple of hours and was beginning to wonder why no one had come to question him further when the door opened and a few men came inside. Without uttering a word they placed handcuffs on his wrists, pushed a kind of cap over his head, blindfolding him effectively. Then he was picked up and carried away and placed in the front seat of a jeep. Others got inside and the vehicle started off. It was a straight drive of over three hours, very tiring and very painful. At the end of it he found himself on the floor of another prison cell, but with a blanket for a covering this time.

Late into the evening Jafa and anguish lay huddled under the blanket. The pain in his back was excruciating and he was drifting into, and out of, sleep or unconsciousness most of the time. In fact, he was not conscious of time any more, except that during the long dark night he woke up again and again to the sound of wailing air defence sirens followed by the unmistakable whine of a fast-moving jet aeroplane, followed by the terrific boom-boom of exploding bombs. This surely was our boys attacking some target nearby, he thought, possibly an airfield. As this went on all through the night he kept applauding the attackers silently ... Good show! ... Well done, boys! ... And he also surmised that he was probably in Rawalpindi now and very close to the airfield. He recalled that he was shot down and captured about twenty kilometres from Lahore and was probably taken to that city on the first night as the journey time was short. The subsequent long journey and proximity to an airfield would indicate Rawalpindi, the capital of Pakistan, well, almost.

The next night he was moved again and when the blindfold and the handcuffs were removed he was pleasantly surprised to find himself upon a soft bed in a dimly lit room. Heavy curtains covered all doors and windows and an armed sentry stood in the open doorway. He was also given a good helping of warm food. He ate all that was placed on the table by his side and then lay back. He was not particularly upset about lying on the concrete floors of prison cells but for the cold and pain it induced, he was not now particularly buoyed by sleeping on a soft mattress except that it eased the pain.

The air attacks went on all through the night. Among the wailing sirens and the exploding bombs he also heard loud groans and shrieks of pain. First he wondered if the bombs had exploded very close to where he lay, but then he realised that these were the cries of badly wounded men possibly just brought back from the front lines. So perhaps he was in a hospital, which held out hope for his own treatment and alleviation of pain.

The Hospital Interlude

Early the next morning he opened his eyes to a vision of beautiful young girls in nurses' uniforms clustering about him and whispering to each other. The soft giggles and the mildly excited conversation were like a soothing balm in the midst of so much pain and trauma. Slowly the laughter became bolder and the whisperings louder, which became too much for the sentry on guard duty in the room.

'Keep quiet!' the sentry commanded. 'And leave the room right away. I had permitted you to take a look at him. I had warned you not to talk or giggle like a bunch of schoolgirls. Now just go!'

The young nurses blushed with shame and quickly shuffled out of the room. But not before Jafa had heard one of them remark, 'Yes, he is the one. It was his picture that we saw in the newspaper yesterday.'

'But they didn't say he was injured. Why have they brought him here then?' wondered another.

Jafa heaved a sigh of relief. If the Pakistanis had announced his capture, even published his photograph in their newspapers, they could not lightly do away with him now. Who knows how many prisoners are killed after capture, there is never any record and no way of ever knowing. Perhaps the only reasonable guarantee for the survival of a captured soldier is the announcement of his name in the newspapers, which happens in rare cases of important catches or for political expediency. He was just lucky, thought Jafa. If he was to be done away with now, his body along with a reasonably good excuse for his death would have to be given to his countrymen. Otherwise, there would be diplomatic, even other repercussions on a quid pro quo basis. He now had a reasonable chance for survival.

A while later he was put on a stretcher trolley and wheeled to a room fitted with x-ray machines of all sizes and variety. A doctor, bespectacled, middle-aged, composed, unruffled, possibly never moved by the sights and sounds of the injured, the crying, the bleeding, and the dying, stood in the way. The trolley halted exactly that he may take a look at the patient without moving a step. He pushed a hand under Jafa's lower back and started feeling around the spinal column. From his wincing and groaning the doctor satisfied himself about what he was looking for. He made some signs over Jafa's torso, which were observed and mentally noted by a nurse who had materialised on the other side of the trolley. And now she took over the trolley and the patient by placing two strong hairy arms on both. She pushed them towards an x-ray platform and walked away. Not a word, then or later, when she returned to take him to another room fitted with other machines, chains, pullies etc. The doctor too returned holding a wet x-ray film in his hand, which he showed to the nurse and apparently gave her some instructions. Jafa heard him ordering a plaster cast for him as the nurse nodded assent.

'Sir ...!' he called out to the doctor. 'What does it look like? I mean, how bad is it?'

'Bad,' said the doctor. 'Four vertebrae badly crushed, others, about six, less so.'

'Are you going to put me on a hard bed or in plaster?' he asked, referring to the now more acceptable form of treatment for this kind of injury.

The doctor nodded his head knowingly, smiled and said kindly, 'Yes, the hard bed is preferable. But you may be living in rather un-ideal conditions. So I think a plaster cast would be a better bet.'

Jafa gaped at the doctor in amazement and gratefulness. He had devised the treatment keeping in mind the 'un-ideal' conditions that he would be living in as a POW and that a plaster cast would give him the best chance for healing. Colonel Hassan had dealt with him purely as a doctor, professional, kind, curative. Much later he met some wounded Pakistani soldiers who had been treated in India and then repatriated. They too had spoken of Indian Army doctors in very laudatory terms. Such acknowledgment of genuine goodness spread a fine feeling all around as it brought to the fore the overweening element of kindness among men as opposed to mere bias and petty hatred.

He was now in the frightening but capable hands of the burly nurse who proceeded, with the help of a puny assistant, to hang or rather suspend him upside down, between two tables. His chin appeared to be resting on the edge of one table and his toes on the edge of another. He had the feeling of being pulled from both ends. At the same time his middle was being lifted, pressed down, and lifted again until the nimble fingers of Colonel Hassan were satisfied about the right curvature of the spine. And with that the Colonel left the scene leaving a moaning and groaning Jafa to the mercy of the Amazon.

'Crying ... eh, fighter pilot?' sneered the nurse. 'Brave soldier of your country, are you? ... Just a little injury and you whimper like this ...?' And with that she poured some lotion on his back and rubbed it down so gently and tenderly that he tried to turn his head to see if it was the same woman who had just taunted him.

'You think you can win against us? ... We are Pathans ... remember? ... We have thrashed you Hindus again and again ... *Insha Allah* ... we shall thrash you yet again,' she spoke in a ringing voice as if speaking from a public platform.

'Does it hurt?' she asked softly as she tightened a bandage and Jafa winced with pain. 'Won't be long. Then you will feel better.'

There was a pause during which she worked on her patient methodically, almost caressingly. As she completed whatever she was doing her hand shot up in the air and the declamation began. 'We are Mussalmans! We shall take your Red Fort apart, brick by brick. You don't know us. We are fighters, we are conquerors ... we shall show you!'

When she set off like that he feared that if her temper rose any higher she might indeed begin the conquest by first breaking him into two. Instead, she would calm down just as quickly and coo ever so sweetly, 'You tell me right away if the bandage is too tight, okay?'

'We are born to rule. *Insha Allah* ... we shall rule over you yet again. We shall drive you into the dust. Alas, but for our own brethren in the East we would have ground you to dust already ...'

He was amazed at this woman, so gentle and perfect in her ministrations and so hard in her convictions and fulminations. Amazing yet more because one side of her nature did not interfere with the other. He felt that while he could not have hoped for a more competent, even benign, nurse, he would indeed by very wary of facing her in different circumstances. She kept alternating between untrammelled gentleness bordering on limitless compassion and the hateful harangues against the perceived enemy who deserved no kindness, no consideration other than total annihilation. And when the job was done to her satisfaction, the plaster solid and firm in the contours she had desired, she ruffled his hair and said, 'You will be alright, *Insha Allah*, you will soon be with your people ...' And in the same breath, without a pause, the tone becoming harder, 'But remember always ... don't ever forget, ... we shall beat you ... we shall finish you....'

During the next few months he was several times taken to the same hospital for a check-up. He looked around eagerly for a glimpse of that extraordinary person, he made repeated enquiries about her, even requested the doctors to send for her so that he could see her just once again, and thank her, and tell her that, for him, she was the perfect image of a mother, so gentle and so compassionate in her actions, yet so hard and so unyielding in her beliefs. May she live long, and live happy ... *Insha Allah*!

5
Myths and Misconceptions

On being taken to his bed he fell into an exhausted sleep and got up several hours later when the discomfort caused by the hardening plaster became unbearable. As he was squirming in bed to find comfortable positions for his limbs there was a sudden scurrying and shuffling in the corridor outside and shortly a senior army officer was ushered into the room by a young doctor. The medico pointed at the prisoner and explained the injuries and the treatment to the dignitary who politely told him to 'carry on,' which in army lingo meant, 'get lost and leave me alone.'

'Received proper treatment?' enquired the Colonel, smoothening the tunic over a potbelly while at the same time lowering himself into an easy chair. He observed that the customary nameplate above the right breast pocket had been removed.

'Yes, Sir,' he said simply, trying to take in the new adversary along with the two subordinates standing behind him. The demeanour, the age, and the commotion that his arrival had created made it quite plain that he carried importance beyond his rank.

'Been treated properly by our people? No problems, I expect?'

'It was okay. Under the circumstances,' said Jafa.

The Colonel was about to say something but then checked himself. After a brief pause he said, 'You were captured ... let me see ... on the fifth, right? So you wouldn't really know about your comrades who were shot down subsequently ...'

Jafa was trying to fathom the drift of the conversation and the line of interrogation the Colonel might be taking, but curiosity and concern for his comrades got the better of him as he blurted out, 'How many shot down? And what about the pilots, Sir?'

'Can't give you an exact number,' said the Colonel. 'But hardly any aeroplane went back. Pilots ... mostly killed, I am afraid.'

There was something not quite convincing about the Colonel's assertion. Again from curiosity, he broadened the question by asking, 'And how is the war going on, Sir? I mean, who has reached where, you and us?'

'How did you expect it to go?' countered the Colonel. 'Yes, you tell me. How do you expect this war to go?'

'I am but an aerial version of a foot soldier, Sir, I don't have a concept of the war as such. As a combatant I am just curious to know what has been happening on the various fronts, who is winning, who is losing, who has reached where,' he said.

'Well, you chaps couldn't have expected to win this fight, this war as you say, could you? And, *Insha Allah* you shall not win,' said the Colonel with a touch of arrogance. 'Or, did you really think that you could win against us?' the Colonel added sarcastically.

'Well, Sir, a soldier doesn't go into battle thinking that he may lose,' said Jafa testily.' All of us, all soldiers on all sides join battle in the full conviction and hope of emerging victorious. Otherwise, there wouldn't be a battle, there would only be a chase by one side and scampering by the other.'

'Precisely,' said the Colonel. 'And it is scampering that your chaps are doing since it all began in the east. Your chaps are just not fighting us, they are dodging us, bypassing us, never coming face to face with us. Why did you start the whole caboodle if you didn't want to fight?'

'We started it?' asked Jafa in consternation. 'You made the grand opening by bombing all our airfields on 3rd December ...'

'Well, we had to. Just to tell you chaps that you can't go on fingering and instigating us in East Pakistan. You will have to pay for it somewhere else.'

'I beg your pardon, Sir. The whole world knows that you instigated the trouble in the east for yourself. And we got laden with ten million refugees, more arriving by the hour, by the minute ...,' he said in some heat.

'Yeah, and then you rush to help those ungrateful, disloyal Bengalis to rise against us. Ha ... the Bengali ... he is okay for agitations, for processions, for occasional Molotov cocktails, but fighting ...? And fighting us, the Punjabis?'

He was relieved and happy that the conversation had taken this interesting turn instead of his being subjected to boring, repetitive questioning. 'You were saying that our troops in the east have been avoiding battles ...,' he put in, not wanting the thread to be broken.

'Yeah, that's what they are doing. On this side of course there is no question of your being able to get away. But in the east your chaps start a build up against our positions but then slink away in the dead of the night like cowards.'

'They may be slinking away towards Dacca, Sir,' added Jafa in the manner of an observation, but also with a fraction of knowledge at the back of his mind of possible alternatives that had been discussed in regard to the well-entrenched and fortified positions that the Pakistani Army had built for itself all across East Pakistan. Later, of course, he would learn, as would the rest of the world, that the Indian Army simply bypassed most of the Pakistani concentrations in their erstwhile eastern part and converged from all directions upon Dacca, the capital, the nerve centre.

'May be so,' said the Colonel, 'but we only have to turn around to crush you like in a nut cracker.' Jafa was amused to note that the Colonel, by his tone and authoritative manner of speaking, had assumed to himself the role of the chief General and policy maker for his country, and that he also seemed to regard him as his principal adversary.

The Colonel was lost in his private thoughts for a while and when he spoke next he seemed to be seething with rage and frustration. 'These ungrateful Bengali bastards, they are not true to anyone, not even to Islam ... helping the enemy, guiding Indian troops across rivers, around minefields, informing them of our positions, our movements, working against Muslim brethren, running into the arms of aliens ... traitors ... we'll fix them ... we shall deal with them ... let us just finish you chaps first ...'

'Finish us first?' he asked in consternation. 'You mean here, on the western front?'. It suddenly dawned on him that the Colonel was fully aware of the situation on the ground but his soldierly pride prevented him from acknowledging his country's reversals. He was now taking refuge in empty braggartism.

'Yes, we will slaughter you on this side,' he ranted. 'You may have gained a bit here and a bit there, in Punjab, in Sind. But that is all part of the game plan. We'll draw you in and then smash you. After that the road would be clear, right up to Delhi.'

The Colonel became pensive again, perhaps savouring the thought of marching in triumph up the road to Delhi, something which everyone in this part of the world seemed to be doing. He then took out a packet of Player's cigarettes and lit one for himself. Jafa had not savoured a cigarette in days and the sight of a whole packet drove him beyond self-control.

'May I also have one?' he blurted out.

The Colonel paused in mid-puff and seemed to deliberate. The gentleman in him got the better of the officer and he proffered the pack to Jafa. He lighted a cigarette for himself, inhaled deeply and lay back with a sigh of contentment. He was already planning to ask the Colonel for the whole pack when the time came for him to depart. Among officers such give and take was a common, everyday occurrence, and while they may give no quarter to each other on the battlefield their reactions in such matters were spontaneous reflections of their upbringing and their regard for their own class. And in any case, whatever the level of hostilities among their countries, at the individual level the Indians and the Pakistanis have never been, nor would ever be, the Nazis and the Jews of pre-war Europe.

'Sir, you were talking about the western front,' he said gently. He didn't want any deviation now, least of all towards any kind of interrogation. As the Colonel seemed to hesitate, he added, 'The fighting has now been going on for a few days. Surely there ought to be a breakthrough by now ... by you or by us ...'

'Breakthrough ...,' mused the Colonel aloud. 'Yes, breakthrough there shall be. In a matter of days. I don't mind telling you since there's no harm you can do to us now ... we are going to cut you into half, west to east, and choke off the northern areas ...' His hand slashed the air in a cutting motion, and his fist tightened in simulation of the choking grip.

'Like in 1965?' enquired Jafa gently.

'Well ... yes and no! Our over-smart tank whiz kids went astray in your Khemkaran sector that time, yes. But not again. You'll see.'

'But, Sir, you mean to say that so far our Army and Air Force have made no gains at all?' he asked incredulously. 'By now they should have been poised with a couple of strongholds to make a dash for a major objective ...'

The Colonel perked up. Here perhaps was some piece of valuable information that the Indian fool might cough up without effort on his part. 'Yes, I suppose your chaps must also have done their planning and must be having an objective in mind. But what objective can they hope to achieve? This is not the darned Bangla land, this is Punjab, boy, Punjab. You chaps can dream ... the weak can only dream against the strong ... that's all they can jolly well do!'

If the Colonel's aim was to provoke him into giving out whatever he knew of plans and projected scenarios, he succeeded admirably. His nostrils flared ever so slightly, the teeth gnashed ever so imperceptibly, the eyes narrowed ever so minutely as he pondered over the silly bravado he had been subjected to ever since he fell into captivity. All the while he could sense a hollowness in their claims, and an irritating element of posturing in their professions of military prowess and superiority.

'I am surprised at what you just said. In fact the position on the ground should be quite different,' he said slowly, firmly.

'How different? What did you expect?' said the Colonel challengingly, teasingly.

'I don't think you are going anywhere, from west to east ... you've tried it before. And in ten days or so, you will see us marching through Rawalpindi ...,' declared Jafa, agitatedly, recklessly, and perhaps wrongly, but he had had enough of braggartism and posturing at every level, from everybody.

'What? ... What are you saying?' shouted the Colonel. 'Your army in Rawalpindi ... in ten days? Are you daydreaming, boy? By God, what nerve ... you Indians have not learnt any lessons ... you know who we are ... we, the martial people ... the Punjabi Mussalman, the Pathan, the Baluch ... the martial races, and you are going to walk into Rawalpindi?'

More of the same nonsense, thought Jafa, as he too became agitated and the mood to demolish a myth came upon him strongly.

'Martial races?' he asked in astonishment. 'Are you deluding yourself? Are you more martial than the so-called martial races on our side ... the Gurkhas, the Dogras, the Sikhs, and the Marathas? ... You name them, we have ten times more of the so-called martial races ...'

'No, no! They don't become martial people just because the British sometimes called them that, for purely selfish reasons of course,' reasoned the Colonel. 'We have overrun the Dogras, the Jats, and the Marathas time after time and routed them in all the battles. And the Rajputs ... ha, they have been good only for providing beautiful women for our people. And who, may I ask, are the Sikhs? Just part of the same stock who have been under our heels and licking our boots? No, young man, the martial tribes live here, on this side. You will have to delve into history for that.'

'Alright. Talking of history, Sir, would you remember the first Indians that were recruited by the East India Company in the so-called native infantry? Who were those Indians, where did they come from, what was their communitywise break-up?'

Myths and Misconceptions

'Suppose you tell me ... propound your theory ...,' nudged the Colonel.

'So far as I know, the *purbiya* sepoy of the East India Company was recruited from the plains of western Bihar and eastern Uttar Pradesh, then known as Oudh. They came mainly from among the Thakurs, the Brahmins, and the upper class Muslims who too were in fact Rajputs who had converted to Islam. These three communities, from these specific areas formed the backbone of the erstwhile native infantry of the British in India. Any dispute about that, Sir?' he asked to drive the point home.

'No ... Given the nature of the British advance from Bengal, this was perhaps inevitable. But what are you trying to say?' asked the Colonel.

'What I am trying to say, Sir, is ...,' Jafa gave a long, deliberate pause, 'that the British used the same troops, recruited mainly from this seemingly docile area, the non-martial area as you may like to call it, for most of their subsequent expansion into the Indian subcontinent. It was the very same *purbiya*s who conquered the whole of India for them, who crushed the Mughal armies at Buxar, then the great and fearsome Rohillas, and then beat the hell out of the Sikhs in three wars, subjugated your so-called martial people right up to Afghanistan. And not only that, these very *purbiya*s conquered Africa for the British and made inroads into China. In fact, the British empire was in a manner of speaking created by them. These are the unpalatable, hard facts of history.'

'No, it is not so simple. There were so many other causes for the success of the British and you can't prove anything just on the basis of one fact of history.' The Colonel was not willing to accept his argument. Or, rather, he understood too well where it was leading and he did not wish to part with the myths he had been brought up with.

'All that it proves, Sir, is that any body of men, properly trained, disciplined and led by capable men becomes a formidable force,' he said. 'The British achieved it with people who lived in relative peace and generally avoided fighting during the Mughal era, and who were again dubbed as third-class military material on account of their role in the 1857 uprising and the subsequent British need to glorify other bodies of men and make them serve their interests.'

The Colonel was thoughtfully quiet. Jafa wanted to go further and demolish, at least as an intellectual exercise for his own mind, this ridiculous theory of martial races, and the airs and posturing some people adopted merely on account of birth in certain communities, and the myths devised and garnered purely for the sake of the psychological advantages they gave to these communities.

'So you see, Sir,' he concluded, 'both the armed forces, yours and ours, have been nurtured in common traditions inherited from the British, the level of training and discipline are also not different. What will ultimately make the difference will be the quality of leadership. If our officers, right from the company and battalion level to the highest echelons remain true to their traditions, true to upholding the motto 'DUTY, HONOUR, COUNTRY,' they shall prevail, they shall earn glory for themselves, for the armed forces and for the nation. If they falter, ignominy shall be heaped upon them, as happened in our war with China in 1962.'

And then he laughed, loud and hard, and said, 'So let's see, Sir, who is better led this time! That's all that ever makes a difference.' His laughter lightened the ponderousness of the moment and left it open for the Colonel to withdraw or change direction gracefully.

After this, when precisely the change-over occurred from an Army Colonel to an Air Force Air Commodore, Jafa never quite figured out. An apparition in blue had suddenly appeared by the Colonel's side, saying, 'And how is the army treating you?' Jafa recognised the Air Force tunic, same colour, same material, the same broad stripes for the rank, similar pilot's wings above the campaign medal ribbons. He felt an immediate empathy and instinctively paid respects due to a higher rank officer by wishing him a good morning. The Air Commodore smiled, lowered himself into the easy chair and faced the prisoner. Jafa now became aware that the Colonel was no longer there, the switch-over had been accomplished so unobtrusively. He began to wonder about the purpose of the Colonel's visit, he had not probed or asked for any vital information, or maybe he was sent only to assess him as an individual and an officer.

'You were flying an SU-7 when our chaps got you?' the Air Commodore asked, steering the conversation clearly to professional matters.

'Yes, Sir,' replied Jafa.

'Rather bulky and heavy, like most Russian equipment,' remarked the officer. 'How does it handle?'

'Handles well. A good platform for firing,' he said , silently acknowledging the fact that he was now speaking with a professional, a fighter pilot of yore, who would be questioning him on some vital aspects of the aircraft and the operations.

'Some of our chaps have flown these Russian aircraft, so we know quite a bit about them. But tell me, how is it for night flying, I mean the version of the Sukhoi you fly? It is properly equipped for night flying as well?' he asked in the manner of a crew-room chat between pilots.

Jafa understood in a flash what was bothering the Air Commodore. The night bombings carried out by the Indian Air Force, night after night, several times each night, over a variety of targets in Pakistan and the inability of the Pakistan Air Force to stop these raids were a matter of great concern to them. Their air defence systems were ineffective against these low-flying aircraft which suddenly popped up over their airfields and adjoining cities and kept dropping two bombs at a time, all through the night. More than the actual damage it was the seeming defencelessness against these night prowlers that had demoralised the military and civilian population alike and focussed attention on the inadequacies of their own forces.

'As good as any other aircraft, Sir,' he said, honestly and sincerely. But it did not carry conviction with the Pakistani officer.

'Like other aircraft?' he asked. 'Come on, boy, the others like your Vampires and Hunters etc. have adequate equipment to help them land after dark. But some of your Russian aeroplanes, some Migs and Sukhois are specially equipped for night operations.'

'Not the Sukhois that we have.'

'Alright, when you say an aeroplane is equipped for night flying, what precisely does it have?' persisted the officer.

'Well, the cockpit and instrument lights, the landing and navigation lights ... what else ...?'

'But how do you navigate at night? I mean, how do you find a particular place or point on the ground? Surely you can't reach from A to B at night without a navigational aid on board, something to show you the position of a city or any particular place, with accuracy, in longitude and latitude ...?'

'If you mean a system like the Doppler or something, no, we don't have any,' said Jafa.

'How are your chaps then popping up over our airfields at night with dead accuracy? How are they finding these targets so accurately that they just have to press a button and drop bombs and vanish? Surely they are not being guided by our beacons and landing aids,' sneered the officer.

'So far as I know it is just the compass for direction, steady speed and a good wristwatch. That's how we do it, day or night.'

'You expect me to believe that, boy?' said the Air Commodore, his eyes beginning to narrow with anger. 'You expect me to believe that you have some very superior, hotshot pilots who can pop up at any place, anywhere, in the dead of a dark night without a target-finding device in the aeroplane? You better tell me what it is.'

'I have told you that we don't have any device of the kind that you mention. You can check for yourself, you have the crashed aeroplanes,' he replied.

'Yes, we have those,' said the officer. 'But I have asked you to tell me. I expect a truthful answer. I'll give you time till tomorrow morning. If you remain uncooperative, you will be handed over to the experts that we have for this very purpose. They may not be quite so patient or kind.'

With these words the Air Commodore was gone. Jafa pondered over the just concluded bout of interrogation. He had told the simple truth but the enemy was not prepared to believe him.

Of course, he hadn't told them that a number of pilots were specially selected and trained for this very purpose, that they had received such intensive and extensive training that they had perfected the art of performing such miracles with the most rudimentary equipment at their disposal. It was a tribute to the professional ability of this select band of pilots—the Brars, the Basras, the Deshpandes, the Kadams—this fear in the enemy, this suspicion that there had to be some special device to guide them accurately to the targets. Jafa was not in the team, but he had closely followed the operational procedures devised for the night bombing missions. It was apparent that the Pakistanis had lost faith in their own information about the capabilities of these aircraft and were now looking for other explanations for the success of the Indian attacks. Anyway, he had been given time till the next morning. They might indeed make it quite unpleasant for him then. But then tomorrow was another day, he thought, and tried to sleep off the present.

6

Compatriots and Colleagues

'Guard ... Guard ...,' called the prisoner. There was no answer.

'Guard ...,' he called again, as loudly as he could, which wasn't quite loud enough for there was still no reply. Possibly the guard was not in his customary position outside the door, perhaps he had gone to the toilet, for a smoke or a cup of tea. The prisoner decided to wait.

The cell was in semi-darkness now. The electric bulb above the bed was switched off at the time of the morning visit to the toilet. Light filtered into the room in minuscule shafts through chinks in the wooden door. Through one of these the prisoner could see a bit of the wall outside. There was nothing remarkable about that bit of the wall except that it was bathed in sunshine. There was light there, and warmth. For many days now he had lived in this cold cell, semi-dark by day, dimly lit by night, without fresh air or sun, the only change being a blindfolded walk to the toilet a few times a day, about ten paces in all. Then, suddenly, two days ago he had been helped out of the bed, out of the cell, into a small courtyard, and allowed to sit in the sun for an hour. But that was two days ago. He wondered if someone would remember to take him out again.

He had been unceremoniously removed from the comfort of the hospital bed to this dingy, semi-dark room, about half-an-hour's drive away, and placed on a sagging string bed with one blanket underneath and one on top of him. The first part of the warning given by the Air Commodore had thus come to pass. With trepidation he had awaited the arrival of the 'experts', some faceless, foul persons, who would extract from him the information he did not have. The minutes, the hours, the days had passed, alternating between anxiously waiting and fitfully sleeping. Then one evening, when it was finally dark, the police corporal had opened the cell door and Jafa was surprised to see that the courtyard outside was flooded with light. This struck him as odd because even at the hospital the nightly blackout was rigidly observed. Did it mean that the blackout was not necessary, not required ... the air raids not expected? Was that why he had lain in wait for the 'experts' and they hadn't come? He had felt a surge of curiosity but had checked himself from asking questions; the guard outside was a taciturn, sour-faced kind, it was better to avoid conversation than invite rude, insulting remarks. But the next morning a rather genial kind of fellow came to escort him to the toilet and he very casually said, 'So, the fighting is over ... Thank God, it is over ...'

In reply the guard merely grunted affirmatively, and Jafa had the confirmation. He then understood why no one had come to question him further. Much later he would know that the defeat had created its own kind of chaos and confusion, and all kinds of uncertainties in the ruling circles of Pakistan, particularly among the officers of the defence forces. For a while nobody was sure of the emerging power equations and the heads likely to roll and those likely to survive, so everything seemed to have been kept on hold.

'Guard ...,' he put all his might in that one word, and soon there was a hopeful crunch of boots outside his cell.

'What is the matter?' enquired the guard in gruff Punjabi.

'Please call the Corporal,' said Jafa. A substantive matter could only be sorted out by or through the Air Force police corporal on duty.

'Bathroom?' asked the guard.

'No, I must speak with the Corporal,' he said firmly.

'Okay,' said the guard, not missing a chance to practise English on the side.

There was a rattle of keys outside, the sound of a key being applied to the lock, the drawing of a bolt, the grating of the heavy iron grill door as it swung back on its hinges, then the unlocking of the wooden door, and the sudden flooding of the cell with light. He wondered if such elaborate locking-up procedures were really called for in the case of a seriously wounded prisoner like him. But, then in the services regulations are regulations, and it is easier and more prudent to adhere to them than get classified as an undisciplined rebel.

'How did you spend your day and your night?' began Corporal Khan in a sing-song voice. He had tried several opening greetings on different days, at different times, and seemed to have finally decided on this one as the most suitable for all occasions. Never over the next eight months was he to begin a dialogue with any but this sentence, except when he was angry, which he often was, when he saw red, looked red, and spoke not at all. Now he waited for his ponderous words to sink in and elicit the usual reply.

'Alright, quite alright,' replied the prisoner.

'I hope you are not getting too much pain?' he asked.

'No, not too much,' he said. 'Will you take me out in the sun today? It's very cold in here and I am shivering. I need to get warmed up.'

Khan hesitated. 'I can't say about the sun, but we will do something,' he said slowly, trying to suppress a smile.

'What will you do?'

'Well, we may take you somewhere else, probably,' said Khan in a manner that assured him that whatever they were planning wouldn't be unpleasant. The war had ended and some change in living conditions was to be expected.

After an hour's wait the elaborate process of the unlocking of doors was repeated, and in walked the squat, portly Master Warrant Officer Rizvi.

'I ... ah ... heard ... ah ... you wished to be taken out?' he enquired.

'Yes,' said Jafa.

'Well ... ah ... we'll take you out ... ah ... but it may not be ... ah ... in the sun.'

'Are you moving me to another camp, prison or hospital?' he asked in a deliberately disinterested manner.

'Well ... ah ... there may be a surprise ... ah ...'

And a surprise it was. He was helped out of the bed and led out of the cell towards another room in the same building. As he neared it he began to hear a loud, excited murmur of voices which reached a crescendo of din as he stepped through the door. All noise suddenly died down as he scanned the faces before him, and then, just as suddenly, the noise began again with everyone shouting recognition and greetings at the same time.

'Jeff, Sir,' cried Dilip from the far corner as he rushed to greet and embrace him.

'Easy, easy, Dilip,' he said as Dilip's strong arms tightened about his chest. Dilip withdrew from the embrace and began to feel Jafa's body.

'Oh, I see. Couldn't make out the plaster under this loose jacket. You better sit down on this chair, here.'

'You should be in the hospital,' said Vikram, the very tall, very thin, very emaciated Mystere pilot.

'Looking at you I may say you should be there yourself,' observed Jafa, 'What happened?'

'Oh, just a bit of bad time, Sir,' said Vikram, playing down the rough treatment and brutal beatings he had received at the hands of his captors.

These were poignant moments. This was the first revelation for each of the downed pilots that those of their friends and colleagues they saw before them were actually alive and living and had not died in battle or shot afterwards. There was Bhargava, the ever-smiling, ever-ready-with-advice, HF-24 pilot who had, after his capture by villagers in a remote area in Sind, successfully enjoyed their hospitality by carrying on as a downed Pakistani pilot. He was in the process of arranging for a camel for a ride south to India when some slip on his part at the time of prayers made his hosts suspicious. He was discovered, dishonoured, mounted on the same camel and sent up north to Rawalpindi.

Kuruvilla, the youngest of the lot, a veteran of three days of hard flying and fighting, quite bewildered at the turn of events in his life, huddled close to Harry, the diminutive Rajput from Kathiawar. The quietest was Chati, lithe and in perfect physical condition, who had survived a rifle shot taken at him by a villager immediately after his touch down by parachute, the bullet just grazing the side of his stomach.

Just then the outer door to the room opened, and in walked Tejwant. He smiled, looked around, fought back tears, and gently lowered himself into a chair. He had suffered a spinal injury and his back needed support all the time.

'Welcome, Teja,' someone shouted. 'When did you arrive?'

'On the 17th,' said Teja, rather sheepishly.

'On the 17th?' asked Brother Bhargava. 'And when did the ceasefire come about?'

'The same day,' said Teja with a wry smile. 'I landed up here just a couple of hours before that.' That must have been during the last hour before the ceasefire when both sides go all out to gain bits of territorial advantages and the fighting becomes very fierce.

'Good, good,' said Bunny Coelho, a cut and dried, no-nonsense Mangalorean health-fiend. 'You just about made it, you know, Teja? Just imagine what all you would have missed otherwise!'

'Come on, let's have the gen, Teja,' said Garry Grewal, the muscular Sikh. 'You must know all that went on right up to the last moment.'

'Wait!' cried Mulla-Feroze, with one arm in a sling. 'Let's check if this place is bugged. You never know about these chaps. They may be taping away while we shoot our mouths off.' The search proved fruitful. A microphone was stuck on the underside of the table. A tug at the wires rendered it ineffective.

Teja had just commenced his account when Rizvi walked in again. He was followed by two men holding up yet another of their comrades. Kamat had sustained fractures to both knees and both ankles. Both his legs from thighs downwards were wrapped in plaster. He was lowered onto a chair and his legs were propped up on a low table. While everyone greeted him and shook hands with him, his physical condition created an air of anguish in the room. Conversation died down, commiseration took its place.

'Well, well, gentlemen,' said Jafa in a cheery voice, 'It's great to be alive.'

'Most certainly, yes, Sir,' echoed Kamy, the most seriously injured of all. The spell of sadness was broken.

The door opened once again. This time it was Squadron Leader Osman of the Pakistan Air Force, in-charge of the POW camp. Whatever Osman did, he did with a smile, and this time he had enough reason to smile for he brought in his wake two men carrying cakes and tea.

'I thought I'll come and wish you all a Merry Christmas,' he said pleasantly.

In the excitement of release from solitary confinement and meeting with comrades-in-arms the festival had been totally overlooked, even by the Christian officers among them. Now, suddenly, there was a hurrah on every lip, hands were clasped and entwined, and greetings and good cheer prevailed all around. The cakes were attacked greedily and tea disappeared as fast as it was poured.

'Are we to go back to our cells after this, or can we now remain together?' enquired Dilip of Osman.

'As you like,' said Osman with the unfailing smile.

'Oh, we would like many things, Sir, but for the time being we would just like to be together,' put in Garry.

'Very well, you may remain in this room, or, if you like, we can take you out into the courtyard outside,' offered Osman. So the courtyard it was, and Osman started to leave after instructing his subordinates.

'Just one moment, please, Osman,' Jafa said.

'Yes, please,' invited Osman.

'Please tell us, Osman, are we the only Air Force prisoners in your custody, or are there any more?' asked Jafa, in a very serious, concerned tone.

Osman paused and then said, 'In my custody, yes. You all are the only prisoners.'

'Elsewhere?' he persisted.

'I wouldn't know,' said Osman. 'I can see your concern, but truly, I don't know.' And with that he exited from the room.

Bunny Coelho then came forward and said, 'Just a moment, everybody. I'd like to say a few words.' All eyes turned towards him.

'I need hardly say, gentlemen, that we all have gone through a particularly bad phase of our lives in the last few days. Some of us are badly injured and have so far endured pain in total isolation. Yet many of our comrades have sacrificed their lives in this war. At least we are sure of someday, sooner or later, returning to our families. More than that, we can be proud that our travails have not gone to waste, that we are here as representatives of a victorious nation, and we, as Indians, shall hold our heads high, no matter what hardships we have faced so far or are likely to face in the near future. Let us therefore first stand in silence for one minute and pray for our country, for the souls of our departed comrades, and for ourselves. After that we shall sing the national anthem.'

They prayed in silence and then lustily sang the national anthem, the notes and words of *Jana Gana Mana* ... floating far and wide in enemy land. There is something very remarkable about the singing of the national anthem in such circumstances, it immediately suffuses one with pride in oneself and in the country, and seems to prepare one for ever greater sacrifices.

On reaching the courtyard they all huddled together and Tejwant was asked to tell all he knew about the closing stages of the war. He recounted all that he was personally aware of, and all that he had heard as crew-room gossip. He held everyone spellbound with descriptions of the surrender by Pakistani Army at Dacca (also Dhaka), the Prime Minister's speeches, the appearance of the United States Seventh Fleet in the Bay of Bengal, the total solidarity and enthusiastic determination of the nation in the face of the American 'tilt' in favour of Pakistan. There were also moments of grief as they heard of the deaths of their friends and colleagues. But as professionals they had learnt to take such things stoically, and look only to the future.

Until shortly before sundown the stories were told and told again. There was so much to say that they kept jumping from one event to another and back again. Such conversations were to fill all their time over the next few days. Even later they would return to the significant actions in which they had taken part, their encounters with the Pakistani interrogators and their harassment after capture.

As the sun went down over the western wall, they were marched off to their cells to await an early meal and a long, cold night. But the feeling of isolation was miraculously gone. There would soon be another day. And companionship. It was good to be alive, as Jafa had said. It was even better to have your own people around.

7

A Yankee Comes Calling

Jafa could not recall later when exactly the American flyer had been brought to his cell by a Pakistani officer. He was introduced as the well-known test pilot of the rocket-propelled air vehicle the X-2, the forerunner of the space shuttle. Jafa recalled vaguely having read about him in the TIME magazine but had no idea what he looked like. But, accepting him to be the genuine person, he nodded at him as a courtesy due to a professional who was involved in a futuristic enterprise in aviation. The American's visit must have taken place after the 25th of December, thought Jafa later, because it was on that day that he had learnt from Teja of the Unites States Seventh Fleet sailing into the Bay of Bengal to pressurise India into stopping its march towards Rawalpindi. And perhaps for that reason he had found the American's appearance particularly annoying.

'I heard you were injured. How you feeling?' said the American.

'Alive and kicking,' said Jafa in not too polite a tone. 'And what is a United States officer doing here? Any old friends among the prisoners here? Brought any chocolates?'

To Jafa he symbolised the Seventh Fleet, the coercive, high-handed, self-righteous aggressiveness of the ugly American. The American was taken aback at his hostility, but quickly recovered himself and said, 'Oh, I was scheduled to be in Pakistan anyway during this period. But then came the fighting between you people. So here I am, travelling around a bit.'

'Been to the front lines?' asked Jafa, again quite offensively. 'Examined the wreckage of all our aeroplanes?'

The American was obviously on a mission and he wasn't going to be sidetracked by the peevishness of one combatant in one corner of the world. With aplomb he said, 'Yes, as a matter of fact I have. Very interesting, these Russian aeroplanes. They have their own standardised methods of building their planes and they never depart from the basic concept.'

He had deftly side-stepped the possibility of a slanging match and opened the dialogue on the subject of his quest. Jafa was impressed. He decided to play along.

'That's an interesting observation, 'he said. 'Undoubtedly, you people must have closely followed the developments in Russian aviation, the Mig series, the Sukhois and, of course, their bombers. I am sure they are all different concepts.'

'No, not really. They come up, say, with a more powerful engine, they put it on the older model, and make just those changes that are absolutely necessary to house it. The same goes for weapons. They don't design a platform for a weapons concept, on the other hand the existing platform is modified to somehow take in the new weapon. You know what I mean?'

He knew; it was so much hogwash. What he didn't know yet was precisely what the American was looking for. So he simply said, 'Well, I don't know, I am only a flyer, the end user, so to say. You'd know better, of course, being a test pilot. But tell me something that I can comprehend in terms of practical applicability.'

'Yes, sure. Take electronics, for that matter. Earlier, the Sukhoi was not provided with any navigational aid to find targets by day or by night simply because the Russians hadn't developed it till then. But later they got it and somehow accommodated it on the same aeroplanes, the ones they gave to you, to enable you to find targets ...'

It was apparent to him that the Americans must have monitored very closely the entire gamut of air operations. And they appeared to be even more bothered about the accurate night bombings by the Indian pilots than were the Pakistanis.

'I don't quite know about that,' he said. 'Unless the Russians put in some equipment inside those aircraft and forgot to tell us about it.'

'Then how come your pilots were finding the targets so accurately by night? Not a single failure,' said the American.

The American and his kind were not daft, thought Jafa. They must have taken all shot down aircraft apart and examined all the bits and pieces to determine just one piece of equipment that would solve the mystery. And if it wasn't on the aeroplane, was it some kind of beam guidance system of which the Americans were not aware? Was there, after all, some truth in the suspicion among their intelligence agencies that the Russians had loaned an AWACS TU-20 aircraft to the Indian Air Force which was used to guide the Indian bombers on to their targets with unfailing accuracy during night attacks throughout the brief war?

'Come on', Jafa taunted. 'Why can't you accept the simple fact that a bit of accurate flying with a compass, a speedometer, and a wrist watch will take you unerringly to where ever you want to go, every time! So tell me, what are you really after?'

'No, no,' said the American. 'We are not after anything as such. Just a bit of chit-chat, among professionals, among fighter pilots that we all are.'

They knew that further conversation would not lead anywhere. The Pakistani officer made a great show of looking at his watch and said, 'Oh, it's getting late. We had better be going.'

As the visitors were saying their goodbyes, Jafa looked at the American and said, 'Are you going to place the Seventh Fleet in the Arabian sea next? For this part of Pakistan?'

There was no reply. The Yankee shrugged his shoulders and walked out.

A Yankee Comes Calling

That day the prisoners were not taken out of their cells. The questions put to the guards drew evasive answers. The police corporals and their chief, Rizvi, remained unavailable. There could only be one reason for this. The American must be going round, meeting every Indian prisoner individually to extract information that would possibly complete some jigsaw puzzle of the American intelligence somewhere in the deep caverns of Langley or wherever. The superpowers played their own games, they were nobody's friends. Alas, the poor, the struggling, the less powerful nations succumbed to their blandishments too easily, too often, and ended up doing all their dirty work. The war between India and Pakistan could have been prevented if the superpowers had been so inclined. That it was actually encouraged to take place could have been for as small a consideration as the testing of the already obsolete weaponry that had been provided to the two sides, or as big a reason as the eventual dismemberment of the sub-continent along ethnic lines.

Garry was the first to speak his mind when the prisoners got together the next day. 'It was that bloody Yank who had us locked up the whole of yesterday. Damned idiot ... trying to create the crew-room chit-chat atmosphere for asking questions. A bit disappointed when he left, he was.'

'What was he after? I haven't been able to guess,' Brother said loudly.

You weren't able to guess, Brother, because he couldn't have been interested in your HF-24,' said Harry teasingly, referring to the indigenously built fighter aircraft, considered to be a disaster all the way.

'I think they are interested in some aspects of the new surface-to-air missiles that the Russians gave us recently. They also feel that the Ruskies have given us some kind of flight guidance system or even AWACS, of which they are not aware,' said Dilip.

Then Dilip laughed loudly and said, 'He wasn't happy with my replies. I think I was a bit rude to him as well. I haven't got over that Seventh Fleet business perhaps. But imagine the access these Yanks have in this supposedly sovereign country. I don't think that on our side the Russians have access to any sphere of activity which is not connected directly with the maintenance of the equipment supplied by them.'

The discussion on the American's visit continued for some time, everyone chipping in with his opinion. But one common thread ran through everyone's mind, they were all angry at the United States tilt in favour of Pakistan. A weak nation, like a weak person, may not be in a position to challenge a mighty opponent, but there is no forgiving either for a manifestly unjust act. One can only bide one's time, for nations, like men, rise to strength, dominate for a while, become arrogant and complacent, then begin the downward slide. It may take a hundred years, a thousand years, but others would be waiting for the right moment with a push and a shove.

8

Some Fun, Some Frolic

Flight Lieutenant Abbas was a young doctor in the Pakistan Air Force. Medicine, and the practice of it, was a sideline in his joyous and ebullient life. He loved the uniform, and the status and privilege it bestowed on him in a country ruled by the military. An ardent admirer of the erstwhile military dictators, the high point of his life arrived when, upon declaration of martial law, he was suddenly called upon to take over as the military administrator of a small town where he happened to be on leave from his unit. He wasted no time in occupying the office of the local magistrate and summoning the senior bureaucrats to his exalted presence. He then proceeded to instruct them on what was expected of them, which was mainly to dance attendance on him, and, at the very least, to report to him twice a day and keep him informed on all that they were doing.

'But, did you have any specific mandate or briefing or instructions on what you were supposed to do?' asked Dilip.

'Like hell I knew what I was supposed to do! And like hell I knew what my powers were,' said Abbas cheerily, and added with a guffaw, 'And like hell did they know what it was all about!'

'You know how these damned bureaucrats behave when you approach them for some work?' Abbas resumed. 'I just wanted to teach them a lesson they would never forget. And, boy, I had them parading before me and generally letting them have it. You understand! It was great fun! Boy, that was the life!'

Abbas lived and re-lived those twenty days when he was the supreme ruler of a small community. He never tired of recounting details of his administrative and humanitarian forays of those days. To him military rule signified propriety, discipline, hard work, responsibility, and, above all, accountability. The civilians had always made a bloody mess of things; only the military could keep things together and keep them going. While the West and the developing countries trying to ape them debated endlessly and attempted aimlessly to harmonise freedom with power, his country and his country's role models debated and disagreed only over systems and modalities of authoritarian rule. They hailed and submitted to men who could conquer enemies, maintain order, render natural calamities less disastrous, and generally enable them, with a mixture of bravado and braggartism, to walk taller.

But Abbas was a good raconteur too, not only of the halcyon days of military rule but also of anecdotes and the personal foibles of the great and the powerful. His repertoire included an endless store of jokes as well, even though most of these were slanted against India and Indians. One such he narrated to us.

This was the time of the General, Ayub Khan, ruling in Pakistan. The Americans were happy, the arms and money were pouring into the country. The armed forces were well looked after, there was plenty of food for the people, everyone functioned under strict discipline and minded his own business. No bitching, no complaints, no agitations. Do your work, take your dues, and shut up. On the other side of the border poor Lal Bahadur Shastri was trying to cope with the mess left behind by Nehru. There was no food, the begging bowls were out and the Americans dictated their terms while doling out food and money to India.

One day two prowling dogs met at the border, one trying to cross over to the Pakistani side and the other heading for India. As is usual with these creatures, they first growled, then inched closer together, sniffed around and settled for a peaceable meeting and parting.

'Hungry?' asked the Pakistani dog by way of polite enquiry.

The emaciated Indian dog stood meekly with its tongue hanging out and its head shaking affirmatively with each laboured breath.

'Okay, okay,' said the Pakistani. 'Go ahead. There is plenty to eat that side.'

The Indian chap began trotting into Pakistan, but after just a few steps he stopped and turning in the direction of his Paki counterpart, barked softly to gain attention. So they both again got together.

'Yeah, I am going into your country obviously because I am hungry; very, very hungry. But why the hell are you going into mine?' asked the Indian dog in some consternation.

'Ah!' said the Pakistani fellow. 'I understand. You see there is plenty of food on my side and all the comforts a dog may want. But there is one thing lacking.' He paused to gather adequate gravity in his voice. 'You can't bark in this blessed country! You've got to take the lid off once in a while, don't you think? And that's why I am going across.'

The Indians laughed at this joke. The Pakistanis laughed louder.

* * * * *

In the prison, life could get very lonely. During the day-light hours the POWs were allowed to stay together outdoors, but at dusk they were locked up separately in individual cells. The long evenings and the nights were the time of nightmarish solitude, relieved occasionally when a pleasant sentry happened to be on duty who could be drawn into conversation.

Iqbal was one such fellow, young, battle-hardened, ever-ready for small talk when his superiors were out of earshot. Jafa would ask him about life in the villages, their food habits, and who made the best *kebabs*. Iqbal would go into rhapsody about the simple fare turned out by his mother and even praise shyly the culinary accomplishments of his young wife. Outside his home the delicacy he admired was the *chappal kebab* made in Pindi.

'But it is made of beef and so of no use to you,' he would say.

Inevitably, the talk would turn to the recent war, their common and intimate experience. Iqbal was acutely aware that his country had lost the war. As a soldier this was a shame he had to live with, a sort of personal inadequacy. Sometimes he would talk excitedly about a particular battle and say, 'Then came your aircraft ... and started firing rockets and guns ... We were in our trenches and they could do no damage.' Going further, he would suddenly stop and slowly mumble ... 'but then we lost ...'

One day when Iqbal had wound up another battle-front tale, Jafa said, 'Iqbal, you are a Pathan. You are among the great warriors of these parts. For times beyond recall you people have launched innumerable expeditions into India and overrun the country almost at will. Tell me, why did you lose so badly this time?'

Iqbal sighed and began a thinking process which allowed the words to come out ever so slowly, but with the weight of conviction. 'Your officers ... yes, your officers.'

'Our officers? What does that mean?' asked Jafa.

'Yes, it was because of your officers that you won this war,' emphasised Iqbal. Jafa looked expectantly at him, almost willing this grass-roots soldier to go on with this exposition.

'You see there is a big difference between our officers and yours. On the front, our Major *Saheb* raises his head out of the trench and tells the Captain *Saheb*, 'CHARGE ...' The Captain peers outside the trench and tells the JCO, 'CHARGE ...' The JCO in turn calls out to the *jawan*s to 'CHARGE ...' The *jawan*s spring out from the trenches and begin the charge. But when they look back, there is no one to be seen.' Iqbal paused, allowing time for this weighty revelation to sink in, also perhaps a little bewildered that his deep perception of the failings of his own people should have finally found expression in words.

'But doesn't it happen like this everywhere?' suggested Jafa.

'No,' said Iqbal emphatically. 'I have seen with my own eyes. On your side the Major leaps out of the trench with a firing sten gun in his hands and bounds forward crying, 'C..H..A..R..G..E..'

The Captain comes behind him, then the JCO and then the *jawan*s, all successive people trying to overtake the ones before them. Finally, of course, the *jawan* takes the lead but he knows that everyone is solidly behind him. This is what wins battles.'

Iqbal was now quiet, mulling over what had just poured out of him; so was Jafa, mulling over the highest compliment an enemy could pay to his class and its character.

'Iqbal, you may be right,' he said.' I do not know how many but we did lose a large number of officers in this war. So many officers killed, many more injured and incapacitated for life. And listening to you fills me with pride. We did our duty, and some of us did much more than that.'

Iqbal was busy with his own thoughts and hardly listened to him. 'Our men are brave fellows, *Saheb*. We don't lose battles; we have never lost battles. We fight like ghazis and we accept martyrdom with pride.'

Emotions were now coming to the fore. Jafa decided to remain quiet. In a musing tone Iqbal asked and himself answered, 'Do you know *Saheb* what would be the greatest fighting force in the world? An unbeatable combination, an army that can beat the Americans and the Russians put together? ... Your officers and our men!'

Jafa was quiet for a while and then said with a smile, 'Iqbal, there is just one other combination that would be even greater in battle ... our officers, and our men!'

Iqbal did not quite listen. He had reached his own conclusions and would not be swayed by any other idea.

*****

Abbas' penchant for recounting jokes and anecdotes was irrepressible. For this, he was always welcomed with eagerness and joy; he alleviated the monotony of prison life.

'Have you heard the one about the eunuchs?' he enquired as a preamble.

Whether we had heard or not was not quite material to the narration that must follow. But Jafa realised in a flash that it would certainly be a joke against India and Indians. In feigned seriousness he asked, 'eunuchs ... what's that?'

'Oh, eunuchs! You know ... eunuchs ... neither here nor there,' clarified Abbas.

'Honestly, no. I am not aware, never seen them,' he said innocently, trying to work out how to turn the tables on Abbas.

Abbas was not one to give up. 'Oh, Brother, eunuchs! Neither men nor women! The *Hijras*, you know, the ones who come dancing and singing when there is a wedding or when a child is born in the family.'

'Ah, the *Hijras*!' said Jafa. 'Yes, of course, I have heard of them. Yes, neither here nor there, as you said. Our old people laugh and talk about them and make all kinds of jokes among themselves.'

'Your old people?' asked Abbas unbelievingly. 'Surely you must have seen lots of them yourself. Your country has plenty, I believe,' he added with a smirk.

With a straight face he said, 'I've heard there used to be lots of them in my country, but they are not to be seen any more. The older people say that there were lots of them up to 1947, and then suddenly they all disappeared.'

Abbas and his Pakistani colleagues slowly turned red in their faces. Anger and helplessness make for strange contortions of the face. But this was the end of anti-India jokes and innuendoes.

9

Courage and Cowardice

A whole year later when Jafa was back in his own country, in his own house, in his own bed, an young officer resplendent in Air Force tunic barged straight into his bedroom with considerable eagerness. He bent over the bed and held Jafa's hands in his own, his mouth open with unspoken words, his eyes moist with deep emotions. Jafa gazed up at him, at the row of medals on his chest, and a look of immense gratification and indescribable happiness came over him. In a gesture of warmth and blessing he put a hand over the young man's shoulder and his own eyes welled up with tears.

* * * * *

Men have always been selected, conscripted, cajoled, enticed, bribed, exhorted, encouraged, inspired to fight wars. The folklore of every people is replete with names of great warriors and heroes and while every fighting man may fancy himself a modern-day Arjun, visions of decimation and death are never too far from his mind. As an impending battle draws closer, the thoughts of achieving battle honours remain constantly interspersed with those of likely annihilation. Most soldiers perform within reasonable and predictable parameters of daring and fear, but every war, each battle throws up some unexpected heroes as well as cowards and even some who suddenly get transformed from one to the other.

Death Wasn't Painful

Just before dusk on 3 December 1971, the Pakistan Air Force bombed seven Indian military airfields in the north and the west. Not a concerted, heavy attack anywhere, merely a declaration of war, an invitation to join battle. The inevitability of this moment on the western front had been apparent for months. On both sides the initial moves, the first strikes, had been conceived, debated, altered, finalised and locked away in top secret drawers. The time had come for these to be brought out and implemented.

At Adampur, in Punjab, as the news of the bombing spread to barracks and mess halls, everyone headed for their flight offices to join those who were already on duty there. A strange calm pervaded the Operations Rooms, there was no longer anything to discuss or muse about. Within the hour strike sections were formed, target maps issued for study, the time of take-off for the dawn attack fixed and crews dispersed with the solemn advice to eat early, sleep well and hit hard.

By nine o'clock Jafa was well tucked in his bed. Earlier in the evening, by courtesy of a kind telephone operator, he had spoken with his wife in another city, another world, another cosmos of hope and fear. The radio had announced the Pakistani attack, she had said, so what will happen now? It's on now, what else, he had said. This was dangerous ground, he knew, yet it had to be traversed. Tomorrow ... you will go in tomorrow? She had persisted. I should think so ... look ... he had changed the subject abruptly, cruelly, necessarily. And then the falsely cheerful, desperate wish from the other end—All the Best, Look After Yourself.

There was very little sleep that night, only fitful dozing with all kinds of disjointed thoughts and images whirring in the mind. Strangely there weren't many thoughts of families, friends; the images were of aeroplanes, formations, tanks, troops, fires and explosions and through them all a peculiar, uneasy feeling in the pit of the stomach that just wouldn't go away. The silent turmoil was eventually broken by a soft knock on the door and someone whispering, 'Jafa, Sir ...', the voice reluctant, afraid to wake up, yet hoping for wakefulness. Jafa climbed out of bed and opened the door. By now he had placed the voice, it was Jaggu Saklani's, one of the youngest pilots in the Squadron, and he expected some important message to be delivered.

'What's it, Jaggu?' he asked. The young lad stood in the chill of the *verandah* and said nothing.

'Well, what is it?' he asked again with an edge in his voice.

'Sir ... I ... I must talk to you,' he blurted out, 'but if you are sleeping ...'

'Well, I am not sleeping now,' Jafa began testily but something in the inflection of Jaggu's voice made him check himself. 'All right, come, come inside ...,' he said gently.

He climbed back into bed and invited Jaggu to sit beside him and gave him part of the blanket to cover himself. And then he smiled reassuringly and raised his eyebrows in gentle enquiry.

'Sir, I ... I ... I am scared,' Jaggu burst out, his desperation close to tears. An youngster of 22, a fighter pilot, a term that presupposes a measure of daring, even recklessness, a good officer with excellent record during training, and a great deal of promise for the future.

The standard reaction in the armed forces to any show of cowardice is contempt. Perhaps this is appropriate for it compels everyone to keep his chin up and to feel brave and, in all probability, to act brave. But this is a panacea for normal times, not when the time to act is already upon you and in just a few hours you may be meting out, or receiving, death and destruction. Jafa felt that the situation was tricky, delicate. He could keep Jaggu out of tomorrow's strike formations, perhaps even for the entire duration of the war. But that would be a colossal waste, both of a fine pilot and a promising officer. As a leader it was for him to carry everybody along, the strong as well as the weak. The weak needed support and posed a challenge, could he ... could he ... first check this weakness from going deeper and spreading wider and then possibly, quite possibly, transform it into a reasonable discharge of duty if not actual courage and bravery? Caution, he told himself. One wrong word, the slightest disparaging remark, even false bravado would almost certainly ruin this fine young man. So nothing but the truth,

Death Wasn't Painful

even the harsh reality of killing and dying, the hopes and fears in every heart, the thin line between courage and cowardice, and transcending it all, one's duty to self, service and the country.

Very gently, very simply, he said, 'To tell the truth, Jaggu, so am I ...'

'Sir ...?' exclaimed Jaggu, and gaped at his commander unbelievingly, at the man who demonstratively flew on all Fridays the Thirteenth and defiantly walked under ladders to rid himself and his boys of superstitious awe.

'Yes, Jaggu, that's true,' he continued. 'And I don't know who is not really afraid before going into battle. Anyone who says he is not, is a liar or a bloody fool.'

'You are not angry or disappointed in me then?'

'I would be wary if you said you were not affected one way or another at the prospect of going into action tomorrow. For, you see, only a rash person is not bothered as he foolishly believes in his own invincibility. And I have seen quite a few of that kind literally going up in smoke, and taking other innocents with them. No, Jaggu, all I can say is that you are not rash, that you are just human, with the normal reactions of any balanced person in the circumstances.'

'But no one else has come to you ...'

'Oh, that is neither here nor there. Most of us live behind facades. You have let down your veil, so to speak, and perhaps you are wondering if there is any abnormality in you. I can assure you there is none.'

'Then, what should I do, Sir?'

'Do? What would you do?' Jafa felt that he was now reaching somewhere and for his own sake he wanted to succeed. 'You see, Jaggu, it is like this. When you see the war coming closer, like it was in 1962, in 1965, and like this time, you lie awake each night thinking of Mianwali and Sargodha, of Sabres and F-104s, and of Mirages now. You are in your bed, and you are not there. You are in a dogfight over Amritsar or Lahore or Peshawar. Or you are in a dive with an enemy M-72 tank lined up beautifully in your sight. And you are firing and coming back a hero. Occasionally, you get shot up yourself, your aeroplane is on fire, you bail out, you dodge the Pakis, crawl under bushes, swim an odd stream at night and make it back home in tatters, in filth, in hunger. Not quite a hero, but a plucky sort, a well-done type.' He paused for this much to sink in.

'So, Jaggu, nothing needs to be done now. Just think of Risalpur, of Chak Jhumra, of the Mig-19s lined up there. And then go out in the morning and shoot them up. That's what you've got to do.'

'Will there be missiles there?' Jaggu was getting to the core of the fear.

'Of course. The missiles might be there. But you'd be flying at tree-top height where you'd be perfectly safe. In any case you have got an excellent ejection seat in this aircraft which will take you out of a wrecked plane every time and bring you down safely. No problem at all.'

According to this formula of course nothing could be safer. But Jaggu was now under a spell and ready to believe all that he was told. All uncertainties were finally laid to rest when he made the final, simple request, 'Sir, may I fly as your wingman tomorrow?'

'Certainly, if you wish,' he said casually. 'I shall make the change in the morning. In fact, we'll do a few sorties together and you better keep a good look-out for me. Okay?'

Jaggu was airborne the next morning on the first operational mission of his career. He flew perfectly and executed all manoeuvres in copy-book style. Even so, Jafa broke radio silence to say an occasional, 'Hold that position, Jaggu,' and again just before commencing the attack, 'Select switches, Jaggu.' It was not really required, yet perhaps it helped to keep alive the vital sense of togetherness. That day Jafa and Jaggu made three forays into Pak territory. A fourth mission had to be given up for want of enough day-light for identification of targets. After each sortie he chatted with Jaggu in the most casual, routine manner. There was no allusion to the dialogue of the previous night, nor any hint of undue concern. At the end of the day Jaggu was suggesting to him how one particular attack could have been more successful! That night Jafa decided that after one more day he could ease the young pilot out on the road to self-dependence. But it had to be done in stages, perhaps a few sorties with someone like Mohan, an officer mature beyond his years and with sufficient self-confidence not to be disparaging about others' shortcomings, helpful to those under his charge. But the next day Jaggu's world got shaken up again. Jafa was shot down during an attack on a very heavily defended target and was listed as missing-in-action, which meant that no one knew whether he was alive or dead, probably the latter. The next day Mohan's plane was hit by very strong anti-aircraft fire and blew up in mid-air. Jaggu was alone once again. The two persons who had helped him to avert a near breakdown and loss of nerve were gone for ever. After some morose deliberation, he decided that he would now have to be what they had set out to make him—a fighter.

* * * * *

The Indian Army had made a breakthrough in the Shakargarh area of Pakistani Punjab. Intense fighting was going on for every inch of the land. Jaggu had just returned from a sortie in another sector when he heard the Base Commander upbraiding some pilots.

'Three missions, six aeroplanes, six pairs of damned eyes, and you can't spot the blasted tanks! What am I to tell the blooming army? That they are imagining the tanks? That my chaps have got holes in their heads and no bloody eyes?'

It transpired that two companies of an infantry battalion, about 600 men, had crossed a river during the night and taken up position in fields and groves on the other side. In the morning the Pakis brought down some tanks and began squeezing them from three sides. The situation soon became desperate and the Air Force was called upon to stop the tanks. Three attempts had been made but the tanks were not spotted. They were taking advantage of the morning fog and natural cover to hide while the aircraft were overhead, resuming the attacks as soon as the aircraft burnt up their fuel and went away. The last message said that the *jawan*s could not hold out for much longer and would be wiped out within the hour if the tanks were not stopped. In a spontaneous reaction Jaggu edged up to the Commander and said, 'Sir, there is still time. Let me try, please, Sir, let me go this once.'

The Commander gave the necessary order for Jaggu to lead two aircraft with rockets and guns. He got a quick briefing from the pilots who had just returned from an unsuccessful trip and realised that it was perhaps a matter of locating one tank and then one would know their hiding pattern. And so it was that within less than twenty minutes Jaggu was headed westwards thinking of the 600 lives that possibly depended on him. A few more minutes and they were in the target area. Jaggu made radio contact with the aircraft controller on the ground, still this side of the river. The controller was in constant touch with the ongoing battle and would guide the pilots onto the targets.

'We are in a bad way, Gold One. You better not miss,' the controller said on the radio.

'Will do,' replied Jaggu. 'Report bogey,' meaning that he needed directions for the enemy, in this case the tanks.

'You have just flown over me, Gold One. Keep straight on. Two o'clock to you, west of the river, look for a cluster of houses.'

'Seen. Just gone past. Turning around.' He had seen the houses half way to his right, perhaps eight or ten dwellings, all without any sign of life. He banked to the right, turning and looking for tell-tale signs of tanks, for the small clouds of dust that should be billowing after them or tracks on the ground if they were moving. There was nothing.

'Look for wooded area 2000 yards south of the houses, Gold One,' said the Controller. 'The tanks are inside there, about eight of them.'

Jaggu searched the ground under him, in front of him, all around him. He turned left, turned right, climbed up for a wider view, came down for a closer look, and called up his wingman in desperation, 'Anything, Gold 2?'

'No joy,' said No. 2, meaning that he was equally at sea.

Death Wasn't Painful

Jaggu kept an eye on the fuel gauge, it was steadily going down. In a desperate measure he reduced speed, the slowing down would give him just that extra second for a closer scrutiny of the ground, it would also reduce the fuel consumption and give him a few more minutes of flying time. But he would also be exposed to much greater danger as at such low speed he would be a sitting duck to enemy aircraft if they came over, even to guns if they opened up from below. But he owed it to the men trapped below, he owed it to his own self as a soldier. And lo and behold! There it was, in the dark shadow cast by a thick tree trunk, a different shape, a squarish silhouette, the unmistakable outline of a tank.

'Found him,' shouted Jaggu over the radio and went into a tight climbing turn to launch the attack. 'Look in the shadows of tree trunks, the tanks are plastered with mud,' he told the No. 2 who was wildly zig-zagging behind the leader and scanning the sky for enemy aircraft. Soon Jaggu had the tank in his gun-sight and was firing off the rockets.

'You've hit him, Gold One. You've hit the bastard,' cried the controller from the ground. Elated, Jaggu lined up again and again for a different tree each time. Some dives were wasted as there was nothing under most trees, in others he often changed course midway when a tank was spotted to the right or the left. Both aircraft were whipping in and out of attacks, sometimes finding nothing, sometimes firing and missing the target, and only sometimes actually hitting the tanks.

'Gold One, check fuel', called the No. 2, cautioning the leader that the attacks had to be given up. As he set course for base, Jaggu calculated that out of the eight enemy tanks, he and his wing man had destroyed or damaged at least five. Our troops on the ground had got the necessary reprieve to consolidate their positions.

After that there was no stopping for Jaggu. He volunteered for the attack missions; he had become adept at spotting tanks and helped our forward troops in many a difficult battle. In thirteen days of the aerial war he flew exactly thirteen missions into Pakistan, each one full of risks, and each one a testimony to his prowess as a fighter pilot.

For his gallantry, professional skill and devotion to duty, Flight Lieutenant J.P. Saklani was awarded the Vir Chakra. He had come a long way from diffidence and fear to bravery and good leadership.

10

Daring and Devilry

The Base Commander walked out of his glass cabin in the Operations Room and stood ponderously in the middle of the hall before asking, 'Who was flying in the Sargodha area at 10:25 yesterday?'

The flurry of pilots returning from attack missions into Pakistan and others leaving on similar sorties came to a momentary halt. Sargodha was the strongest base of the Pakistan Air Force, its soul and heart. Anything to do with Sargodha had to be important.

'Who was ...?' the question was repeated in ominous tones. Obviously, it was some bad show, someone chickening out and turning away from battle, or not pressing the attack, or throwing away his bombs in the wilderness and running back home, or not rushing to help a fellow in trouble with the enemy. Such things did happen. So ... who ... who ... who ...?

Precisely at that moment Flight Lieutenant S.S. Malhotra walked into the Operations Room and everyone turned towards him as if the riddle had been solved, almost even before it had been posed fully. Malhotra (Mally) looked from face to face, unable to comprehend the accusing looks. He had encountered those looks on many occasions. But now it was war; they couldn't accuse him of breaking their god-damned rules for now the bloody rules did not apply anyhow. Now it was war. He could twist his aeroplane into a knot and they could do nothing about it. Now he could go all out and really hit ... hit ... and hit. This was what pilots like him were waiting for. Even the Base Commander couldn't hamstring him now. This was the time of the soldier, the fighting man, not the chair-borne General with his damned rules and dos and don'ts.

'Who was ...?' the question was repeated, this time to Mally directly. A moment's hesitation, a lowering of the eyes, an uncertainty of thought and reply....

* * * * *

Mally was a straight fellow, but otherwise it was difficult to define him. He could not really be disliked, yet he was not quite loveable. He could be fiercely loyal to a friend, a colleague, a superior, yet his devotion could often become an embarrassment. He never shirked work, in fact the problem usually was to stop him from doing too much. While flying he would take his wingman through the most difficult and risky manoeuvres ostensibly to prepare him for war regardless of whether he survived the peace in the first place. On the sports field he would lead the warming up exercises and often go on until everybody, himself included, almost collapsed with fatigue even before the game got going. Alas, he always slipped while always trying for the perfect outcome. Even those most sympathetic to him agreed that if there was one hole anywhere in the ground, poor Mally was most likely to fall into it.

The squadron had just moved into a new location in an area that had remained untended, unkempt, uncared for, overgrown with dried grass and crass vegetation. One morning the CO arrived in his jeep and stood before the flight office surveying the grounds. Then he walked up to the road saying, 'Can't live among these brambles!' And when he walked back from the road his mind was made up. 'Must have a garden here,' he announced to the full complement of squadron pilots gathered there.

'Yes, Sir, right time Sir, for the winter annuals,' said Mally. And that is how he got the task of creating a garden in that water-starved patch of earth where even cacti refused to grow. Perhaps Mally had not heard the old adage, 'Never Volunteer for Anything.' And even if he had heard it, men of his ilk were not hamstrung by advice that preached inaction. Mally was a warrior, which also being the emblem of his squadron, meant that he was concerned only with the outcome of battle, not its hows, whys and wherefores.

Now, there were two fighter squadrons on the station euphemistically known by their emblems as the Warriors and the Falcons, two teams of young, hot-blooded fighter pilots engaged in intense rivalry. If the Warriors put up parachutes over the dance floor for their party the Falcons would at the very least build a ship's deck for their party, if not actually bring over a ship into the plains of Punjab.

Now when Mally surveyed the entire station in preparation for his horticultural task he discovered that the Falcons were already well advanced in their gardening endeavours. They had a full-fledged nursery going with strong, young seedlings which seemed to be awaiting just a drop in temperature to burst forth with buds and blossoms. Well ... well ... well ...!

On one particular afternoon fifty men gathered outside the Warriors' flight office with fifty shovels, spades, buckets and Mally in the lead. The digging, clearing, re-digging went on until late in the full moon night. The evening meal was served on the spot and cigarettes were on Mally. About midnight half a dozen men went for a walk and when they returned they had enough seedlings to plant half a dozen gardens. Mally's garden was ready well before the next daybreak.

The operation had been planned with tactical care. The night planting was to be followed by a Sunday and a closed holiday on Monday precluding any immediate hue and cry. But Mally had no way of knowing that the two toddlers of the Falcon Commanding Officer (CO) might desire to be given an airing on Sunday afternoon. And what better place for them to run around than the unit grounds where Daddy could spend time fraternising with the airmen on guard duty. Along with them came the First Lady of the Falcons, who regarded the unit garden as her personal contribution to the grandeur of her husband's command. So, naturally, all hell broke loose on that Sunday afternoon. The Falcons CO reported a theft in his unit lines of perishable items and insisted that the other CO, of the Warriors, carry out a search in his area before the material evidence perished altogether. The Falcons called it an act of blatant moral turpitude—stealing—and demanded the strongest disciplinary action. Mally's detractors in his own unit immediately recalled his other crazy activities, how he had once picked up a fish knife from the dining table and brandished it at the Falcon boys who were making fun of his CO, and how he had blocked the exit door and kept brandishing the knife until full apologies had been rendered. Even how he had upbraided an air traffic controller over the radio with the whole wide world listening simply because the chap had been late in acknowledging Mally's radio call. And look at his flying discipline, they said, he did not merely bank the aeroplane while turning it, he damn well stood it on its side! And now stealing, that too from a lady as surely everyone knew that the wife of the Falcon CO had developed that garden with personal care and tended the seedlings like babies. Enough was enough, the chap had to be thrown out, at least grounded immediately in the interest of everyone's safety in the air and on the ground. As everyone knew, keeping a pilot on the ground was, of all the informal punishments available to the senior staff, the surest means of reining in the boisterous, youthful indiscipline among young officers.

Among the Warriors Jafa alone said nothing and even the CO finally turned towards him before pronouncing the judgement. Jafa was known to have a soft corner for Mally and had condoned his many escapades saying that even a bad coin could get you excellent return in certain circumstances. In any case, he was convinced that Mally would surely put up a spectacular show someday, even if it was to be his own funeral. No fighting unit had ever achieved glory without a few daredevils in its ranks. So he once again came to Mally's rescue by suggesting gently that he would personally speak with the First Lady of the Falcons and then see what had to be done.

The matter was as good as closed; where women were concerned Jafa got what Jafa wanted.

* * * * *

But ... who was flying in the Sargodha area at 10:25 yesterday ...? ... Who ... who?

* * * * *

Mally had been detailed for a photo reconnaissance mission over an airfield to the south of Sargodha. Such tasks are important for getting the latest information on enemy's dispositions and for the planning of subsequent attacks. Mally had planned the mission with care, he would make a feint run towards Sargodha and shortly before reaching it he would turn south towards the actual target and make the photo run. That way he would hide his real intention from the enemy radar and observers until almost the last minute. Mally was also given an escort for safety and success of the operation. However, soon after crossing the border the escort plane developed engine vibrations and Mally ordered him to return home. Now Mally was alone and reaching deeper into enemy land. In the absence of an escort plane he could have given up the mission without being faulted for it. But he also knew that he could not be faulted for carrying on alone either. In air warfare the outcome of such a decision is either total success or total death, and no faults are ever found after either.

Coming closer to Sargodha all Mally's faculties were on maximum alert. Any moment now the anti-aircraft guns would be opening up on him, even an odd missile getting launched against him. Every second he was getting closer to the heart of the enemy Air Force but as yet there was no sign of resistance. Strange, deceptive, suspicious ... and then ... a flash in the sky to his right, a speck, a passing shadow in the distance. Almost in a reflex action Mally whipped his aircraft into a turn to the right towards the shadow, the phantom that could be stalking him. Of course, there would be no firing from below because the bullets and the missiles could not differentiate between enemy and their own aircraft when they were flying close to each other. In an instant the two planes passed head on and both turned sharply again towards each other in a dogfight that surely must have been watched by the entire Pakistan Air Force at Sargodha. A dogfight is perhaps the supreme test of a pilot's flying ability, courage and ruthlessness and here it naturally became an India vs. Pakistan contest. A series of sharp, harsh manoeuvres, an orange flame emanating from the engine behind him as Mally used the afterburner on his engine and took out that little bit more out of his steed, and then he was inching forward behind the enemy aeroplane. A little more turning and twisting and he was in a position to press the trigger. The greatest moment of a fighter pilot's life had arrived, the culmination of years of rigorous training and, in plain language, the final realisation of the moulding of a killer's character. Mally pressed the trigger and a continuous stream of lethal 30-mm shells poured out towards the victim. The Mig-19 ahead of him let out a wisp of smoke, which got darker and thicker until it turned into a huge ball of fire. The deed done, Mally broke sharply away, shook his dazed head and turned homewards.

Ah ... the photo mission! He glanced at the fuel gauge. No, there wasn't enough fuel for that work, the dogfight had consumed a great deal of gasoline. In fact he could just about make it back to the home base and any kind of diversion would mean disaster. Of course, they would be at his throat for not bringing back an exposed film, they would criticise and deride him. But there was nothing he could do about it now. Possibly even during a photo run the camera could malfunction, he could press the button and the odd circuit might fail to carry the right message to the shutter or the motor or whatever. Anyway, he would have to wait and see and in the meantime keep his mouth shut.

*****

'Were you in the Sargodha area yesterday, Mally ...?' Now it was a straight, direct question at him and while he could avoid telling the truth he could never utter a lie.

Death Wasn't Painful

'Sir, I ... the photo recce ... I mean ....' More confusion and more stammering. 'The camera button, Sir ... I mean I don't know, Sir....'

But what was that? The Base Commander's expression had changed, there was a glint of mischief in his eyes and he was laughing. 'You stupid fool ... ha ... ha ... ha ... you damned idiot ...' and he seemed to go into a paroxysm of laughter. 'What are these photo runs for, my boy, except to find out where the enemy is hiding its aeroplanes and then go out and shoot them? And you ... you have done your bit without the damned photos ....'

The Base Commander sobered up eventually. He put on a serious face again and glared at an uncomprehending Mally. In his most officious tone he said, 'The President has been pleased to award you the Vir Chakra for your singular act of bravery deep behind enemy lines. Some wireless messages and telephone conversations of the PAF intercepted by our intelligence boys have confirmed that a PAF Mig-19 was shot down over Sargodha by an Indian SU-7 at 10:25 yesterday.'

Congratulations were on everyone's lips. The erstwhile detractors were in full-throated praise. Only Jafa said nothing, he walked away with an amused smile on his face.

11

Kala Sandhu

One rainy, lazy, humid day in the prison camp, time hung heavy. The Indian officers sat around listlessly whiling it away. Brother sat in one corner, lost in his private thoughts. Suddenly he bestirred himself, turned towards Jafa and said, 'Sir, how well did you know Kala Sandhu?'

'Why, Brother?' asked Jafa, taken by surprise.

'No, just tell me. I know that he was once in your squadron, but how well did you know him?' persisted Brother Bhargava.

'Well, I knew him since the days of our flying training in Secunderabad. After that we were together in 14 Squadron for many years. Again, we served together in 2 Squadron when the Gnats were introduced. That's knowing someone well enough, I suppose,' said Jafa.

'Were you at Pathankot on that day during the 1965 War when his father came to meet him?' asked Brother.

'No. But I know about that visit of his father. And all that happened before it and afterwards,' said Jafa

'Then you tell us what exactly happened that day ...'

'Yes, do tell us about Kala Sandhu,' added Kuru. 'We have heard so many versions of that incident. We want to hear the truth.'

Death Wasn't Painful

Jafa sat pensively for a while, wondering where to begin, how to put across the love, the pride and the expectations between an old man and his son. Then, in slow, measured tones he narrated the story they wanted to hear.

* * * * *

Squadron Leader Amarjit Singh Sandhu was unusual in many ways. The tribe of Sandhus boasts of tall, well-built, fair-skinned Jat Sikhs, aggressive in manner and fierce in battle. He had inherited most qualities of his clan but had lost out on his complexion, which was as dark as an Indian could be. Hence, the nickname. On the ground, he was never aggressive or deprecating in manner, but in the air his indomitability was well proven. He had come up from the ranks and while acquiring the polish and grace of the officer class had retained the loveable simplicity, humility and directness of the village lad. His family were farmers, again very simple village folk quite alien to the westernised culture of the Air Force in which their brightest son had gained a place. Secretly perhaps Kala Sandhu felt some embarrassment whenever his village folk visited him in an officers' mess, and it was after many years' of persuasion by his friends that he finally called his simple, rural wife and children to live with him among the English-speaking and ballroom-dancing families of the Air Force fraternity. But again, with rustic sensibility and simple good-heartedness Kala Sandhu's family broke all the artificial barriers of language and anglicised social etiquette, and quickly became a part of the larger family that was the fighter squadron.

Whenever Kala Sandhu was posted in Punjab, a frequent visitor to his house was his old father. Dressed in impeccable white clothes, turban, shirt, *lungi* and a white walking stick in his hand, he proudly walked down to his son's house from the nearest bus station. Not for him the pickup in a military transport or a pillion ride on his son's motorbike, only the sturdy legs and the grace of a tall, erect, white-bearded man walking down with a good walking stick in his hand. He stayed for only a couple of hours during each visit, observed everything minutely, upbraided his son for any lapses in the running of the household or the upbringing of the children and left without ever displaying softness or emotion of any kind. The father and the son both understood each other perfectly. While there was abundant respect, care and concern from the younger Sandhu, there was immense pride and satisfaction in the old man's heart over the achievements of his son, even though he was convinced that it was his own hard mien that had kept his progeny disciplined and on the straight and narrow path of progress with honour. He was not going to let up for there was much to achieve yet.

Kala Sandhu was an outstanding fighter pilot. He had begun his flying career with the renowned Spitfire of Second World War fame, then moved into the jet age with the Vampire fighter and finally graduated to the coveted, dreaded Gnat, the dream of a fighter pilot in those days. He was in fine fettle and form when the war with Pakistan broke out. As expected, Pakistan's main thrust came in an area which was vital for the defence of the rail and road links of India's northern state of Jammu & Kashmir. The Pakistan Air Force launched practically its entire fleet of sabres against the Indian Army and the Air Force, subjecting the forward airfields to an almost hourly attack. Faced with this situation, the Indian Air Force moved half a dozen Gnats to Pathankot to beat back the Pakistani Sabres.

Early next morning, four Gnats were airborne, waiting to be called up to deal with the enemy aeroplanes as soon as they showed up. In a little while the army asked for help, the Sabres were attacking our forward troops on the ground. The Gnats swiftly descended in that direction and the battle was joined in a series of sharp turns, dives, pull-ups, spirals with each pilot attempting to get behind an enemy aeroplane in a shooting position.

These manoeuvres continued in their fullest intensity for a while till one Gnat pilot found himself closing in upon his prey from the right quarter. The enemy was well placed in his gun-sight. He slid his index finger on to the trigger but then decided to close in a little more before squeezing it. And just then, through a corner of his eye he saw another Gnat, one of his companions, in pursuit of the same

Sabre from the left. Being slightly ahead, the Gnat on the left did not notice the one on the right, and even as the latter was reaching the ideal position for opening fire, the other had already started firing. The one on the left fired a long burst, saw the enemy aircraft being hit and beginning to spew smoke. His job done, he pulled up and away from the quarry. Just at that moment the Gnat on the right, finding himself in the perfect position for firing, also pressed the trigger on his control stick. The 30-mm cannons from his aircraft too poured out innumerable rounds of lethal ammunition in the direction of the Sabre which almost instantly was seen emitting thick smoke that changed into a huge flame. His job done, he too turned away sharply and headed homewards. The cameras fitted in the Gnats had recorded the evidence, the first Gnat's camera showing the Sabre with a thin stream of smoke indicating a definite and, ultimately, lethal hit, the second Gnat's camera showing the same Sabre emitting thick smoke changing into a huge ball of fire.

'I have shot one Sabre,' announced the pilot of the second Gnat gleefully to the air traffic controller at the home base.

'I too have shot one enemy aircraft,' announced Kala Sandhu, the pilot of the first Gnat that had fired on the Sabre.

Little did anyone know that they were talking of the one and the same Sabre. In a further twist of fate the second Gnat landed back first and was personally received by the Station Commander who had been sitting in the control tower waiting to hear some such news and who did not wait long enough to hear the radio call made by Kala Sandhu. So, as our hero of the second Gnat landed, taxied back into the dispersal area, switched off the engine and stood up in the cockpit, the flag car came to a screeching halt beside him. The Commander leapt out of the car and looked questioningly at him.

'I got one, Sir. I shot him,' shouted the pilot exultantly. 'It blew up before my eyes.'

'Are you sure?' asked the Commander, who wanted to be doubly sure himself. This was too important a matter. 'Of course,' assured the pilot.

'A Sabre?' asked the Boss, hoping that it could be a Starfighter, the F-104, which would have lent greater glamour to the achievement.

'Yes, Sir. One Sabre, F-86.'

The Commander shot back into his car and told the driver to take him to the Operations Room, fast. Once there, he lunged for the hotline and immediately got on to his superior in far away New Delhi.

'We have shot one Sabre in air combat,' he announced proudly. He also gave the name of the pilot, with whom he had just spoken, as the one who had done the deed.

A Commander in disgrace for having got a number of his aeroplanes shot up on the ground by the enemy in the previous days, and extremely anxious to redeem his pride and prestige, did not wait for corroborating evidence such as the films or the testimony of other pilots. Even the radio calls by two pilots, each declaring a 'kill', had not registered upon his mind which was simply looking for one quick success. And in faraway Delhi, the higher commanders and planners, starved of any good news from the battle fronts and having to explain away the awesome losses inflicted by the enemy Air Force with impunity in the last few days, wasted not a minute in letting the media know of this singular achievement. Within minutes the news was on the air waves, on radios in millions of homes, on transistors in the farmers' fields. The second attacker became an instant national hero, his name in every news broadcast, his photograph on every newspaper's front page.

Kala Sandhu withdrew into himself, unable to comprehend how he had got totally sidelined. Yes, the other chap had definitely fired upon that Sabre, but it had already been shot by him. The film taken by the camera in his aeroplane clearly showed the stream of smoke emanating from the Sabre, a sure sign of a lethal hit. Even the other pilot admitted having seen it. The Squadron pilots ran the two films again and again and came to their own conclusions. Whispers began to circulate regarding the authenticity of the real claimant to glory. A sense of unfairness, even injustice, began to pervade the atmosphere, snide remarks and scathing comments flew fast and loose. The reports floated upwards and the commanders began to worry about the effect this might have on aircrew morale. The leader of the Gnat detachment was then asked to sort this out with the pilots. He took Kala Sandhu aside and spoke with him at length.

'You and I both know the truth,' he began. 'The kill was rightfully yours even though it cannot be denied that the Sabre was also fired upon by the other pilot as well, and quite accurately too. But do you realise what has happened?'

Sandhu maintained a stoic silence. The detachment leader continued, 'He landed back before you did. He announced the outcome of the battle as he perceived it. Possibly, in his excitement, he recollected nothing other than his own firing and the blowing up of the Sabre. You understand what I am trying to tell you?'

'Yes, Sir,' said Sandhu dejectedly. 'Still...'

'But now I come to the other factors which perhaps contributed more to the compounding of an error.' He paused to collect his thoughts and continued, 'Here was the Air Force, and the whole nation, waiting to hear of one success, one achievement in the air battle after the debacles of the preceding days. And the shooting down of the first Sabre was that success, that achievement. Who shot it—that was incidental really, as it always is. The individual glory, the lionising of a soldier, the awards, the publicity, these are all incidental to the basic achievement which the nation wants first and foremost and without any frills in the first instance. And therefore this information, this news, had to be conveyed to the nation urgently, without a moment's delay. The incidental part, the man who did it, was not important at that stage, and that's how, that's where the error got made.'

'Where does that leave me, Sir?' Sandhu said with a wistful smile.

'Exactly where you are now, where you were yesterday or the day before! Rightly or wrongly, one name has been given out for this deed. The whole country, the whole world, now associates this happening with that one name, and that one only. The Air Force or the nation cannot retract what has been put out with so much fanfare.'

'So someone else walks away with the credit that should have been mine?'

'Yes. In the interest of the Air Force and the country, it has to be left at that. All I ask of you is, Be A Sport! The war has just begun. You are in the forefront of fighting. Each day, several times a day, you will have a chance to do it again. A person of your grit and guts and mastery over battle manoeuvres will do it again. You cannot be stopped.'

And so on and so forth! Kala Sandhu accepted the need to make a personal sacrifice and not rake up the issue. After that he never spoke of this matter though the others who were part of that action and knew the truth intimately and explicitly never tired of talking about it. Kala Sandhu gained in respect and stature what he had lost in glory. The young pilots and the airmen on the station pointed him out to each other with reverence. But, for this, there were other reasons too.

The elder Sandhu had heard of the outbreak of the war during the evening gathering at the village *chaupal*. His first instinct was to immediately proceed to Ambala where his son was posted and personally, and quietly, invoke the *Wahe Guru*'s blessings upon his son. But that could also be seen as emotional weakness at a crucial time. So he sent a distant nephew to get news of his son. He learnt that the son had been sent to a forward airfield where fierce battles were raging between the opposing forces. After that he tied himself down to the transistor radio and was constantly changing channels to hear news broadcasts from anywhere and everywhere. He heard claims being made of great successes by both sides. He heard names of individuals who had shown great bravery and courage in battles. He heard with great attention the names of the gallantry award winners, the ones who were awarded one of the three *Chakra*s for bravery beyond the call of duty. He also heard the names of those gallant warriors who had sacrificed their lives in the defence of the motherland. Each day new names were coming up on the radio. The old man was becoming edgy in expectation of hearing his son's name too, in the one or the other context, during such announcements.

'Where is your son, *Bhai*?' asked Banta Singh one evening at the *chaupal* where the villagers gathered to exchange the news of the day.

'He is at the front, fighting. Where else?' said the old man. 'Why do you ask?'

'Nothing, really. Just wondered if he was sitting out in the rear area,' commented Banta.

They expected the old man to make a retort, but he said nothing. None of the people gathered there that evening spoke either. The Sandhus were proud people. They had a son who was a senior officer in the Air Force, whereas others in the village could only show other rankers in their families. This was their chance to pull down the haughty old man a notch or two. They kept making such seemingly innocent enquiries every time they ran into him. The old man silently heard the aspersions they were casting upon the honour of his son and himself, and daily he grew more tense as he listened to the names of the heroes and the martyrs on the radio.

The next evening again the village folk gathered together and listened to the news broadcasts. At the end of it Banta addressed the old man, saying, 'We haven't heard your son's name on the radio yet.'

'The radio gives out names of brave people only, those who fight courageously, whether they live or die,' commented Natha Singh in a scathingly sarcastic tone.

The old man heard and understood. He did not speak. He picked up his stick, stood up, and walked away. He went to his house, spoke to his wife briefly, took out some cash from a tin box and walked out again. He went to the bus station and took the first bus departing in the general direction of the air base where his son was placed at that time. He changed buses twice and at dawn he stood before the Guard Room of the air base, at Pathankot.

'What do you want, Baba? Why are you standing here?' asked the Air Force policeman on duty there.

'I have come to see my son. He came here from Ambala a few days ago,' said the old man.

'Who is your son, Baba? Please give me his particulars,' demanded the police corporal.

The old man gave his son's name and added that his son was a very senior officer and a Gnat pilot who had been called there to deal with the Pakistani Sabres.

'Okay, Okay, Baba!' said the policeman who had heard tall tales from many a relation before this. 'You know there is a war going on? Your son, the great fighter pilot, we all know about him of course, is busy. Very busy. He is at this very moment flying in the air, looking for Pakistani airplanes to shoot them down. We can't disturb him. So, Baba, let him do his work. You go home, Baba. We will tell him that you had come. Any message? Anything else that we can do for you?'

'You don't understand!' said the old man gently but firmly. 'I told you that I have come to meet him. I need to speak with him even if for just a couple of minutes. If he is busy I shall wait. I shall leave only after I have seen him.'

The police corporal turned back to consult his colleagues. They decided that the matter involved an officer and his father and so at the very least the unit adjutant should be informed. That they did forthwith.

'What the hell!' exclaimed Kala Sandhu when he received the information.

As the other pilots looked at him askance, he said, 'My old man! Why can't he leave me alone!'

'What's happened now? What's the matter with your old man?' asked a colleague.

'He is at the Guard Room, wanting to see me.'

'If he has come all this distance, it has to be something important,' opined the other officer. 'You better go and see what this is all about.'

Death Wasn't Painful

Sandhu stood there debating in his mind whether he should go to meet the old man at all, a father who understood nothing of military protocol and cared even less, a father who was obviously worried about his son's well-being but would take great pains to hide it. After all, there were other sons of other fathers who were possibly facing greater risks. But the dread that his father might create a great deal of fuss persuaded him to make the trip. The old man was seated in a chair when he reached the Guard Room. The two quickly exchanged formal greetings. The old man at once opened the dialogue.

'I have been hearing news of the war on the radio, just like the others have been doing in the village. I have come to see if you are also taking part.'

'What else would I be doing at this forward air base?' asked the son, incredulously. 'Is that all you have come here for?'

The son had raised his voice while speaking and that attracted the attention of a dozen airmen and civilians who heard the ensuing dialogue between the father and the son with astonishment.

'Yes,' said the old man. 'I came for that, and a little more. You see, in the village everyone also listens to the names of those who get the *Chakras Shakras*.'

'So ...?' asked Sandhu.

'They listen very attentively to all the news about the war, as do I, waiting and wanting to hear some familiar name.'

'How many people in the forces do you know? And whose name are you wanting to hear?' said Sandhu in gentle exasperation. But some doubt about his father's intention was beginning to sprout in the back of his mind.

'The villagers only know you,' said the elder, simply.

'I see,' said the son sombrely. That simple statement, that yearning of the father to see his son among the brave, the gallantry award winners, went through him like a knife. He felt a physical pain at the thought that he had already achieved it but was unable to show it, that it had to remain unrecognised, unacknowledged, that some other parent had usurped the pride that should have been his father's. He fought back the urge to tell the old man how he had been deprived of the credit that should have come to him, that, in the larger, vaguer, interest of the service and the country, he could not openly claim it.

Sandhu put on a stern face and said, 'It's not something that I can go and get at will. It will come only when I am able to accomplish something great in battle. It's not in my hands; I am doing my best.'

'But then you will have to do more than that,' said the old man. 'You see, people like Natha Singh go around voicing doubts whether you are at all taking part in the fighting or whether you are hiding somewhere.'

'I can't be bothered about fellows like that coward Natha,' said Sandhu angrily. 'You know what I am doing and that should be enough for you. Go back to the village now and stay there. I shall come and see you after the war.'

'That's the problem, son. I cannot go back to the village. In fact, I have decided not to return to the village like this. You see, they taunt me about you. They say, 'Your son's name should either be among the Vir Chakra winners, or, among the martyrs, if he is fighting on the front. It ought to be in the one or the other list if he is active in the war.'

'You listen to such nonsense?' asked Sandhu with some heat. 'And you've come to bother me with this crap without realising that I am so busy, so occupied, so laden with responsibilities?'

'The village people keep saying such things, son,' said the old man pensively. 'And I too have been thinking. After all, there are only two things that bring honour to a soldier in the service of his country—either a great triumph in attack, or great martyrdom in defence. So the village folk are not entirely wrong, my son.'

Sandhu understood for the first time in this encounter what his father had been leading to. The realisation stunned him, left him speechless and stirred to the core of his being. The picture of the great Guru Govind, flashed across his mind and the exhortation he had made to his sons during a crucial battle.

'What ... What do you want of me?' he blurted out.

'Son,' said the old man, with feeling, with affection, with eternal love. 'Get a Vir Chakra. I want to walk in the village with my head up. And, my son, even if you attain martyrdom, I shall still be able to walk in the village with pride. God Bless You, my son.'

Eyes moist with unshed tears, hand shaking in mild tremors over the cane, the legs a bit wobbly, the old man placed a hand on his son's head, turned and walked away, out of the Guard Room, out on to the road, without once turning back.

Sandhu stood rooted to the spot. He made no attempt to turn towards the old man or walk after him. The flurry and movements of others in the room brought him out of the reverie. The men were running after his father. He would learn later that they accompanied the old man to the bus station, arranged a comfortable seat for him for the return journey, piled him with fruits and sweets, touched his feet and bade him an emotion-charged farewell. They had seen, they had heard the father and the son in the Guard Room. They knew that they were unlikely to see or hear such heroes ever again. In simple, straightforward terms, the father had demanded from his son supreme valour, or the other, supreme sacrifice, in the service of the nation, either of which shall get talked in the countryside from generation to generation, and adorn the family with glory.

Kala Sandhu walked out of the Guard Room immersed in deep thought. He returned to the crew room and sat by himself for a long while, evading polite enquiries about his father's visit. Whenever he was called up for an operational sortie he went out with a different kind of determination. He took chances, he threw caution to the winds. On the third day after the old man's visit a fierce battle raged on the ground for the control of a vital area. The Air Forces of the two sides were launched against the ground troops as well as against each other. Sandhu flew sortie after sortie and during one encounter chased the enemy airplanes deep into their own territory and, there, surrounded by four foes, he shot two of them, one destroyed totally, the second damaged. The announcement of the award of Vir Chakra was heard on the radio by his father. It was heard by all the village folk. When the old man next walked up to the village *chaupal*, Natha Singh was the first to greet him with respect.

Not much later Kala Sandhu died a martyr's death.

Dressed in a spotless white turban, white shirt and white *lungi*, the old man walked through the village once again, eyes a bit moist, legs a bit wobbly, hand shaking a bit over the cane, but the head held high, the gaze fixed in the distance, the countenance bewildered at the ways of the *Wahe Guru*. He was going to catch the bus to attend to the last rites of his son.

The entire village walked behind him.

12

The Times, They Were Bad

In May the war was six months in the past. Zulfiqar Ali Bhutto was firmly ensconced in the seat of power in Pakistan. That nation now seemed embarked upon introspection and debate on what had led to the break-up of the country. In similar mood a larger number of Pakistani officers began visiting the Indian prisoners incarcerated at a Pakistan Air Force facility in Rawalpindi. They discussed the recent conflict, the earlier wars, the partition of the sub-continent, and the yet deeper malaise of Hindu-Muslim disharmony. It was as though unhinged in their moorings by the outcome of the war they were seeking some explanation, some justification, some re-affirmation of the decisions and deeds of their fathers and the causes of so much trauma in their lives.

Kamy listened to the views of both Pakistani and Indian officers but seldom spoke. He was a man of the present, the past had only skeletons that did nobody any good. After listening to one such long discussion, he said in exasperation, 'why do these chaps bring up the Partition and the riots again and again? That was done and over with twenty-five years ago. Why don't they think of what needs to be done now, today?'

'I think they are a bit lost,' said Kuru with unusual perspicacity. 'They asked for the Partition, for separation from the mother country. They expected to be better off than us, stronger and more well-knit with the cementing force of Islam. But none of this happened. On the other hand, everything seems to be falling apart.'

'Yes, but why blame us for it?' asked Dilip. 'If you've noticed, they are always trying to find faults with us, I mean with India, with Hindus. We haven't done too well ourselves but it seems that we have done better than them. Anyway, even Bangladesh was of their own creation. Only if they knew how hopelessly incapable we are of creating problems for others ...' Dilip laughed at his own humour.

'Or ... solving our own,' added Jafa.

As the laughter died down there was a sound of footsteps outside. Three Pakistanis in civilian clothes were walking up to Cell No. 5, the largest in size where the prisoners usually sat together in daytime and where Jafa alone was locked up during the night. The police corporal on duty ushered them in.

'Good Morning!' said the one in the lead. 'I am Ashraf, Wing Commander Ashraf.'

'My colleagues,' he said, introducing the other two, a tall one and a short one.

The Indian officers had already risen from their seats. Hearty Good Mornings were exchanged. Extra chairs were brought in by a guard. The Pakistani visitors were invited to take their seats first and made welcome with smiles and cheerful noises. The air was light with the expectation of a pleasant and interesting morning to be spent in conversation, in banter, in polite digs, in sexy anecdotes. Also in the happy anticipation of a couple of rounds of tea that were always provided by the establishment during such visits, possibly paid for by the guests themselves, and certainly the fine English cigarettes that the Pakistani officers offered around generously.

After the pleasantries were over, Dilip asked, 'Are you all flyers?'

'No,' replied Ashraf. 'I am an education officer. These, my companions, are in the engineering branches of our Air Force.'

'Ah! The intellectual types,' remarked Garry.

'In the Air Force the pilots got recruited at very early ages, soon after finishing school. They were regarded as cerebral lightweights and dandy playboys by the officers in the other branches who came with higher academic qualifications. There was always a pleasant banter going on between the so-called intellectual types and the playboy types.'

'I don't know about that,' said Ashraf, making light of Garry's comment. 'But we are never able to drill any sense in the likes of you.'

'Anyone from that elephantine state of yours—Uttar Pradesh—here?' asked Ashraf, looking around and changing track.

'Yes, of course, Jafa Saheb is from there,' said Brother.

'I too am from there,' piped up Garry the Sikh. 'Not much to be proud of, but there it is,' he added smilingly, taking a dig at Jafa.

Garry was voicing the unconcealed, over-expressed opinion of the Punjabi settler who regarded the U.P. *bhaiya*s as lazy, lethargic layabouts, tolerable as farm labour, provided that you could dope them with a bit of opium and drive them like slaves round the clock.

'Don't say that,' exclaimed Ashraf. 'That was my home province too!'

'Really?' exclaimed Brother in delighted surprise.

'I too am from there,' piped up the short one. 'Bareilly, that's where my family came from. Ashraf *Saheb* hails from Moradabad.' Then turning to Garry he asked, 'Your family settled there after Partition?'

'My father was in Amritsar. But the rest of the family moved from Lahore and from this area, Rawalpindi,' said Garry. 'And now we live not far from Moradabad, near Rampur in fact, in the Terai.'

'You remember your days back in India?' Brother asked Ashraf. 'And how do you find it here?'

'Yes, I remember that place and those days very well.' Ashraf's voice dropped a few decibels. It was not the tone of nostalgia alone, it contained a hint of hurt, of anger.

'Ashraf *bhai* lost three members of his family coming here,' said the short one. 'We too lost some people. I was much younger though at the time.'

The Times, They Were Bad

'Very sorry to hear that,' sympathised Bunny Coelho. 'In fact, living in the South, in the depths of Tamil Nadu, Karnataka, we don't even come to know, much less get shaken up with, what goes on in the North. You chaps must have suffered a lot.'

'Suffered?' said Ashraf with sudden vehemence. 'Those were days of sheer terror, of madness, of blood and gore, of pieces of human flesh and limbs and skeletons, of the cries of women and children. All the way from Sirhind right up to Wagah, after which we entered this country and took the first breaths in safety and deliverance after seven days of hell in your country.'

The short one took up the narration. 'All trains bringing us Muslims towards Pakistan were set upon by Sikh mobs in Punjab, not once, but several times, again and again. They went on a killing spree, sparing not a child, not an old man, just sometimes taking away the young women. Only those mistaken for the dead made it to Pakistan.'

'You ask what I remember of those days?' said Ashraf. 'I remember the send-off of blood and loot given to us by your people.' Ashraf was beginning to perspire with the pain and anguish of recall as he continued, 'And you ask how I find it here? I'll tell you. I arrived here ragged, beaten, broken, with a torn shirt on my back. And see what I have today...a coveted job, a house, a car and total security. I don't have to live in fear. This is my home, my country. It has given me so much.'

'But who asked you to set out for Pakistan in the first place? Who asked you to leave your home and hearth in Moradabad?' asked Kamy sternly.

'How could we live there, surrounded by Hindus on all sides?' countered the short one. 'It was better to take a risk once rather than get beaten up every day.'

'And what about the relatives, the cousins and uncles and the rest of the Muslim brotherhood whom you left behind? Those who chose to stay back in the land of their birth? Any news you have of them, of how they are faring in Hindu India?' persisted Kamy.

'They are living in terrible conditions, we hear. No jobs for them, no food, the women being made to wear *bindi*s on their forehead...,' said the short one.

'Nonsense,' admonished Kamy. 'For God's sake do not repeat the propaganda that has already caused so much bloodshed. Look at the statistics, the population figures. At the time of Partition the non-Muslims formed about twenty percent of your population, mainly the Hindus among them. Today they are under six percent, even less. And in India the Muslim population has increased from about ten percent at the time of Partition to about twelve percent today. Who is doing better, where? The minorities in Pakistan or the Muslims in India?'

Jafa looked in amazement at Kamy reeling off such figures. He didn't know how accurate the percentages were, but there had to be some substance in them as they succeeded in stopping the Pakistani onslaught.

'You said you arrived here with a torn shirt on your back. How do you think the Hindus and the Sikhs who were driven out of West Pakistan arrived in India? In suits and neckties?' This came from Garry many of whose extended family members had to flee from Pakistan during the turmoil of Partition, and the survivors had been direct witnesses to the holocaust.

Jafa realised that the discussion had taken off on an issue which touched raw nerves on both sides. Even after twenty-five years the Partition of the country excited such ferocity of emotions as if it had occurred just last week or the last month or the last year. Those who created Pakistan and migrated to the new country felt that they had been driven by the Hindus to make that choice. The Hindus in India felt that a handful of Muslims in the heart of the country had stabbed them in the back and walked away, like errant, grasping children, with part of the ancestral property. Yet, the discussion needed to be controlled and guided.

'Let's not get excited about it,' said Jafa to Garry and to all others. 'The Partition uprooted ten million people and killed one million in communal rioting. It left very traumatic, very sad memories for people like Ashraf *Saheb* here and Garry on our side. But it would be incorrect to say that atrocities were perpetrated by one side only, or that only one side suffered. Don't you think that our fathers, I mean people in that generation, just went berserk and caused such communal frenzy and havoc that it continues to affect our lives even today? Even to the extent of the three wars that we have fought and the fact that we are sitting in your prison today?'

As Ashraf and his companions pondered over these thoughts Harry took out a pack of K-2 cigarettes, the cheapest in Pakistan and the staple smoke of the prisoners and offered them to the guests. They in turn pulled out the finer English cigarettes and offered them in a reciprocal gesture. Harry's day was made.

'Our fathers had no choice really,' said the short one, resuming the discussion. 'We couldn't have survived with dignity in Hindu-dominated India. We would have been smothered, forced to forsake our culture, our way of life, even our religion.'

'Look, there are fifty Muslim members in our Parliament,' retorted Brother Bhargava. 'Of course, you would remember Dr. Zakir Hussain, the former President of India. Also there are any number of Muslim ministers in the Indian states. Brigadier Usman and Abdul Hamid are our heroes. In India the Muslims participate and proliferate equally. It is not like your Pakistan where power must remain in the hands of Punjabi Sunnis alone. The others must conform or get smothered.'

'Then how do you explain the hatred and the violence that we were subjected to?' asked the short one.

Garry coughed gently to draw attention. The others left the field to him. 'Incidentally several of my relatives migrated from this very area, Rawalpindi, from a village which is perhaps a few miles from where we are sitting. I have heard the details of their travails from elders in the family. And I can tell you that the hatred and violence they were subjected to and the suicidal acts they had to inflict upon themselves are beyond imagination too.' Garry's eyes were red and beads of perspiration shone on his forehead as he recalled the unspeakable, indescribable cruelty and barbarity meted out to his family members.

'What suicidal acts?' asked the short one.

Garry spoke with a voice flat and heavy with emotion. 'About thirty members of this part of my family, a grand uncle, sons, wives, daughters, children, were surrounded by a huge mob of Muslims. They were inside their large house. The end seemed imminent. The women begged the men to kill them with their own hands. They preferred to die at the hands of their own men than be taken away by alien men to be dishonoured, converted to Islam, used mercilessly while young, and thrown away later. My grand-uncle understood the fears of the women folk and took the desperate decision. He unsheathed his sword and cut off the neck of his own wife. The other males fell similarly upon their wives and daughters. After this suicidal slaughter they went out and died fighting the attackers. Only one male member, a child survived. He lives near Delhi, alone, with his memories.' Garry wiped the tears that had now welled up in his eyes.

'We did hear of such occurrences but this is the first time I've heard it from someone who was so close to it and it is very saddening indeed,' said Ashraf nobly. 'But perhaps our women feared equally being taken away by Hindu mobs. Take the Garhmukteswar riots. The sight of the women was heart rending, breasts cut off, their private parts spiked with swords and spears. And this with those that could not be taken away immediately. I have seen with my own eyes the young women being pounced upon and dragged away, their cries haunt me even today. I don't know how many of our women are still there, and in what condition...'

Kamy bestirred himself, rather his memory cells, once again. 'About women on both sides,' he began. 'The Viceroy's office had set up a committee to search for and to reclaim the abducted women from both sides. About fifteen thousand such Muslim women were discovered in India of whom about twelve thousand were returned to their families in Pakistan and in India. On the other hand, in Pakistan only one-tenth of this figure, just about fifteen hundred such Hindu women were identified. Out of these only about two hundred were repatriated. The Pakistani officials claimed that the rest refused to leave their new-found homes. You can interpret that as you like...'

Jafa again looked at Kamy in amazement. Another set of facts and figures, delivered with aplomb and confidence, and going unchallenged. Or perhaps everyone knew that though the numbers might not be precise, the message was irrefutable. Yet, something about the exchange of women stirred a thought, a string of memories in Jafa's mind. The abduction and kidnapping of young women was an ancient preoccupation in these lands, the strong preying upon the weak, taking away their most prized possessions—beautiful young women. But when this happened between Muslims and Hindus there was a greater sense of defilement and dishonour. Both fought hard over their women, yet both reacted differently when it came to reclamation.

'There may be some substance, Kamy, in the Hindu women opting to stay back with their Muslim masters,' said Jafa. 'Mostly, Kamy, the Muslims take back their women. The Hindus don't.'

'That is simply to snatch them back from the Hindus. But what they do with them afterwards, well, there are gruesome stories...' Kamy retorted angrily.

The three Muslim officers turned towards Jafa, expecting to hear a more balanced view on their social mores.

'No, Sir,' said Jafa. 'To us Hindus, a woman who cohabits with or without consent, with an outcaste, even worse, with a Muslim, becomes a *patita*, a fallen woman. There is no longer a place for her within the family, within the class and caste; she gets relegated to the fringes and is forced to slowly, but surely, vanish from the scene. On the other hand, the Muslims take back their women with greater grace. A reclaimed girl is usually fixed up with a groom in a distant place to shield her from her past and to give her a fresh chance. They may be harsh with her, but she is not abandoned.'

'That's interesting,' said Ashraf with a smile. 'You are not influenced by the propaganda in your country about the plight of

Muslim women? About how they are exploited sexually, about the four wives and the *talaaq*?'

Dilip was not to be left behind on a subject close to his heart. 'Well, for that matter, no people, nowhere, can boast of too good a record in this matter. We Hindus pat ourselves on the back a great deal about the status of women, but have you noticed amongst us the plight of a spinster or a barren female, a widow or a divorcee, or one who cannot produce a male heir? And those who are powerful in money and in muscle, do they ever confine themselves to a single woman?'

Dilip grinned mischievously at Kamy and said, 'Only that these people do legally what we do surreptitiously.' The grin broadened as he continued, 'And let's keep on doing it, I say! And as regards the difference between men and women—*Vive la* difference, say the French! Long live the weak female, say I'. And he burst into a loud guffaw.

As the laughter died down Jafa said, 'Ashraf *Saheb*, getting back to the original topic, you people, I mean your ancestors in U.P. and Bihar wanted and created Pakistan. Today, after the separation of East Pakistan, would you say that the creation of Pakistan was the right decision, the right step?'

'What makes you say that the people of U.P. and Bihar created Pakistan?' retorted the short one. 'All Muslims everywhere wanted Pakistan and we all together made it.'

Jafa explained, 'What I meant was in the sense of the intellectual and emotional thrust for the idea. It was the highly educated Muslims, the writers, the scribes, the thinking bureaucrats, the lawyers and the landed gentry in the heart of the country who provided that thrust. Pakistan was in that sense created by people like you, by the so-called *Mohajirs* from U.P. and Bihar, who conceptualized the two-nation theory and disseminated it among the masses, who actually ran Jinnah's campaign from behind the scenes. You people also suffered, got uprooted, and are perhaps a bit disillusioned today. But it was your doing, not of the Pathan, the Baluch, the Sindhi, or even the Punjabi. They only provided the muscle, the gun fodder, as they have been doing from times beyond recall.'

Ashraf deliberated over this. He said slowly, 'I will not dispute this entirely. The Muslims in U.P. and Bihar were perhaps more perceptive and more communicative. The intellectual, even the religious, thrust undoubtedly came from us. But do you think that only the Muslims created Pakistan? I would say that the Hindus were equally responsible for it. Even more so, for, we feel that you Hindus forced us to seek Pakistan.'

'This is a strange notion,' observed Dilip. 'There was the Mahatma going on fasts to coerce Hindus and Muslims into giving up violence, into living together in freedom as they were doing during the struggle. And there was Jinnah, giving the call for direct action, meaning violence and bloodshed, to show that Hindus and Muslims could never live together.'

The short one rejoined, 'But Gandhi, however great, was quite in the minority. Hindus in general were not tolerant of us. Moreover, you are talking of incidents during the culminating phases only. You do not realize that Pakistan was not made in ten days or ten years. It was not created between the rout of the Muslim League during the 1937 elections and the massive support it got just nine years later in 1946.'

'It was also not created during the period between the first resolution demanding Pakistan in 1940 and its achievement in 1947,' he emphasised after a pause.

The short one left it at just that. The Indian prisoners looked at the Pakistani officers and at each other as if to say that there was something amiss, the argument was not complete.

Ashraf took it upon himself to elaborate the idea. 'You see, when we talk of Pakistan we go back to just the last ten or twelve years of British rule, and for Partition we think of only the 14–15 August 1947. At best we think of the period of a few months before and a few months after the event when communal rioting was at its worst. But when did Partition really begin, when did it germinate in our minds, in our conscious thoughts? And, I ask, when did it finally occur, when was it consummated, when did it end? Or, is it still continuing? Like an ever-swelling river of mistrust, fear and hatred which keeps pushing further and further apart its two banks! I therefore also ask—Has the Partition ended?'

Ashraf's well-modulated voice delivering the well-formed argument cast a spell on all listeners. There was silence in the room, everyone silently absorbing the thought. Jafa looked at Ashraf with a new-found respect. Here was a person from his own area, one who had breathed the same air, lolled about in the same mud, absorbed similar joys, hurts and perceptions, then similarly subjected to a sudden erosion of trust, of bonhomie, of mutual concern, and then having to withdraw within a community, within a religious entity, bewildered at first and then washed down and away rapidly in a tide of jingoism and bigotry, only to be caught later, firmly and irrevocably, in separate, sectarian, communal nets. It was as if a massive wave had washed over the sub-continent and, subsiding, had taken away the top soil, the veneer of tolerance and good neighbourliness, of civilised behaviour and the respect for life and property, exposing the insecurities, the mistrusts, the religious mindsets, the perceived injustices of a thousand years which had remained embedded deeply and firmly in the sub-cutaneous consciousness. Ashraf had provided a glimpse of it from the other side of the fence.

'Please go on, Ashraf *Saheb*,' said Jafa earnestly. 'You will have to carry this idea forward.'

'You see, gentlemen, the Partition has been described by some as the division of hearts. Personally, I think that's exactly what it was. In matters of the heart the minutest perceptions of disregard, disrespect, humiliation can become great impediments in the flow of good blood among peoples. We discuss such things among ourselves and we can give you scores of instances.'

'Let's hear some,' said Brother.

'All right,' intervened the short one. 'Take the matter of social intermingling. Whenever we visited a Hindu household during festivals or weddings we were given excellent food and generous helpings. But do you know how we were served? We were served in dishes that had been stored in some untouchable corner of the house specifically reserved for the Muslims and brought out and placed before us by some untouchable minion. We knew that the dishes would again go back to the same untouchable corner until the next such occasion. And the higher caste hosts poured food into those dishes from a good height, afraid that the serving spoons, even their bodies, might get polluted by a closer contact.'

The short one resumed after a pause, 'I tell you...the things that we hear from our elders. In some houses the Muslim guests were even asked to bring out the contaminated crockery themselves and put it back after use. The hosts apologized and blamed the social and family customs for it. And the funny part was that our fathers complied with such requests, perhaps out of the desire not to spoil someone else's festivities.'

'The very same Hindus spread themselves on the ground in abject fawning and grovelling before the British masters, and accommodated those beefeaters and porkeaters in every manner possible,' put in the tall one.

The short one said further, 'The impression gained over generations, centuries, was that the Hindus would at best tolerate us but not take us into their hearts, and never accord us equality as human beings unless we ruled over them. Therefore, separation was a better option. If we could have a part of the country for ourselves, we would be kings there.'

Dilip retorted, 'But you did not think for all Muslims. You thought only for yourselves, the elites, the landed gentry, the civil and military officers. The poor, illiterate masses who were used for the demonstrations, the rioting and the killing, were ditched and left behind to fend for themselves among the horrible Hindus. Moreover, as you said, you have to rule anyhow. As long as you ruled over the Hindus you were content to live in India. But when you could rule no longer, you were not happy. It is you who don't want to live as equals with Hindus.'

'No, you are not entirely right there,' said Ashraf. 'The educated class as well as the landed gentry felt disturbed and apprehensive about Nehru's socialism and the threat of *zamindari* abolition. You see, the godless socialist and communist ideologies are anathema for us Muslims, rich or poor. Also the Islamic society is based on a system of chieftains and a strong, central ruler, which our people understand and feel comfortable with. Too much talk of democracy and socialism, Panchayati Raj and Ram Rajya of Gandhi was very unsettling, if not outrightly frightening.'

The short one added, 'You must understand that we Mussalmans have a different psyche, different from yours. The customs and thoughts of our ancestors govern our thoughts and actions.'

'Your ancestors?' asked Garry, a bit perplexed.

'Yes, all the people from Ghazni downwards, the Arabs, the Turks, the Persians, and the Central Asians, our forefathers who invaded India and settled here,' replied the short one.

'Ah, that's the kind of talk one sometimes hears among my tribe, the Sikhs, when they try to convince themselves that they are different from the rest of the Indians,' said Garry. 'But look at me, my fair complexion, light eyes, and my build. Perhaps my ancestors too came from Persia or Turkey. That should entitle me to claim a different ancestry, and to be inspired by their customs and traditions. And, by the way, the Turks have in any case gone far ahead of all of us in such matters.'

'Even if we go by your argument,' mused Brother, 'What would be the percentage of pure-blooded central and west Asians among the Muslims in our areas? One percent? Two percent? That too among those who have been marrying strictly within their own families.'

'Difficult to quantify, but what point are you making?' asked Ashraf.

'All the Ranas and the Lambas and the Vaderas and many more that we both have in common,' replied Brother.

'That's a very small percentage, insignificant in this context,' insisted the short one.

'On the contrary,' said Jafa. 'This is a very significant matter. If for a moment you take away the codified religions from our lives, we shall appear to be what we actually are, brothers under the skin—the same families, same common ancestry, same bloodlines. Who are these so-called Pathans all over the Indian heartland if not the Rajputs of just a few generations ago? The Syeds are erstwhile Brahmins. The Yadavs became Ghosis and Chaudhrys, the Chamaars got the appellation of Chamara Karigars, the leather workers, when they embraced Islam. And there are Bengali and Assamese Muslims. You will have to decide which part of Arabia they came from.'

No one disputed the argument and Jafa continued, 'You see, there may be regional variations but on the whole our ancestry is the same. The thought and the propaganda that the Mussalmans are some special people, descended from Allah's backyard, that they are totally alien to the Hindu, to the traditions and ethos of Hindustan, that they are ethnically and emotionally descendants of other races is fallacious and dangerous. It was such ideas preached from pulpits and political platforms that divided the hearts. Not that bit of untouchability that the Hindus practised with you, for they have been practising it among themselves for times beyond recall.'

The tall Pakistani had been following the freewheeling discussion with rapt attention but had hardly spoken till now. He coughed and joined in.

'If indeed we are brothers under the skin, as you say, then how come brothers slay brothers without a second thought?'

'Come again,' said Garry, inviting him to explain further.

'Communal, rather anti-Muslim, riots take place in your country with unfailing regularity. The Muslims get slaughtered in their hundreds and thousands. Hardly a week passes without such happenings. We have sources and we get to know,' said the tall one.

'In that case we should have finished with all the Muslims by now,' commented Kamy. 'But...riots are a regular feature all over India. There are Hindu-Muslim riots, of course. But the Keralites and the Maharashtrians fight it out in Bombay, the Assamese and the Bengalis in Gauhati. The hill people fight the plains people, the Sikhs fight the Hindus, the upper castes fight the lower castes. So what is great about riots in India?'

'You are very right, Sir,' said Dilip. 'These people get terribly excited over riots involving the Muslims. Riots involving others do not register with them.'

'Very well,' said the tall one. 'You fight among yourselves as much as you like. Why fight and kill the Muslims who are in a minority and weak and insecure in any case?'

'You mean violence is condonable as long as it takes place between the sects of one community, as between Assamese and Bengalis, as between Shias and Sunnis, but not among two separate religious entities?' asked Kamy.

'You are talking of surface appearances only,' said Ashraf, shifting the focus back to Hindu-Muslim riots. 'If you go deeper you will find that communal riots in India occur mainly in those areas where the Muslims have established their businesses and where they are doing well financially. Maybe just to uproot them and push them back into poverty and want.'

'Precisely, Ashraf *Saheb*,' intervened Jafa. 'You have identified the main cause of such conflicts. It is economic. It is survival, it is possessiveness, sometimes disguised as upper and lower caste troubles among the Hindus, at other times as Hindu-Muslim problems, and getting exacerbated with increasing populations. The real issue is that of two neighbours fighting over a common wall, two farmers fighting over a common embankment between their fields. Starting with survival and going onto baser instincts of acquisitiveness, greed, avarice, possession and dispossession through wile and violence, these are the causes. You can give them fancy names such as social inequalities, financial imbalances, religious bigotry...'

'You would perhaps also ascribe the ferocity of violence on both sides during the Partition to material and financial greed,' commented the short one.

Before anyone on the Indian side could reply, Ashraf said, 'I am inclined to agree. Even when we were attacked it was our luggage, our possessions that attracted attention in the first place, our women next. Islam was only an excuse. The killing too seemed to be incidental, like a corollary.'

'It was the same syndrome here, in West Pakistan, where the Muslims were in a tearing hurry to drive out the Hindus and the Sikhs so that they could grab our lands, houses and goods and, of course, the women. Killing for the sake of just killing was seldom the aim,' said Garry.

Kuruvilla stopped puffing at his cigarette and observed, 'That may be true of Punjab, but it doesn't explain the killings in U.P. and Bihar. Perhaps, it was more the anger and hatred of hundreds of years coming out.'

'Muslims were always aggressive and out to kill,' said Kamy.

'And the Hindus out to loot, by guile preferably, by force if necessary. That was always their first aim. They killed when they were frustrated in that aim,' said the tall one.

There seemed to be no meeting ground between the Hindus and the Muslims, thought Jafa. Even in the microcosmic representation of the two communities in the prison camp the prejudices and perceptions of aeons gone by immediately came to the fore. It was brother against brother, the breakaway parts ranged against the parent community.

'I don't understand,' said Bunny the Christian. 'Don't all your religions teach you to be tolerant and to respect humanitarian values?'

'Certainly,' said the tall one. 'There is no religion as tolerant as Islam. The great Prophet allowed the Jews and the idol-worshippers to follow their own ways of worship right there in Mecca. In Islam there is perfect equality among men and compassion the highest virtue.'

'The Hindu is no less tolerant,' said Kamy. 'Go to any Muslim *mazar*, you will find more Hindus praying there than Muslims. It is the Hindu who keeps such places alive and flush with funds. It is the Hindu taxpayer who pays for the Muslims' haj in India.'

Kamy paused, looked at the Pakistani visitors, and continued, 'Mind you, many a Hindu will happily pray inside a mosque if it were thrown open to him. For a Hindu there is just one God, not his alone or somebody else's but everybody's. He can find him in a *mazaar*, in a mosque, in a church, in a temple, even in a piece of stone.'

These were unanswerable, unresolvable questions, like philosophical riddles, thought Jafa. Everyone agreed on the sameness of all religions, and swore by its values, yet everyone flouted the principles and plundered the neighbours, again in the name of the same religion.

'Well, people do not judge a religion by its prophets or its scriptures,' said Jafa. 'They judge a religion by the way the followers put those preachings and sayings into practice. Christians are not judged today by the conduct of the Inquisitors or the excesses of the Crusaders because those were deviations in the remote past and not repeated. They are judged today by the soft-spoken priest, by the nun who brings up small children in orphanages, by the kind, unfleecing doctors in missionary hospitals, even by the just and even-handed conduct of the erstwhile Christian British administrators. So are the Muslims judged not by the exalted Ayats of the Quran but by the violence that accompanied its spread, by the unashamed despoiling of others' religious shrines, by the coveting of others' women, by the resort to fundamentalism and the call for bloodshed in the name of religion for the achievement of mere political aims. And the Hindu is judged not by what is written in the Vedas and the Gita, but by the deviousness and greed of its priestly class, and the cunning, the self-serving, self-debasing, acquisitive, exploitative endeavours of the rest. Perhaps the only saving grace is that the Hindu does not take his religion to anybody, he bears the travails with infinite patience, and finally gets the adversary in the end.'

Ashraf smiled broadly and said, 'We better watch out then!'

They all laughed, Dilip the loudest as he said, 'For all my Hindu deviousness let me ask our guests again—Was Partition right? Was the creation of Pakistan the only course open to the Muslims?'

'One moment, 'said Ashraf. 'This matter of violence accompanying the spread of Islam... that certainly is a widespread belief about Islam, but, in our context, in the sub-continent, this was not quite the truth....'

'You mean there were no forced conversions? No demolitions of temples?' asked Brother.

'The conversions to Islam were more out of fear, rather, out of the desire to curry favour with the new rulers,' Ashraf continued. 'This was particularly true of the Rajputs who calculated that that was the easiest way to retain their fiefdoms and their fortunes. In that sense they were willing converts. Others of their ilk bought the same privileges by offering their women in marriage to the Muslim princes and rulers. Yet, I would say that these conversions were in small numbers and couldn't have accounted for the vast population of Muslims at the time of the Partition, about a quarter of the total.'

'So ...?' queried Kuru, inviting Ashraf to go on.

'So ...,' said Ashraf. 'The bulk of converts to Islam from among the Hindus came willingly, of their own accord. And that was not through the efforts of the diehard Mullas and Maulvis, but in spite of them. That was accomplished by another set of people without deliberately setting out to do so.'

'The Sufis ...?' asked Jafa.

'Yes, 'said the short one. 'The Sufis were more effective in carrying the message of The Book to the masses. They were more in line with the traditions of the gurus and the ascetics in Hindu society, and the main thrust of their religiosity, simply the love of God, found a ready echo in Hinduism. Combined with this were the strongest tenets of Islam, social justice and equality, the emphasis on egalitarianism. These were powerful magnets for people who had known only the oppressive caste system in their religion and society.'

'You mean that the Muslims we see today had become Muslims simply out of greed and out of the desire to escape the caste system?' asked Kamy unbelievingly.

'Absolutely,' said the short one. 'The maximum number of conversions occurred in areas where the caste discriminations were the worst. Bengal, parts of Bihar, the present Uttar Pradesh. Entire villages of the so-called lower castes turned to Islam. In Kerala, an area ruled by Hindu kings, it was the same syndrome.'

There was silence as the Indians absorbed the ideas thrown up by Ashraf and his companions.

'I wonder,' said Ashraf after a pause, 'I really wonder sometimes as to what would have been the state of things in India if the over-zealous Mullas and some impatient rulers had reined themselves in, if they had desisted from propagating Islam with sword in one hand and mallet in the other, and, instead, left the field to the Sufis...?'

Ashraf turned to look at Jafa, urging him to suggest an answer.

Jafa took time to reply. Then, in a measured, slow tone he said, 'In that case we Hindus might have been where the Muslims today are... a minority in India...'

They all stared at him, Pakistanis with a measure of disbelief, Indians wondering if he had spoken in jest, but seeing the hard look of conviction on his face they refrained from protesting. Only Kamy decided to take up the issue later, separately.

After the brief silence that followed, the tall one looked at Dilip and said, 'You asked if the creation of Pakistan was the only course open to the Muslims... I would say that was the only way....'

'You see,' continued the tall one. 'In Pakistan we created a focal point, a point of reference, a centre of power for all the Muslims of the sub-continent. Even if all the Muslims could not be accommodated in this area, they knew that there was Islamic power here, their own brothers and co-religionists, to whom they could turn for help whenever needed. Ask any Muslim in India, he may be afraid to say so in public, but he is happy that there is a dreamland for him called Pakistan where Muslims rule and where the injustices perpetrated in India can be challenged and avenged. That is justification enough for Partition.'

'Even though half of Pakistan broke away and negated the very basis of Partition by coming under the wings of the mother country once again?' asked Dilip.

'No, not quite like that,' argued the tall one. 'We have no worries about Bangladesh. They are our people and when the chips are down again, sometime in the near or the distant future, they will stand on our side, not against us, and never with India.'

Ashraf took up the main theme. 'Bangladesh came into being not because of the weakening of the Islamic bond, nor as a negation of the concept of Pakistan. Contrary to the propaganda in your country, mind you, Bangladesh was the result of the pursuit of power by individuals.'

'You mean *kissa kursi ka*? The fight for the throne?' asked Harishsinhji.

'Well, draw your own conclusions,' intoned the short one.

'The Punjabi strongmen in the west and the Bengali majority in the east? Mujib denied his right to power by Yahya Khan, backed by Bhutto, the ultimate contender for power in Pakistan...?' observed Dilip.

There was a lull as nobody spoke. After a pause Dilip continued, 'This only shows that religion is not the strong binding force that it is made out to be, that the lust for power among individuals shapes the destiny of the multitudes. Distinctions of religion and culture, social and economic inequalities, genuine and perceived injustices, these are the tools in the hands of the modern day conquerors in pursuit of power. Suitable demagoguery to inflame the passions of the gullible, unthinking, illiterate masses—and you have a country, a kingdom of your own.'

Kuruvilla looked at Ashraf and said, 'You said something about individuals trying to grab power....'

'That may be as it is,' said Ashraf quickly, perhaps wanting to steer clear of any comment on his country's ruler. 'But look at the way the Quaid was treated at the Nagpur session of the Congress. He felt positively insulted. Nehru didn't accommodate him, possibly for fear that the resoluteness of Jinnah's great intellect would eclipse him. The Mahatma was the only one who understood the fire and the determination of the Quaid. He offered him the prime ministership of an undivided India, but it was too late by then.'

Yes, thought Jafa, it was individuals, always individuals who created countries and empires, democracies and dictatorships, using differences in faiths, inequalities in wealth, or the arrogance of racial superiority to enthuse their followers, and subjugate others. In the same vein, sometimes it looked as if the story of India's Partition was the story of two men, both totally British in their outlook and upbringing, one in Indian clothes, the other with a Muslim name, one a high-caste Brahmin and a self-proclaimed agnostic, the other keeping a long distance from Islam and meeting only the Islamic norms in dress and rhetoric in tune with the needs of the moment. Both individually tolerant and imbued with secular values and the burning desire to uplift the masses and drive them into the modern times of science and technology, yet both also imbued with such arrogance of personal superiority that brooked no tolerance of each other, much less allowing any sense of equality and therefore of participative action. Nehru, the darling of all Indians, the undisputed heir to Gandhi, the confident Brahmin assured of his place at the helm of an independent India. Jinnah, the modern liberal aristocrat, piqued at Hindu superciliousness, repugnant of being smothered by the vast Hindu majority, finally harking back to the medieval idea of religion as the basis of nationhood. Nehru and Jinnah, the two men driven by their destinies to rule over parts, if not the whole of India, one abandoning Gandhi in the process, the other abandoning more Muslims than he professed to have salvaged in the new country.

'Can this ever be undone?' asked Kuru with honest simplicity.

'No,' said Ashraf without hesitation. 'Never. The best we should hope for is not to fight wars. We should look inwards, at our poor and the needy, and fulfil the aspirations of the founding fathers.'

Ashraf looked at his watch and stood up saying, 'My... didn't realise it's been a couple of hours here. But very nice, very illuminating, speaking with you gentlemen.'

The Pakistanis shook hands with each Indian officer, lingered a bit longer with Jafa, and stepped out.

'God bless you,' said Jafa.

'*Khuda Hafiz*,' said the Pakistani officers.

The Times, They Were Bad

Jafa sat back in the chair, in a pensive mood. One people, three countries, he thought. When did Partition begin, when did it end? Could exact dates, even boundaries, ever be demarcated? Wasn't there a bit of India in the hearts of all those who went away to Pakistan, as indeed in the hearts of all the other Muslims there? Wasn't there a longing for bits of Pakistan among the Hindus and Sikhs in India? Partition may have been caused by a division of hearts, but the divided parts ached with memories and longings.

As Jeet Behn, who, as a child, had witnessed the slaughter of her family in West Pakistan, and still felt bewildered as to the cause for so much sudden hatred among the same people, was to say later, 'That atmosphere was bad. The people were not evil. The times, they were bad.'

13

Tigers in the Cage

As the end of the year 1971 approached, and the New Year appeared around the corner, vague hopes of going home stirred among the Indian prisoners in the camp. The exciting tales of the war were already wearing a bit thin. Brother and Teja, the indefatigable talkers, continued to spin sporadic yarns in one corner while the others simply sat on the few available chairs or lay about on the cement floor, their eyes staring fixedly straight ahead and their thoughts far away. Rizvi's arrival broke the reverie.

'I ... ah ... have brought ... ah ... some indoor games. I ... ah ... thought ... ah ... you have nothing much to do.' And he produced a chess set and a pack of cards.

'This is alright for six. What about the others?' enquired Mulla who was adept at discovering a discrepancy in any given situation.

'Ah ... well ... ah ... more will come, *Insha Allah*,' assured Rizvi with a promising grin.

Mulla and Brother Bhargava commandeered the chess set right away. A foursome for cards was quickly formed. The rest gathered around as onlookers first, then turned into advisers and finally formed into two opposing blocks. The games were not played, as they never can be played in such circumstances, merely between two players, but between two teams, each jeering and cheering to the eternal chagrin of the actual contestants.

Only Garry paced up and down the courtyard, hands locked behind and head cast down in deep thought. Whether in deep thought or otherwise, when Garry walked about like this there was just one impression he gave—that of a caged tiger. On this occasion, even in thought, he was not far from this comparison.

'I say, when do you chaps think we'll go back?' he asked, stopping abruptly and addressing no one in particular. All eyes turned towards him, all minds weighing the question.

'Shouldn't be long,' said Kuru. It was more a wish than a considered opinion.

'I'd say very soon. Any day.' Another wishful outburst, this from Mulla. And finally there were as many opinions as people. Vikram's gambling instinct was quick to discover the possibility of a good wager. He offered half-a-month's salary to any one forecasting the correct date for repatriation and began to talk others into sealing the bet.

'That's too much money,' said Bunny Coelho. 'If I know my wife, she would have burst up my next year's salary too by the time I get back.'

And so a token bet of fifty rupees was decided upon, the house going to the person whose prediction came closest to the actual date. Harry borrowed a stub of pencil from a guard and wrote each forecast on an empty packet of cigarettes. He saw that all dates fell within a span of two months, except one.

'Why must you be awkward?' he asked Garry. Harry liked to think pleasantly and act pleasantly. An unpleasant thought was like a pain one inflicted on oneself, unnecessarily.

'Why, that's my feeling. Nothing is going to happen for six months. Just wait and see.' And with this Garry resumed his pacing. He had wagered on 31st July.

'Pessimist!' countered Harry, but with some uncertainty.

A little while later Dilip walked over to where Jafa was lying down in the sun and sprawled alongside.

'I see that you have placed your bet on 10th January. You think we might go back so soon, Sir?' he asked.

Death Wasn't Painful

'We don't know what's happening outside, in politics, in diplomacy. So, perhaps like Garry, one date is as good as another,' said Jafa.

'I have doubts about any rapid cooling down between our countries,' said Dilip.

'Yes, Dilip,' said Jafa thoughtfully. 'The arrogance of victory and the defiance of defeat ... there is little common ground between the two. It'll take just one face-off, one minor incident to be perceived as an affront, to delay settlement for ever.'

Dilip was quiet for a while and then he said, 'Sir, if our repatriation remains uncertain and keeps getting put off indefinitely, then we have to think of something, some way of getting out of here. Even though it is going to be difficult and risky.'

Jafa's mind went back to the twilight period before the war, a period of waiting, seemingly endless waiting for something to happen, something to start, nerves on edge, the athlete waiting for the gun to go off, the hound on leash and the scent of hare strong. Curiously, no one talked of the danger of death, which was a very likely certainty for many. The conscious mind went only as far as the dreaded possibility of having to bail out over enemy territory and being captured by the enemy. Thus, in the crew-rooms and operations rooms a lot of time was spent on discussions regarding evasion and escape. Everyone seemed to be firming up his ideas on the subject. Jafa remembered a south-Indian officer whose linguistic skills were limited to English and his native Malayalam, being given a crash course in Hindustani by a Punjabi officer. Questions and answers were devised as between a suspicious Pakistani and an evading Indian. The whole exercise was so hilarious that someone seriously advised the officer that the safest thing for him in Pakistan would be to find the nearest police station and surrender.

'If I can't talk my way out, I can always leg it out,' said the Malayali officer in final repartee. 'I will hide and run, hide again and run faster.'

'But there can be no hiding in Pakistan,' said someone else. And that was the truth. In the heavily populated areas of West Pakistan an attacking aeroplane was almost constantly in sight. The troops on the ground would hardly miss a parachute descending from a burning aircraft, and even if one was fortunate in getting away from them, there could not be any escape from the vast civilian population which was just as keenly involved in the war. There were absolutely no pockets among the populace where one could expect help or even silence on being spotted. There was no question of any one from the majority community extending help to an Indian. And, unlike India, the minorities were too scarce and too scared not to run to the authorities with the slightest suspicion and information of this kind.

Fighting men consider capture by the enemy as humiliating, mortifying, something to be avoided, resisted, endured, and, if possible, overcome through escape. Escaping from the enemy signifies defiance, a testing of one's wits and courage, an act of daring, a challenge to the power and might of the enemy from within his captivity. The penalty for failure is usually death. The thrill of success is like coming through a winner in a particularly dangerous sport, like climbing the Everest, like sailing the oceans alone. There are such restless, even reckless young men in the armed forces all over the world who cannot abide the crushing confines of a prison camp and who must attempt a breakout if only to defy the enemy.

Dilip was one such. During a particularly lively discussion in the crew-room he had once declared, 'If I am shot down and captured, I shall escape. By God, I'll not sit in their jail. I shall escape.'

And now Jafa smiled at Dilip, the smile of an indulgent elder, and said, 'What you can dare, you may will; and what you can will, you may achieve. And that's how, Dilip, sometimes great things get done.'

He did not elaborate. He had his own reasons for encouraging this young, intelligent, dashing officer to attempt a very difficult feat.

14

Freedom Beckons

And now, a few months later, as the winter was on the wane, though a bit of sun in the morning hours still a balmy and enervating experience, the Indian prisoners thought longingly of home, but with increasing uncertainty and despondency. Dilip and Garry huddled in one corner of the courtyard, the thought of escape uppermost in their minds. Their patience with the politicians and leaders in the three countries was wearing thin, and as the possibility of repatriation receded, their hunger for freedom began to gnaw at them like some living thing. One morning they sidled up to Jafa, who was reclining back on the warm cement floor, determined to thrash out the matter of the escape.

'We better finalise the escape plan, Sir,' Dilip spoke in the manner of a child who has been denied his favourite chocolate far too long. 'There is no point in waiting indefinitely and simply ageing up on ennui and half rations.'

Jafa smiled at Dilip's and Garry's irrepressible need to be occupied mentally and physically all the time. The escape plan had already turned into an obsession and a pre-occupation with them.

'Alright,' said he, 'Tell me, how will you get out of here in the first place?'

'Getting out of the camp may not be difficult,' said Garry. 'But the problem is that we are in the heart of Pakistani Punjab. One can't go through unseen, unobserved. It may be easier in the Sind desert or the hills of the north-west. But how to get to those areas in the first place?'

'We don't have our flying maps anymore. In any case they wouldn't have the details we shall require. We have to collect information on the countryside, the rail and road connections leading towards India, the rivers and other natural obstacles. In other words, a trekker's guide book, that's the kind of information we need.' Dilip was coming down to the specifics.

'Dilip,' said Jafa after some deliberation. 'The Pakis have acceded to our request for books, English novels, biographies etc. These would be coming from Unit and Station libraries going back to the British times. In my estimation there should be an odd travel book somewhere in some old library, written by some British crackpot who might have taken a marathon walk across the sub-continent and later recorded it fondly for posterity. Amazing that no Indian ever did it. For information about the ancient times we have to fall back upon a Hiuen Tsang or an Ibn Batuta, and for modern times it is always a Kipling or a Cunningham. There is never any Ram Sevak or Allah Baksh to refer to.'

'You mean, Sir, that we should try to lay hands on a travel book, in English, which is likely to be available at an old military station like Rawalpindi,' cut in Garry, who knew that Jafa had a habit of going on and on whenever there was an occasion to pinpoint the inadequacies of our own people.

'Precisely,' said Jafa. 'Now it is up to you fellows to wheedle such a book out of Wahid or Rizvi.'

Squadron Leader Wahid-ud-din had now taken charge of the POW, a good man, but a vain man, whose vanity could be played upon to wheedle things out of the Pakistani establishment. So, during Wahid's next visit to the prisoners, Dilip and Garry thanked

Death Wasn't Painful

him profusely for all the books he had procured for them and which had helped to alleviate the tedium of long hours in the lock-ups.

Dilip then said, 'In fact, Sir, we are also very keen to read some books about the people of this area, particularly the north-west. Those are rather the wild areas, we understand, inhabited by fiercely independent tribes. Our generation has had no interaction with these people—the Pathans, the Baluchis, the Pakhtoons. We have only seen their caricatures in our Hindi films. So, if there are any books in your libraries about these rugged areas, the tough, rifle-wielding tribes who, I believe, buy and sell cartridges by weight, we would love to read those.'

'Yes, those are indeed wild areas,' said Wahid. 'In most of the tribal areas you are safe only so long as you stay on a macadam road. You leave the road at your own peril. They fire first and think later, if at all. They also live by their own customs and laws.'

'That should be very interesting,' said Garry. 'Now you have to find for us some books about these people and these areas. Maybe, a book written by someone who has personally been there and met the people.'

And that is how within the next week, among the many Charles Dickens', Thomas Hardys, and Jane Austens, Dilip found a copy of Murray's travel book on India, Burma and Ceylon. It was an old book, which perhaps had not been opened since the British departed. But it was the very thing they needed, a record of Murray's trek across the sub-continent, containing brief descriptions of the topography including natural obstacles like hills and rivers, notes on the people in different areas, the routes to all parts of the country with rail and road connections right up to the Khyber pass, the medieval gateway to India, and for Dilip and Garry, possibly the doorway into Afghanistan and freedom.

'We shouldn't think of going through the Punjab,' said Harry who had been avidly studying the book. 'That would be too dangerous.'

'But that's the shortest route,' said Garry. 'If we can hit a railway line going south-east towards Wagah or Kasur, we simply walk along all night and hide during the day. We are bound to hit the border and hopefully, our own forward troops.'

'Very smart!' sneered Harry. 'We keep walking leisurely for three or four nights while the alert is out and the whole of Pakistan is looking for us. And then we manage to dodge the Pak Army and meander through all the minefields that have been spread out both by them and our army just for the likes of us, and suddenly pop up before our own Gurkhas or Sikhs in these funny clothes and they welcome us with a volley of machine gun fire! Yeah, Garry boy, you can then happily breathe your last breath on home soil! But not me! I am going north-west, that's the route to take.'

They argued on the north-west versus the south-east route for days but Harry was implacable. Dilip and Garry patiently explained and tried to argue him out of his obstinacy.

'See, Harry,' said Dilip for the nth time. 'It's the shortest route. The shorter the route, the lesser the chances of our being discovered and the quicker our escape into India.'

'No. I will not go via the Punjab,' was Harry's final word.

'Oh,' said Garry. 'I think he doesn't want to escape at all! So why are we wasting our time with him?'

Harry jumped in his seat. 'Look, let's get one thing clear,' he said hotly. 'If anyone escapes, anyone, it will be me. I mean I shall be the first to break out of here, ahead of all of you. But I shall not go through the Punjab.'

Patiently Dilip argued, pleaded, shouted, threatened, and begged, at least to be told the reason for such monumental obduracy. But Harry neither explained his stand nor came around to agreeing with them. A couple of days went by without anyone yielding an inch.

Jafa was amazed at Harry's determination to escape as well as his stubborn opposition to the Punjab route. While Garry and Dilip were well-built youths, Harry was puny. He was so short that another couple of centimetres less and he wouldn't have made it as a fighter pilot and so thin that Garry often picked him up and walked about the courtyard just for exercise. He wore a smile on his face, always and in all circumstances, and if caught in a predicament or a particularly difficult situation he would first say something to invite laughter at himself and then deal with the problem after putting everyone at ease. But his easy manner and innocent looks belied his clear-headed intelligence and the sheer grit and guts of his personality.

Jafa had grown fond of this small fellow whom he had met and observed for the first time in the prison camp. Yet he too could not understand this obduracy on Harry's part. So one day he asked, 'Harry, why are you so adamant in your opposition to the direct south-eastern route? After all, why not keep all options open at this early stage?'

Harry's smile did not wane. He puffed harder at his cigarette and seemed to be weighing several things in his mind all at once. Suddenly, almost on an impulse, he took Jafa aside and whispered into his ear, 'Sir, you know, if we go across Punjab we will have to cross at least one major river and possibly several smaller streams?'

'Yes, go on,' prompted Jafa.

'Do you know, Sir, that I cannot swim?' blurted out Harry.

In great agitation he began to puff at the cigarette again. Jafa gaped at him, trying to grasp the significance of this revelation. Then, as the cause for so much mayhem and unending, unpleasant arguments became clear to him, he began to laugh. He laughed loudly and uncontrollably. Everyone turned towards him and Harry wondering what had caused so much mirth.

'Dilip,' said Jafa, trying to control the laughter. 'You are not going across Punjab. Harry has clinched the argument. It's going to be the north-west route.'

'I don't understand,' exclaimed Dilip. 'What has he said to convince you so thoroughly?'

'Simple, Dilip. Harry is going with you. And he can't swim,' pronounced Jafa. They all stared at Harry in consternation, and then burst out laughing.

'That was a googly I didn't expect,' said Garry angrily. 'He doesn't have to come with us. After all, we can't put limitations on ourselves right at the beginning.'

'No, Garry boy, I am going with you. Even ahead of you,' said Harry. Then turning towards Jafa, he continued, 'What is the meaning of team spirit, Sir, if this fellow is unwilling to accommodate me?'

'Team spirit doesn't mean that we allow one incompetent fellow to lead us all into hell, does it?' asked Garry.

'What makes you think that there won't be rivers on the other route? Have you seen the map, Harry?' interjected Kamy.

'Maybe not,' said Harry. 'But I do know that the north-west is a totally dry area; they don't even have enough drinking water.'

'Between here and Peshawar, Harry, you could be swallowing the waters of the Indus, and going down among the stones at its bottom,' said Kamy in his usual, mildly sarcastic style. 'Of course, you have the choice of going down into the more comfortable, sandy bottom of Jhelum or Chenab or Ravi, if you take the south-eastern route. Either way you will finally be resting in the Arabian sea.'

When the laughter died down Dilip said, 'Harry, if you are so keen to come with us, we'll find a way, man. So don't upset yourself, let's just get going.'

'I trust you, Dilip,' acknowledged Harry. 'But this chap Garry will let go of me in mid-stream and he'll be laughing while I bob up and down and hit my watery grave.'

'I am not all that bad, Harry,' assured Garry. 'In fact I have the greatest concern for you. As soon as I reach India I shall go straight to your parents and explain how bravely, though tragically, you passed into the Great Beyond. I shall, in your everlasting absence, offer to undertake your filial duties, which, by the norms you have followed, shouldn't be much of a problem. I am sure they won't miss much.'

'Don't worry, Garry, I won't give you the chance for such a courtesy,' said Harry. Then turning to Dilip he said, 'Dilip, I am somehow going to get hold of a strong string. I'll trust you to tow me across. Not this chap Garry, I won't trust him with my old shoes.'

This exchange of views and arguments brought out one thing very clearly—the escape team would consist of three persons—Dilip, Garry and Harry. The others were either physically handicapped for

Death Wasn't Painful

the time being, or just lacked the urge, the daring, and the recklessness required for such an attempt. Most of them were enthusiastic and eager to work towards its accomplishment, though a few were wary, even discouraging.

The first issue was getting out of the camp itself. The prisoners were kept in eight cells, seven of which were the regular, strongly built lock-ups. One was a room which was part of an old building that had been converted into Cell No. 5. This was the weakest in construction and had quite appropriately been used to lock up the injured Jafa. The rear wall of this room, if dug through, would open out into the compound of the main building which housed the Pakistan Air Force Recruiting Office. Once into the compound, a six-foot wall would be all that stood between an escapee and freedom. Kuruvilla had learnt from a civilian employee in the camp that the building and the compound were not guarded by armed men, which meant that some odd, lackadaisical civilian watchman would perfunctorily be walking or sleeping around the place. Thus this was the most appropriate room for a breakout. A hole, approximately twenty-one inches by fifteen inches, would have to be dug into the rear wall for this purpose. Since this was an old construction of about fourteen inches thickness, it meant the loosening out of about fifty-six bricks by scraping away the cement plaster holding them together. This had to be done silently, slowly, painstakingly with the help of things like nails, strong wires etc.

They looked around and pulled out quite a few nails from the walls in the courtyard and the toilets. Kuru stole a screw driver from an electrician who had come to repair some faulty line, the finest instrument for this purpose. All these were carefully hidden away by Dilip in Cell No. 5. This was the largest room in the campus, airy and bright, and now that the weather was rapidly turning warm, the natural place for all prisoners to gather during the day. Since activities in the room were clearly visible from outside the scraping of the wall for loosening the bricks could only be done at night under cover of darkness and the deception of pretended slumber. For this purpose the escape team had to be somehow moved to this room.

Jafa's plaster cast was removed in April and he was advised to consistently exercise his back muscles as taught him by the doctors. He pretended to be sicker than he actually was, whimpering and simpering with pain he did not have, and requested the assistance of another person in the room. Dilip offered to help and was allowed by the kind Rizvi to shift to this cell.

A few days later, while playing in the courtyard, Dilip slipped and fell heavily, hitting his head on the concrete floor. He suffered some convulsions but soon came around to full consciousness. The guards had witnessed the incident and the police corporal came quickly to enquire if medical aid was required. This was politely declined but Dilip was immediately brought to Cell No. 5 and made to lie down. Later he pretended to be afflicted with a severe headache and shooting pains in his limbs. He said that he may need to see a doctor next morning but in the meantime Garry may be allowed to minister to him during the night. Thus, Garry came into Cell No. 5.

Events had moved rapidly in Pakistan after its military defeat. General Yahya Khan was removed and Zulfiqar Ali Bhutto took over as the new ruler. His demagoguery inspired confidence among a battered people. All eyes were now turned to him to get India to vacate the occupied lands and to get back the hundred thousand Pakistani prisoners in India's custody. The government-controlled newspaper, *The Dawn*, which was now being supplied to the prisoners, also gave the impression that a settlement leading to the exchange of prisoners was around the corner. The incessant talk of repatriation being imminent and the bonhomie created in the camp as a result of this perception lulled the Pakistanis into believing that the Indian prisoners would rather go home in comfort and safety than attempt a tough and risky escape. They became less vigilant about the activities of the Indian prisoners and so long as the head count was correct and all the prisoners were locked up in the evenings it did not quite matter if there were more than one to a cell.

Soon the presence of three prisoners in one cell began to be taken for granted. The new guards coming on duty stopped asking questions about it. The three people then started to lament the boredom of the long hours between supper and going to bed each night. They talked politely with the guards and very courteously with the police corporals, requesting all and sundry to allow one more person into the cell at nights so that they could form a foursome for bridge and tide over the long, tedious hours before falling asleep. The persistent request gradually got floated upwards till one day the nod of approval came down and a fourth prisoner was allowed into Cell No. 5. For form's sake everyone was offered this chance, and everyone declined except, of course, Harry.

In addition to the escape team comprising of three persons, there was need for a fourth able-bodied person to help with the digging of the hole, the looking out for the guards, and, importantly, to finally provide the cover-up for the escape. Their choice fell on Chati who had at one stage shown an interest in joining the escape team. Chati was an agile and a very quiet person, well-suited to a task requiring reticence and economy of words. He was in Cell No. 1 and a straight exchange of places between him and Jafa appeared to be the best solution.

Dilip hatched a plan and during Wahid's next visit to the cell he addressed a squirming and obviously uncomfortable Jafa, 'Sir, I am telling you again that your pain will not go away unless you sleep on a hard bed. This string bed is no good for you. You must get down and sleep on the floor.'

'No, I won't sleep on the floor if I can help it. I am scared of the little creepy insects that keep crawling all over here,' said Jafa.

'In that case you should shift to a regular cell which has a raised concrete bunk,' advised Bunny Coelho.

'Well, if it's okay by Wahid *Saheb*, I might as well shift to a cell. But I would like one near the toilet,' said Jafa.

'It's alright by me,' said Wahid. 'You may change places with the chap in Cell No. 1.'

And that is how Chati and Jafa changed places. The escape team was now in place in Cell No. 5.

Murray's book had been read over and over again. A great deal of their time was now spent on discussing the requirements for the escape. These were summed up as civilian clothes, emergency rations for at least three days, and money in Pakistani currency. While thought was being given to other items, the question of hard cash could possibly be tackled right away. The prisoners were being supplied with essential toiletries and cigarettes on a regular basis; there had to be some fund, some source of accountable finance for this purpose. They decided to confront the man in charge of such provisions, Master Warrant Officer Rizvi, to see if they could lay hands on cash in the first place instead of goods.

'Mr. Rizvi,' began Dilip during the very next visit of this dignitary. 'Mind you, there is no complaint from our side. Please understand this. You have been supplying us with all our requirements of soap, toothpaste, shaving items etc. You also bring for the smokers a reasonably adequate supply of cigarettes. We are all quite satisfied as far as that goes. But, Mr. Rizvi, where does it all come from? And how much of each item can we get? I mean, if I ask for an expensive thing like after-shave lotion, will you be able to get it for me?'

'I ... ah ... don't understand,' said Rizvi. 'You are ... ah ... prisoners ... there are ... ah ... some entitlements ... I mean ... ah ... you can get things ... ah ... within your ... ah ... allowances.'

Bunny took over. 'You mean, Mr Rizvi, that we, as officer prisoners, are entitled to some allowances, on a monthly basis or whatever? And that you bring these goodies for us out of the funds allocated individually for us?'

'Well ... ah ... yes, there are ... ah ... funds for you,' acknowledged Rizvi.

'Then each of us must know his entitlement so that he may also know how much of toiletries and how many cigarettes he can get during a month,' argued Brother.

Rizvi thought for a moment and apparently decided that such a disclosure would not amount to giving away a State secret. 'Our authorities ... ah ... have ... ah ... fixed your allowance ... ah ... at ...

ah ... sixty rupees per month ... ah ... irrespective ... ah ... of ... ah ... rank,' he disclosed.

'Ah, if it is my individual entitlement, Mr. Rizvi, then I'll have to think,' said Teja, articulating the well-rehearsed line. 'As you know, I don't smoke. But you can't let Jafa *Saheb* have two packs of cigarettes a day while I don't even get a bottle of Fixo for my beard.'

'Well ... ah ... gentlemen ... ah ... we don't have ... ah ... Fixo ... in this country,' said Rizvi laughingly, referring to the glue-like substance Sikhs use to dress their beard.

'I don't smoke either, Mr. Rizvi,' said Brother. 'Why can't I get additional eggs or biscuits out of my allowance?'

To Rizvi this smacked of selfishness, greed and intolerance among the Indian prisoners, which rather pleased him. With a straight face he said, 'I ... ah ... thought ... that all the money ... ah ... could be pooled together ... ah ... and ... ah ... used for all ... ah ... your combined ... ah ... needs, but ... ah ... as you like. I ... ah ... will have to ... ah ... maintain ... ah ... separate accounts ... ah ...'

'Why should you maintain accounts for us?' asked Bunny. 'Why can't we get our money in cash every month? And then we shall pay you for whatever we wish to buy. Personally, my expenses don't exceed twenty bucks a month and I may want to get some extra things for myself. Why should others use my money?'

'Absolutely right,' piped up Brother. 'I also want my money in my hands and I'll pay for whatever I wish to get.'

Everybody joined in the demand for the allowance to be handed over in cash every month on an individual basis. There were veiled hints of the possible misappropriation of funds which rather upset the honest, upright, fumbling Rizvi and caused a greater stammer in his speech.

'Ah ... well ... ah ... your money ... ah ... gentlemen ... is ... ah ... your money. I shall ... ah ... speak with ... ah ... authorities. I'll ... be happy ... ah ... to be ... ah ... rid ... of this.' Then turning towards Jafa and Kamy he said, 'The loss ... ah ... is yours ... ah ... if ... you ... keep smoking ... ah ... at this rate ... you won't ... ah ... have a ... a piece of soap ... ah ... to wash ... your hands after latrine.'

'*Insha Allah*,' said Rizvi finally. 'I shall ... ah ... do ... as you like. *Khuda ... ah ... Hafiz.*'

On the first day of the following month Naqvi came with a notepad and jotted down everybody's requirements. He gave a sympathetic shrug to Jafa and Kamy and muttered, 'Let's see'. And after he had delivered the goods he handed over various amounts in cash to all the prisoners. This represented the balance of money left over from their allowances, and it came to a tidy sum of about three hundred rupees. Jafa calculated that if the preparations for the escape took two months, each escapee would have two hundred rupees in cash to pay for the available transportation or food on the way. He instructed every officer to hold the cash in trust. On his part he decided that he would have to give up smoking in order to contribute his share. It would be difficult, very difficult, but it had to be done. So when Wahid-ud-din visited the prisoners next, with Rizvi in trembling attendance, he decided to make the move.

'Wahid *Saheb*,' began Jafa, 'Flying Officer Vikram is not well at all. His cough persists and there is blood in his sputum. The doctors in your hospital say it will get all right, that there is nothing seriously wrong with him, but he seems to be getting worse by the day. We are quite worried about him.'

'I have seen the specialist's report,' said Wahid. 'There isn't anything to worry about, really. He should eat and rest. In any case there is nothing for him to do here.'

'You know the kind of rations we are on,' said Jafa. 'Do you think we could get for him an extra egg and some butter out of our allowances?'

'That's up to you,' said Wahid.

Jafa let the silence that ensued hang for a while. He then took a long puff at the cigarette he was smoking and said, 'Here it goes!' flinging the cigarette into the fire place. Then he added, 'Vikram is buying butter out of his allowances. I would like one egg to be provided to him every day out of my allowances. I don't want any cigarettes anymore.'

Wahid and Rizvi stared at him, as did the other prisoners. Giving up smoking is never easy, more so under the stressful conditions of a prison camp. No one was in doubt that Jafa would do what he said he would. There was a lesson in it for everyone, that of care and concern for a junior colleague as well as the tightening of belts for the achievement of a common purpose. Even after buying an egg a day some cash would still be left for the escape team.

As these preparations were going on, Kamy called everyone's attention to the matter of clothing for the escape.

'Jafa, Sir,' said Kamy. 'We must think very carefully about what these chaps are going to wear when they break out of the camp. Mind you the common people mostly wear a shirt coming down to below the knee and a *salwar*, usually with the footwear called the *Peshawari chappal*. Our chaps have got just shirts and trousers and canvas shoes. They will stand out like sore thumbs in the civilian milieu outside.'

'Even shirts and trousers may pass, for that matter, in any part of the world. But these faded out uniforms of the PAF will definitely draw attention. This may even prove to be the Achilles heel,' said Kuru.

'Sir, what about the clothes that Dilip received in the Red Cross parcel from home? Can't those be used for some purpose?' asked Teja, who always called attention to small things, even if he never solved a major problem.

'Ha ... ha ... ha ...,' guffawed Dilip. 'Yeah, I can dress up in the blue woollen suit and the terylene shirt and the necktie that my dear sister sent me and walk out like a real gentleman heading for a social night in the officers' mess. Only problem is that my canvas shoes would give me away.'

This was a recurring topic of mirth at the expense of Dilip's family. A month earlier the Indian prisoners were pleasantly surprised to see Pakistani guards walking into Cell No. 5 with ten cardboard boxes. Following them was MWO Rizvi.

'Good ... ah ... news ... ah ... for you ... ah ... gentlemen,' he began. 'These parcels have come ... ah ... from your ... ah ... country.

Our government ... ah ... has ... ah ... kindly ... ah ... allowed these to ... ah ... be ... ah ... handed over ... ah ... to you.'

The boxes were sealed on top with cellophane tapes and had no markings other than the logo of the Indian Red Cross. But it was like receiving something from home. They all picked up a box each and held it in their hands with tender sentiments. The parcels yielded a great many toiletry items, cotton vests and underwears, *hawaii chappals* and more canvas shoes. There were also plenty of copies of the Gita and the Bible. They searched in vain for items of food like cheese, chocolates, jam, butter and biscuits, pickles and chutneys, particularly as the food served in the prison camp at this stage was still meagre in quantity and poor in quality. But there were none. Perhaps even petty things such as food and clothing also became major issues across diplomatic and political conference tables where the peevish denial of such items to the helpless prisoners of either side could be hailed as significant triumphs. The Indian prisoners understood that what they now held in their two hands must also have been cleared at some international conference in Geneva or New York. Yet what they held in their hands were not mere items of physical comfort, but pieces of warmth, of affection, of remembrance by their countrymen.

Kuru who was still rummaging in the boxes suddenly pulled out a plastic bag with Fl. Lt. Dilip Parulkar written on it in big letters, and held it up for others to see, exclaiming, 'What's this?'

'Oh, those are my things,' shouted Dilip as he lunged forward, grabbed the bag and started pulling out the contents. There was one woollen lounge suit, a necktie and two smart terylene shirts. Dilip's eyes turned moist as he quickly wore the coat and held the other clothes close to his chest. Just then two other parcels were discovered containing two woollen jerseys, one marked in Bunny Coelho's name, the other in Brother's. Nostalgia and emotions got them too, while the others looked on longingly.

'How come only you chaps have received things from home?' asked the disappointed Teja.

'Only their families may have come to know that the Red Cross was sending parcels across and they somehow managed to smuggle these items with the help of some sympathetic official,' observed Garry.

'My sister in Delhi is a very persuasive kind of young lady,' said Dilip grinning broadly. 'She must have hung around the Red Cross office for days for this purpose. But look at what she has sent me, my best lounge suit. She might have thought that her brother shouldn't remain poorly dressed in a foreign country.'

Now in the month of June their minds went back to that parcel of clothes. The boxes were pulled out from under the bed. The clothes were tried out for fit, Garry selecting a brown shirt and the blue trouser, Harry contenting himself with just a grey shirt. Dilip let them commandeer his clothes, and, as an afterthought, took out the two woollen jerseys as well and packed them all together in one box and put it in its place under the bed. In front of the boxes were lined up all spare *chappals*, shoes, blankets etc. in order to effectively hide that portion of the wall.

Kuru had in the meantime established a good rapport with Aurangzeb, the all-purpose Man Friday in the camp. Now that the prisoners had cash in their pockets, Kuru often got this good Pathan to buy for them delicious *chappal kebabs*, meat beaten flat and cooked over slow fire, and even the sweet dish called *phirni*. Kuru had also discovered that Aurangzeb was an accomplished tailor in civilian life before joining government service. When Dilip heard of it he got a new idea into his head.

'This *salwar kameez* that you Pathans wear, Aurangzeb, is a very fine dress, elegant and manly,' he initiated the conversation one day. 'Did you tailor it yourself?'

'Yes, of course, I stitch all the clothes for my children as well,' said the Pathan.

'I wish I could get a suit made for myself,' said Dilip longingly. 'We don't get such clothes in India. How much cloth does it take?'

'Only seven metres,' said Aurangzeb with a smile. 'And for you only five,' he joked looking down at Harry from his great height.

So the exchange of ideas on a Pathan dress, the cost of material, the choice of colour etc. went on for a few days with Kuru joining Dilip in persuading Aurangzeb to arrange for one such outfit as a memento of their stay in Pakistan and the fine people they had met there. Finally, the good man Aurangzeb at a minimum cost for the materials stitched a green Pathan suit for Dilip, even foregoing the tailoring charges. Dilip was overjoyed at having managed one more item that would be of great help during the escape. But this achievement also pained and moved him.

'I don't feel happy,' Dilip confided to others after a few days. 'I have sweet-talked a good, simple man into arranging for me a dress for the purpose of escape. After our escape this is bound to come out and the poor fellow may get into serious trouble. And this, after the generosity he has shown by even foregoing the cost of his own labour.'

'Yes, the poor are always more forthcoming. They trust more easily, calculate more sparingly, react more positively, and give more generously. People of our class do not measure up to them, really,' Jafa said. Then noticing that Dilip was still disturbed he continued, 'Dilip, it is the poor, simple folk who always get hurt more. It's true of wars between nations, it will also be true of your attempt to escape. So you do what appears right to you, and let God be the final judge.'

'Don't start getting soft. And that goes for all of you,' Kamy admonished Dilip and all the other younger officers, with sudden vehemence. 'They are all enemies. You just worry about achieving the objective. Who gets hurt in the bargain is not your concern.'

Kamy was seldom confused in any given situation; for him the lines were clearly drawn as between black and white, between good and bad, the desirable and the undesirable, the honourable and the reprehensible, the performance of duty and the shirking of it, the preservation of one's own and the annihilation of the enemy, physically, morally, emotionally. He spoke little, and had hardly participated in the discussions on the escape. But he had observed and listened to all that had been going on. He intervened only to draw attention to some vital detail that might otherwise have got overlooked, and was always thinking ahead to devise things that would be helpful in the escape. In his mind two things had been well taken care of under the circumstances—availability of some cash and a semblance of civilian clothes. He now advised Dilip to try to procure dry fruits such as figs, dates, peaches etc. as well as packets of biscuits. These were arranged and a rough calculation of calories showed that the escapees would be all right for two days, but would have to fend for themselves after that. Kamy then asked Bunny to gently prise out the rubber tubing from his flying overall in which he had arrived in the camp and which was still in his possession. This consisted of a fairly long rubber tube with a non-return valve at one end.

'You will fill up this tube with water and carry it in a bag,' Kamy instructed Dilip. 'This much water, if used sparingly, will see you through for almost twenty-four hours. Of course, you must replenish it at every opportunity.' Then turning to Harry he said, 'If you have to cross a river, Harry, empty out the tube and blow air into it. Wrap it around your chest and you won't drown.'

Kamy had also set about constructing two very important items for the escape team. One was code-named the 'bazooka', a contraption of wire about three inches long which could be safely inserted into any electric socket to effectively fuse the entire circuit. This was to be used for ensuring total darkness in the camp during the breakout. The other was a masterpiece of engineering accomplished within the confines, the limitations, and the total lack of resources inside the prison camp. It was a direction finding compass in the shape of an ordinary fountain pen. When the cap was unscrewed the hollow bottom part of the pen yielded two long parallel needles fastened on to a shirt button, and two smaller sewing needles, all wrapped together with sewing thread. As the button was held aloft, balanced on the tip of a small needle, the two longer needles were free to rotate through 360 degrees. Kamy had devised another contraption with pieces of wire stolen from here and there to repeatedly pass electric current through the two long needles tethered on to the shirt button. He had thus succeeded in magnetizing them, and when free to swing, the points of the needles rotated towards the magnetic north and the eyes towards the south. So here was a home-made compass to determine direction, in light and in darkness, for marching homewards.

The procurement of three bags or rucksacks to make them appear like ordinary travellers was next on the agenda. All eyes again turned towards the great inventor, Kamy. After much thought and scratching of heads for a few days however they were still not close to a solution. Then, one morning sitting on the western-style water closet—which he was allowed to use in the Commandant's personal toilet on account of his peculiar injuries—Kamy noticed the two curtains hanging over the only window in the room. He had never seen them drawn, possibly because the window looked out over a little used part of the camp, and the window had already been provided with strong steel rods and wire gauze. These curtains were unlikely to be missed, thought Kamy as he removed one, folded it under his shirt and returned to his cell. Late at night he cut up the cloth with a shaving blade and stitched together a passable bag. The second curtain was stolen after a gap of a few days and turned into one more bag. For the third, Kamy had to use cloth from Chati's parachute, which, quite inexplicably, had been left with him in the cell. Kamy also made a few smaller bags for carrying provisions, water tube etc. But as he did the cutting and stitching together of the pieces of the parachute cloth in the dark, Kamy did not notice the deep red stains on parts of this parachute which Chati had used to staunch the flow of blood from the gun wound he had received during his capture.

15

Preparations and Doubts

'Tom is getting ready,' whispered Dilip to Jafa during the evening stroll in the courtyard. He had, of course, named it after the first of the three tunnels, called Tom, Dick and Harry, that were dug by Allied servicemen to escape from a German prison camp during the Second World War, as described in the book and film *The Great Escape*.

'Are you still determined?' asked Jafa.

'Absolutely,' said Dilip.

'The others?'

'Some softening of the will, whenever there is news of a possible agreement on repatriation. Otherwise, they would go with me.'

'Approximate D-Day?' asked Jafa.

'The 27th or the 28th.' Dilip was fairly certain of the time it would still take to complete the digging of the hole.

It was Dilip and Garry who worked alternately from about 10:30 p.m. in the evening until about 1:30 a.m. in the morning, every day, at scraping out the cement plaster and loosening the bricks. The modus operandi was to begin playing cards immediately after supper and put the transistor radio on high volume for any kind of music from any corner of the world to cover up the noise during the scraping of the wall. At about 10 pm they would ask to

Preparations and Doubts

be taken to the toilet, and, on return, ask the guard to switch off the cell light from the outside. The radio would keep blaring. Chati and Harry would then lie down on the floor close to the door and the window while Dilip and Garry pulled the bed slightly away from the rear wall and moved the cardboard boxes around to create working space. One of them would then get down and begin scraping, while the other collected the loose bits of plaster, sand and brick and hid them inside the empty cardboard boxes.

It was for Chati and Harry to watch over every movement of the guards. If any of them came too close to the cell a 'bogey' call was whispered, and the scraping stopped instantly. For anyone peering from outside there would appear to be four bodies in deep slumber inside the cell, three real and one dummy representing whoever was down at work behind the cot. But for Dilip the preparation for the escape was not merely a serious and desirable endeavour, it was also a great deal of fun. Little things amused him and he merrily laughed away at all the peccadilloes. Now he was bent upon testing out Kamy's bazooka in spite of all the assurances by the inventor and others that it was an unfailing device and needed no experimentation. So one night he positioned the bazooka over the electric plug, waited until the young guard, a new face, had gone furthest from the cell, called 'ready' and pressed it inside. WHOOSH! There was noise like a whisper heard through a 200-watt amplifier at maximum volume, and the room was bathed in a neon-like illumination for a brief second. Dilip leapt on to his bed a moment before the guard pressed his head against the iron bars of the cell door.

'What happened?' asked Dilip innocently of the guard.

'There was a strange kind of noise here. What was it?' enquired the guard.

'Noise? What noise?' Dilip countered and continued as with afterthought. 'Oh, that noise ... I was just changing the band on the radio and perhaps the volume was too loud.'

The guard retreated slowly. It did not occur to him to put on the light switch for this cell which was on the outside. That would have solved the mystery of the noise. But he remained very alert after that, so alert that Dilip and Garry had to give up the digging work for the night.

The young Shamsuddin was a clever and properly suspicious guard. The escape team had to be very careful and alert when he was on duty. One night as Dilip and Garry were at work behind the cot, Shamsuddin tiptoed to the cell from one side, but the even more alert Chati noticed the shadowy approach just a couple of seconds before he reached the door. Chati gave a frightened 'bogey' call and leapt up towards the door just as Shamsuddin clicked on a torchlight. Harry too sprang up and they both effectively blocked the light from penetrating deeper into the room.

'What's up? What's happened?' Chati called out to Shamsuddin in the manner of a rudely awakened person.

'I didn't ask to be taken to the toilet. Did you, Chati?' Harry piped up in mock surprise.

'No ... nothing,' said Shamsuddin as he retreated with uncertain steps. For him suspicion was not enough; concrete proof was needed to justify the raising of an alarm.

The next morning they discussed the narrowly missed detection by Shamsuddin the previous night. Chati observed that the guards did not seem to relax so long as the music blared from the radio in Cell No. 5. The guards positively took it more easy once the radio was switched off for the night, possibly because the silence assured them that the prisoners were peacefully asleep. After that they made fewer rounds and even sat on an odd stool or on the *verandah* steps outside other cells and, possibly, even dozed a bit. In any case, it was now necessary to divert attention from Cell No. 5. So Kuru was asked to take the radio to his cell at the other end of the camp every night after supper and keep the music blaring until the early hours of the morning, which he did meticulously. The guards' attention was divided, but greater care had also to be taken to suppress the scraping noises in the cell and the 'bogey' call had to be given on the mere suspicion of an approaching guard.

Preparations and Doubts

A few days later luck again favoured them and they were saved from discovery. The pack-up call was given by Dilip at 1.30 in the morning. He and Garry quickly put the loose bricks back into the hole, then scooped up the dirt and poured it into the cardboard boxes, covered the hole with the same boxes, and placed shoes and other things in front of them. Dilip lay down on his bed and everyone relaxed. But Garry, before pushing the cot back to the wall, wanted to take another look at the closing arrangements. He peered down in the direction of the hole and began to re-align and re-adjust the boxes. At this time his torso was reclining sideways on the bed, the two legs jutting out like two ivory tusks, while the head and shoulders were buried in the cavity on the other side, the whole apparition only dimly visible in the reflected glow of outside courtyard lights. Suddenly, the click of the electric switch outside the door came on like a thunderclap and the room was flooded with light. On one side was a pair of ivory clubs sticking out of a body with no head, on the other the stare of a young guard fixed on this ostrich-like apparition. Then even as the guard blinked to clear his vision, Garry's massive head with the hair just sprouting after a recent haircut, swung on to the bed. Garry blinked, his forehead furrowed and lips compressed as with disgust he said in Punjabi, 'Can't a man even get a night's sleep in this damned place?'

The guard stood there, unable to decide whether he should blow the whistle, get the keys and have the cell checked out, or whether he was letting his imagination run wild. Then he switched off the light and walked away, Garry belching forth the obligatory growls of discontent and the others barely managing to stifle the alarm as well as the chuckles. The guards were young and diffident about their own conclusions as well as afraid to make mistakes. Or, the Indian prisoners were simply very lucky.

During the walk in the courtyard the following evening, Dilip caught up with Harry and Jafa and whispered, 'Two nights work left.'

There was silence for a while. Then Harry said, 'We were talking just now, of the need to finalise the route and take a firm decision about it. It is not just my personal inability to swim or undertake an arduous cross-country march. It is much more than that.'

Jafa looked at Dilip, inviting his comments.

'Sir, until now we seem to be agreed that on breaking out of here we shall get out of the city fast and head in a north-easterly direction. We shall avoid Wah and Islamabad to the east, which are more or less government areas and where suspicion may get aroused more easily. Also, there would be fewer places to get lost in, like crowded market places, *dhaba*s etc. So, going north-east, we hit the hills and then turn eastwards, get down and cross the Jhelum and climb back into the hills on the other side. The idea would be to cross the border somewhere between Kotli on this side and Poonch on our side.'

'The total walking distance would be seventy to a hundred miles,' observed Jafa. 'Do you think you chaps can make it in, say, three to four days? Mind you, you've been living rather a lazy life here.'

'I think Garry can make it, he'll be quite up to it,' said Dilip. 'And so long as Garry keeps going I would too, if only on willpower and little else.'

Their eyes turned to Harry whose thoughts at this moment had flashed back to an English film in which a grotesque thing, a skeleton covered in tattered skin with the blood in his veins almost congealed due to dehydration, staggers across a border onto home ground and takes an year to recover. Bleakly Harry accepted the impending fate of similarly staggering across and perhaps taking forever to recover. But to voice any self-doubts would not only disqualify him at this late stage but also get him branded as an LMF—one with lack of moral fibre, a man without courage, therefore without honour, the most derogatory epithet among fighter pilots.

So, drawing a deep breath, Harry said, 'Sir, one radio announcement about our escape and every man, woman and child would be looking for us, in trains and buses, in hills and valleys, in *bazaar*s and *dhaba*s, even in drains and rabbit holes. This is not India where half the people may yet not know that a major war was fought recently.

Preparations and Doubts

Sorry about this, but in this country our safety will lie in covering as much distance as possible in the shortest time.'

'What's the alternative?' enquired Jafa.

'Kuru and I have been collecting information on buses from the civilian staff in the camp. I understand that the bus station for Peshawar is very close from here and we should be able to reach it in just a few minutes. I have also learnt that buses for Peshawar leave every half-an-hour, around the clock. The same holds good for Lahore. But, Peshawar may be a safer option than Lahore,' Harry concluded.

In silence they kept walking up and down for a while. Jafa then called out to Garry who joined him as Dilip and Harry fell back. He repeated Harry's argument against the cross-country march and added that he himself tended to agree with him. Then Jafa went over the Peshawar route with Garry and the possibility of taking a fast bus ride almost up to the Khyber Pass.

'That's okay by me so long as you have considered all aspects and are convinced about this route,' said Garry simply, trustingly. He was indeed the chap to go into the jungle with, thought Jafa. If he trusted you, he did not ask questions, he did his assigned job faithfully and fearlessly and did not even wait for thanks.

They both slowed to allow Dilip and Harry to come closer. Jafa looked at them and said, 'Garry seems to be convinced about the north-west. Aren't you, Garry?'

'Yes, okay by me,' affirmed Garry.

'That makes three of us,' said Dilip as he burst into loud laughter. The other prisoners as well as the guards turned towards them. They saw all four laughing and assumed that Dilip must have cracked a good joke.

Jafa kept walking up and down the courtyard by himself, thinking about the impending escape, and the tensions, hardships, harassments, punitive actions by the enemy, even loss of life, that were bound to follow. But ... there could be no going back now. It was not some children's imaginative games that they had been playing so far, and what had appeared to be right during the long preparation could not turn out to be wrong at the moment of execution. Yes, the decision was already made, in bits and pieces, in moments and months, only the deed remained to be done.

'Dilip,' Jafa called out.

As Dilip came closer Jafa whispered, 'You have to pass word now to everyone that the D-Day may be the day after tomorrow. Tell them that whatever happens, no one is to open his mouth during questioning for at least twenty-four hours. This is the minimum time that they will have to endure even beatings and other third-degree. Even afterwards they should not give out the route if they can help it. Let everybody sleep over it tonight; may be someone will come up with some ideas about the cover-up.'

Dilip fell back and was seen walking with each prisoner in turn for a few minutes, conversing in subdued tones and whispers. Jafa walked alone, others in pairs, and soon it was time for supper and return to the cells for the night.

The next morning there was palpable tension in the room as all the prisoners gathered there after breakfast. Dilip and Harry tried to say funny things to induce laughter but their attempts did not go far. And then Bunny Coelho, an elder officer with a serious mien coughed gently to draw attention.

'The newspapers are again coming up with hints of a possible agreement for our repatriation ... ,' he began.

'Of course,' affirmed Brother Bhargava. 'Even the TV news and interviews with journalists, politicians etc. give the same strong impression. I'm sure that an agreement would soon be reached and we shall be home before we know it.'

'So ... ?' asked Kuruvilla, a very pointed and pregnant question. 'We have been hearing these rumours for the last six months,' he added by way of explanation, possibly also to snub any soft thinking at this final stage.

'No. It's not as simple as all that. And it's a serious matter,' said the older officer. Then turning towards the door he looked around furtively to check if any guard was within earshot. Finding the coast clear he addressed Dilip and Garry. 'Even if the repatriation takes some days, even some weeks, isn't it better to wait for it rather than rush out madly and ... Kaput?' He ran his hand in front of the neck in the known gesture for beheading.

'It's totally foolhardy and unnecessary,' emphasised the elder after a pause. 'I don't think you chaps should go ahead with the escape.'

'Isn't it rather late in the day for that, Sir?' said Dilip a bit sarcastically, a bit irritated.

'Nothing has been done. There is no commitment of any sort. No harm if you just drop everything, as of now, as it is now,' added Brother.

The elder turned towards Jafa and addressed him directly, 'You better tell these chaps to call it off, and not be rash.'

It was like an order from him, in his capacity as the elder, the eldest. Yet, Jafa quickly thought that the circumstances did not warrant a command of this nature, and therefore, its obedience was not called for either. He began fingering the pack of cards lying on the table before him, his mind on several things. Instinctively he knew that this was the moment for assuming responsibility or withdrawing from it, this was the moment for decision on execution or abandonment, this was the moment that would make heroes of men or cast them in the moulds of cowards forever, this was the moment that would inspire future generations or make mice of them. In any case this was the moment of decision that would be etched in their memories for ever.

'It's up to these chaps really,' said he gently, matter-of-factly. 'It's not for me or anyone else to take the position of a decision maker in this matter.'

Then he narrowed his eyes and spoke harshly through his teeth. 'But, By God, I shall abide by whatever these three fellows decide and I shall back them to the hilt.'

In the stunning silence that followed all eyes slowly turned towards the trio. In soft, weighty words Garry said, 'If Dilip goes, I go with him.'

'The same for me,' said Harry, firmly.

Dilip broke out into a loud laughter and said, 'Sir, the decision was made even before I landed here.' He patted Garry and Harry on the biceps, elated by the faith reposed in him by the other two, and said, 'So, there we are, partners!'

The die was cast.

The elder was unhappy. 'Well, I still don't approve of this,' he said finally. 'I will not take any responsibility for it, now or later.' And with that he walked out of the room and asked the guard to take him to his cell.

'I hope he will remember to keep his mouth shut from now onwards,' said Kuru behind the retreating figure of the elder.

The day passed in desultory conversation. Even the games of bridge and chess failed to incite the usual noisy disagreements and recriminations. The four cellmates, Dilip, Garry, Chati and Harry mostly slept or dozed during the day, the others too whiled away the time. In the evening they were taken out to the courtyard where the fitter people played volleyball and the others watched. Soon the game was given up and everyone joined the promenade in twos and threes. After a while Brother came up to Jafa and Kamy, making it obvious that he had something on his mind.

'It shouldn't have happened this way,' he began. 'I mean it shouldn't have been said like that. Of course everyone is entitled to his views, but don't you think there is at least some truth in what was said?'

'Yes, of course, there is truth, pure and unalloyed truth in what he said,' intervened Kamy. 'Who doesn't know that a great deal of risk is involved in this attempt? Who doesn't know that in all likelihood they will be shot if captured? And that we all will be harassed, humiliated and beaten up in either case.'

Brother entirely missed the drift of Kamy's comment. He felt encouraged to press on with his views.

'Then why don't you stop them?' he asked.

'But you heard their decision, Brother. I am with them, all the way. I only wish I was in a condition to go myself. My bloody luck!' Kamy displayed such intense frustration and helplessness at

Preparations and Doubts

his physical disability as Jafa had rarely seen. He placed a hand on Kamy's shoulder and gently held him. Words were not needed.

But Brother was not one to give up. His was that middle-of-the-road kind of persistence that takes a man determinedly forward without ever taking too strong a position on any issue. But in this instance he was mainly motivated by genuine fear for the safety of all.

'I ask you, Jeff, Sir,' said Brother. 'Will you let Dilip go if he was your son?'

Jafa halted, turned and looked at Brother. 'That's a difficult question, Brother. All I can say is that if my son was placed in this position, I wouldn't like to be around when he made his decision and carried out the plan.' With this he resumed the slow walk. Brother kept pace with him.

'But to return to your question,' continued Jafa. 'I would explain the pros and cons to my son, definitely emphasize the cons more than the pros, as I hope I have done with Dilip and Garry and Harry, and leave him to reach his own decision ... And I shall live with a trembling heart and dry tears and silent prayers while he went ahead ... as ... as ... I am doing right now.'

Kamy was visibly moved at these words as he turned to look at Jafa approvingly, adoringly. Brother only said, 'I see!'.

After a little more walking in silence Brother again brought up the subject. 'I am only wondering, Sir, if it is at all worthwhile. After all it is not an operational necessity, our country's well-being doesn't depend upon it. It is not essential, it is not even desirable. Even if they go through successfully ... so what? What would they or the country or the Air Force gain? So, why take the risk?'

'Ah! We now come to the issue—why take the risk, for this or for any other such enterprise! Why climb the Everest? Well, to become a Hillary! Why sail around the world? Well, to become a Columbus!' expostulated Jafa. Teja and others edged closer to listen to this conversation which they sensed was an interesting expression of the issues raging in everyone's mind.

'We have a Douglas Bader as our hero in the Air Force, a British fighter pilot who flew operational missions with artificial legs. We have a Steve McQueen leading the breakout of Allied prisoners during the Second World War. For the Army, Rommel, McArthur and Patton are the heroes. And our Navy harks back directly to Nelson. Do you see who our heroes are? Do we have any of our own?'

Jafa paused until everyone had come within hearing distance. 'Yes, we can hark back to the ancient times, to Arjuna perhaps. To Rana Pratap? ... Rani Laximibai? Yes. Netaji Subhash? Yes! But are we going to stop and simply bask in their glory? Aren't we going to carry on and set newer examples in bravery and daring? Isn't modern, resurgent India going to have newer heroes?'

All stared at Jafa. No one spoke.

'Yes, risks have to be taken. Lives may have to be lost in the pursuit of such objectives. Mercifully for the nation, there are always, in every generation, men of daring, men of vision, men who brave hazards, men who challenge the demons of death. Such are the men a nation needs, such are the men we hope and pray for. Such are the men who mostly come through with flying colours. Such are the men who get to be looked upon as heroes. By God, we need men like that!'

In the silence that ensued Harry sidled up to Jafa and said, 'I now understand. That's why you have been encouraging us all this time! Yes?'

Jafa smiled. There was nothing more to say.

The events of the day, the discussions and Jafa's final harangue had helped to put everything in perspective, that the impending escape was not a haphazard, ill-planned, ill-conceived, foolhardy enterprise, that it had a noble, an honourable purpose. They were all now inspired to contribute their best moral support and physical help and fervent prayers for its success.

B.A. (Bunny) Coelho

Dhirendra S. Jafa

A.V. Kamat (Kamy)

Dilip Parulkar receiving Vayu Sena Medal from Marshal of the Air Force Arjan Singh

J.L. (Brother) Bhargava

M.S. (Garry) Grewal

A.V. (Vikram) Pethia

V.S. Chati

K.C. Kuruvilla (Kuru)

Harish (Harry) Sinhji

H. Mulla-Feroze (Mulla)

Prisoners-of-war alighting at Palam Airport: Returning home on 1 December 1972
1st row: Dhirendra S. Jafa, Harish Sinhji, B.A. Coelho, A.V. Kamat
2nd row: J.L. Bhargava, K.C. Kuruvilla, Tejwant Singh
3rd row: Dilip Parulkar, V.S. Chati, M.S. Grewal

Arriving at Palam, 1 December 1972
Bunny Coelho, Dhirendra S. Jafa, Tejwant Singh, Harish Sinhji, V.S. Chati and M.S. Grewal

Bunny Coelho being received by his wife at Palam, 1 December 1972

Author, Dhirendra S. Jafa, being hugged by his mother Smt Prakashvati at Palam, 1 December 1972

Brother Bhargava being received by Air Marshal T.S. Virk at Palam,
1 December 1972

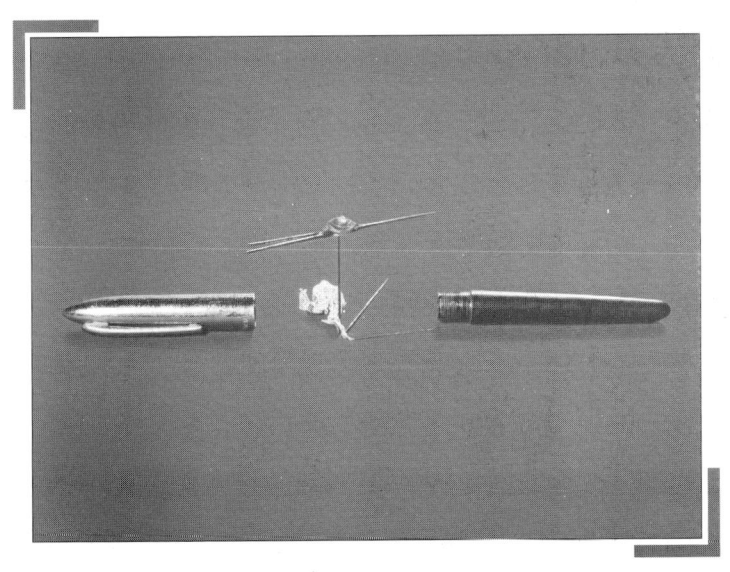

Pen compass made by Squadron Leader A.V. Kamat

Postage stamp issued by the Government of Pakistan in April 1973 to garner international sympathy for release of their 90,000 soldiers who surrendered to the Indian Army in December 1971

Indira Gandhi, the architect of India's greatest military triumph, greeting the author and his family on the award of Vir Chakra to him

16

The Breakout

The following night, all the bricks were finally out. Only the outer layer of cement plaster remained in place. Dilip and Garry ran their hands over it with great satisfaction. They tapped on it and heard the hollow sound, like that of an empty container.

'Now we leave it like this, Garry boy,' whispered Dilip. 'One gentle push when we are ready, and out into the open! What do you say, partner?'

'I only say, put the damn bricks back properly and neatly, and hope like hell that nobody gets wise to it,' said Garry.

After covering up the hole, they all went to sleep and got up next morning to begin another day in the prison camp. Jafa was quietly informed that the exit hole in the wall was ready. Equally quietly he asked Dilip to mentally go over all the items needed for the escape and to once more pass the hat around for the very last penny in cash still lurking shyly in someone's pocket.

'Be ready to go, but the final decision shall be made at supper time,' advised Jafa.

So the day passed quite normally, with card and chess games going on apparently as usual with arguments and jokes and laughter. The evening in the courtyard was also whiled away in a normal, everyday routine manner. Only Harry came up to Jafa and whispered, 'Tomorrow is Saturday. If we get out tomorrow, we may have the initial advantage of slower reactions on the part of the enemy on Sunday morning.'

Jafa acknowledged the value of this idea by nodding his head vigorously a couple of times. But he continued walking silently, weighed down by his own thoughts. At eventide as the day light began to fade and give way to the gathering darkness, Jafa spotted a flash of lightning on the horizon. In the next few minutes the western sky began to get covered up with dark clouds. Perhaps a rain storm was in the offing, he thought. That could be helpful to the escape team. Jafa sought Dilip out and told him, 'Looks like a storm coming up. You may start getting ready after dinner. If the storm hits this place, go. If not, you may go tomorrow as Harry has suggested.'

Dilip simply nodded to confirm that he understood perfectly and went away to speak with Garry and Harry. Later during the dinner the distant rumbling of thunderclouds became clearly audible. Dilip, Harry and Garry began to whisper farewells; the others pressed their hands and arms and wished them well. Soon it was time to move off to the cells. On reaching his cell Harry quickly fished out the rubber tube from under the bed and wrapped it around his body under his loose shirt. He asked to be taken to the toilet and there he filled it up with water, wrapped it around his body once again and returned to the cell. This was the only item for which an outside trip was required. All the other things were to be put together inside the cell.

They made a pretence of playing cards and in whispers went over the list of items to be packed for the escape. They then talked to Chati about the cover up he would have to provide in order to delay discovery of the escape for as long as possible. At about 10:30 p.m. the light was switched off in ostensible preparation for going to bed. The radio in Kuru's cell at the other end of the camp blared on maximum volume. While Chati and Harry lay down near the door, Garry and Dilip began to pack foodstuff and the woollen pullovers in two bags. The water-filled rubber tube was put in the third bag.

The Breakout

One by one they changed into the clothes for the escape and wore the canvas shoes. The cash was distributed among the three. Dilip picked up the fountain-pen compass and kept it carefully in his breast pocket. Chati who had developed a toothache a couple of days earlier and was on medication, took out the painkiller pills and passed them on to the three. 'Just in case', he said.

Around midnight the storm broke over the camp. Loud thunder was followed by heavy rain. Dilip removed the light bulb from its holder, the device called the 'bazooka' having been given up for the noise it made. Garry pulled back the bed and quickly removed the loose bricks from the hole in the wall. He pushed against the outer layer of the cement lining to break it and clear the hole for the escape. The plaster held firm. Dilip too tried his hand, again to no avail. Dilip eased back and kicked at the layer of plaster with his foot. It did not give way. They were now getting desperate. The thunder and the rain were ideal for the breakout. It was a summer storm which could move away as rapidly as it had arrived and they would be deprived of its protective noise and low visibility. In desperation Garry grabbed the cricket bat lying under the same bed and shoved it against the plaster. Nothing happened. Another harder blow. And a hole the size of a tennis ball appeared. Yet again, one more blow, but there was no further effect on the concrete plaster.

'Bogey', called Chati urgently. He had seen Shamsuddin running towards the cell in the heavy down pour.

Shamsuddin reached for the light switch ... click ... click ... click ... but no joy. The bulb just wasn't there. If the light had come on Shamsuddin would have been shocked to discover two human forms sleeping huddled together on each of the two string beds and on Harry's bedding on the floor, one real and one dummy each. He would also have noticed three bags in the middle of the room, and the cardboard boxes lying in a jumble under the bed and spilling over beyond it.

Chati, by now used to handling such a situation, rose from his bed as if awakened suddenly. 'What's the matter, Shamsuddin? Why are you getting wet in the rain? Is there any problem?' he enquired.

'There was noise here. A few hard knocks actually. What happened?' demanded Shamsuddin.

'No, there was no noise here, you must have heard the thunder,' Chati suggested earnestly.

Shamsuddin looked like a cat who has smelt her favourite mouse under the sofa but can't get to it. Very reluctantly, very slowly he walked away in the rain. Dilip jumped out of his bed and quickly grabbed a piece of cloth, rolled it into a ball and stuffed it into the hole in the wall. All the bricks were quickly put back. The bags were unpacked and their contents returned to the cardboard boxes. All other items were rearranged under the bed. Then they changed back into camp clothes and lay down in their beds. Lucky to have escaped detection, thought Dilip. A few more days of work to further scrape and thin down the plaster and they might be out.

No work however could be done on the concrete plaster for the next few nights as the guards were unduly alert. Undoubtedly, Shamsuddin had aired his suspicion that the prisoners in cell number 5 could be up to some mischief. In the meantime they were worried about the hole in the plaster and the piece of cloth jutting out from it on the other side. It could be noticed by any one of the dozens of employees who parked their bikes on the other side of that wall. But, as usually happens, most men see but do not observe. The only one to notice that piece of cloth and take an interest in it was a tom cat that owned the territory. It happened one night about a week after the failed attempt when Dilip felt safe to restart the scraping work. He noticed that the cloth was being pulled by someone from the other side. Gently but firmly he held on to the cloth on his side and a tug-of-war ensued. The cloth was getting pulled out and getting pulled in repeatedly, though gently, as if two adversaries were playing a teasing game. Dilip feared that discovery was imminent and warned Garry in a whisper that there was someone on the other side trying to pull the cloth away. Just then he heard a soft 'meow'.

'It's that damned tom cat,' said Dilip, barely able to suppress his laughter. Then he pulled out the cloth and peered outside. There was the tom cat, looking perplexed. He saw that the compound and the boundary wall were clearly visible in the moon light.

'Lovely ... yaar! The glimpse of freedom!' he sighed, and went back to work.

It was now the beginning of August. The repatriation of prisoners of both sides had got linked with the recognition of Bangladesh by the Government of Pakistan. For two or three days in succession Bhutto hinted that Bangladesh would be recognised by August 15th. The prisoners' expectations of going home began to rise, some even saw the hand of Providence in the aborted escape attempt and strongly prevailed upon the trio to postpone their plan indefinitely. On the other hand, the concrete plaster had been scraped to a delicate thinness that would yield at the slightest pressure. All other preparations too were as complete as they would ever be in the prison camp.

Then on the evening of August 11th Bhutto addressed the people of Pakistan on the national television. On Bangladesh he said that the question of recognition shall not even be discussed in the National Assembly as Mujib-ur-Rehman was acting tough and putting up unacceptable demands. The Indian prisoners had watched this announcement and in the silence that followed they could see Dilip's features hardening into a kind of grim determination.

'There never was any point in waiting,' he said.

'Tomorrow then,' added Harry. 'Ideal timing. The 13th and 14th are holidays. Slower reactions. Better chances for us.'

The drill of the previous attempt was repeated after supper on the night of August 12th. At 00:15 hours on the 13th morning Garry had the hole completely open before him. He invited everyone to take a peep at freedom on the other side. Then he said goodbye to Chati and slipped out. Harry went next, Dilip last.

There was again a storm brewing and dust was swirling about when they got out. They quickly sat down against the rear wall of the furthest cell to take stock of the surroundings. The storm gathered speed and clouds of dust began to rise everywhere. The Recruiting Office *chowkidar* was sitting right in front of them about thirty yards away, huddled under a blanket to save himself from the swirling dust. Garry eased himself up the boundary wall to take a look at the road outside, The Mall. A large number of men were scurrying away rapidly in the dust storm; perhaps a late night movie had just got over. Garry sat down under the wall and waited. After a few minutes he again peeped over the wall, and, finding the road clear of people, he signalled to the others to follow him. In a jiffy they were all over and across the wall, walking the hundred yards down The Mall towards the Pindi-Peshawar highway. The time was 00:40 hours.

Just before they came onto the highway, Harry exclaimed, 'Freedom! How Lovely!' And began to dance a jig on the open pavement.

Garry turned around and placed a sound kick on Harry's bottom, saying, 'Hold on, you bugger! There's a long way to go. Else our freedom will end right here.'

The sobered Harry tried to recall what he was supposed to do at this stage of the escape. One was to act casual, so he took out a cigarette and lit it with great relish. The other was to address each other by their new identities. Dilip was now John Masih, a lowly Christian airman of the Pakistan Air Force, from Lahore. Garry, who looked like a tough Pathan, was to be called Ali Ameer, again an airman from Lahore. Harry who was the most anglicised of the three and could not speak Hindi or Urdu even passably, was now Mr. Harold Jacob who played drums in a band in Karachi. The three were friends and had joined up for a sightseeing trip to the north-western frontier area.

'Ali,' whispered Harry from behind.

'Ali Ameer!' he repeated again.

'What's happening to you?' demanded Garry.

'I am calling you and you don't listen. Have you forgotten your bloody name?' Now Harry was one up.

As they passed the Odeon Theatre, big drops of rain began to come down. This was a good augury, considered auspicious by some but helpful to them in any case. A couple of hundred yards further down the road, and the street lights went out, a common occurrence during storms all over the sub-continent. They felt hidden from the world and hoped that luck would continue favouring them.

'I am worried about Chati,' said Dilip, a while later. 'I can't imagine what they'll do to him when they discover that we've escaped. Might even shoot him to show that they had downed one prisoner while the others escaped. That may lessen the charge of negligence on their part.'

'He'll definitely be questioned about the escape route. May even get roughed up a bit, but I doubt it'll be more than that,' observed Garry.

Then they talked about the support Kamy had given them, the items he had produced for the ease and success of the escape. And the regrets Kamy will always have for not being with them, all due to his injured legs which as yet could not support him adequately. And the sustained, single-minded encouragement and guidance provided by Jafa. Like Kamy he too could not join the expedition, but unlike anyone else he was for it from the very beginning without wavering even once. But, wondered Dilip, in the pursuit of an objective did individuals matter to Jafa? He picked men for specific tasks, groomed them and set them on the path to some desirable achievement. Success usually crowned his efforts, but when things went wrong and ended in disaster, or in the context of military operation, in death, he was quick to derive useful lessons but was never seen to grieve over anybody. What if he and the others in the escape team lost their lives in this attempt, Dilip wondered ... well, he would never know the synopsis of errors that Jafa's mind would work out for future wisdom. He would certainly write a touchingly beautiful letter of condolence and then go on to groom someone else. Yet they all found him faultless, even adorable, because, as with others, he never spared himself, never shirked from the most dangerous missions and they were sure that if he met his own end the first thing he would do up there would be to sit down with his chin resting on his hand and begin working out the mistakes he had made.

They walked through the town for nearly an hour and came to a *tonga* stand. One by one the *tongawallah*s turned to look at them as they passed, a question mark hanging on their faces.

'We are not as inconspicuous as we thought,' said Garry.

Another half-a-mile and they came upon a bus parked on the side of the road, its engine idling. The driver peered over his window and yelled out at them, 'Peshwar ... Peshwar.' He was soliciting passengers to fill up the bus.

They looked at each other in amazement at their luck. Dilip climbed aboard and took a seat on the left of the aisle. Garry took the seat behind him and dragged Harry to sit on his right. Garry pointed at his *kara*, the iron wristband that all devout Sikhs wear, which he had been unable to remove and which now protruded below the shirt-sleeve. Harry put a hand over Garry's right arm to hide the *kara* which could be a certain give-away if spotted by anyone. To make matters worse the driver put the cabin lights on. They thought of stepping down from the bus to while away the waiting period in the dark outside. But that might have given rise to suspicion, so they spread their limbs and partly hid their heads into their shoulders feigning sleep. They were not disturbed by anyone till the bus started moving at about 02:30 in the morning, after which a youth came around to collect the fare which was paid out by Dilip. The bus ran non-stop for nearly two hours during which they actually dozed off and felt quite refreshed when a halt was made at a wayside *dhaba*, an open air restaurant. Everybody was getting down from the bus, so did they, and, like others, they too first went round the corner. Whatever the westerners may feel or say, this open-air toilet facility in the orient has its own peculiar advantages. One doesn't have to seek directions for a loo and one doesn't have to pay for it. This is what Harry was thinking when he heard Dilip say, 'You know what? I find the sense of adventure totally missing. I don't feel a thing.'

'Exactly,' said Harry. 'It feels like going from Delhi to Ambala by bus! I think I know what is lacking—the background music of a James Bond movie!'

The Breakout

They laughed softly and headed for the benches laid out in the open by the restaurateur. Garry greedily eyed a *paratha* that was being gobbled up by a youth this early in the morning. But Dilip only ordered tea. He later got one more glass for Garry.

At sunrise the bus entered Peshawar and they got off at the very first stop in the city, and headed for the nearest tea shop where they could sit and take stock of the situation. A small boy served tea in an ancient Chinese pot which seemed to have served many generations and many tea shops. It was in fragments but each fragment had been put back again with all kinds of glues and adhesives and held together with a netting of thin steel wire. It did not leak and poured out strong, hot tea. In different circumstances Harry the collector would have tried to strike a bargain for it. But for now he only admired the original beauty of the piece and the ingenuity of the local people to keep it going.

'Can't believe we've already made it to Peshawar, in just five hours,' said Garry softly and with a smile of satisfaction.

'Yes. But let's hurry and move on before the Pakistan radio comes on with the morning news about us,' Dilip cautioned.

They crossed the road and stopped a cruising *tonga*. Garry moved forward to bargain with the *tongawallah*. Dilip and Harry spotted a few three-wheeled autorickshaws on the side of the road awaiting passengers. The drivers wore belts of ammunition and a rifle lay along the handlebar of each vehicle. This was an unexpected sight and they had no wish to hire a vehicle that may get involved in an exchange of fire.

'Where to?' asked the *tongawallah*.

'We have to go to Jamraud Road. How much will you charge?' countered Garry.

'Jamraud Road or Jamraud *Chowk*?' asked the *tonga* man.

'Yes, yes, Jamraud *Chowk*. That's the address,' affirmed Garry.

The driver looked at them quizzically but decided that his first task was to begin the day with a good fare. 'Four rupees,' he demanded.

'Four rupees?' asked Garry in mock surprise. 'That's too much. You should charge not more than three, a rupee for each of us.'

'The best *tonga*, the best horse in Peshawar, it is. Also you won't find another *tonga* at this time of day. Hop on. Four rupees,' declared the cabbie.

'Alright, but take us fast,' Garry said because he had to say something while capitulating. He climbed up alongside the driver in the front, Dilip and Harry occupied the seat in the rear. One swing of the whip and the horse trotted forward.

'Jamraud *Chowk*! Where do you want to go in Jamraud *Chowk*?' asked the driver as he launched out to satisfy his curiosity that had been gnawing at him from the moment he had set eyes on this bunch of men.

'There is a newspaper office in the *Chowk*,' said Garry, matching Punjabi with Punjabi, and hoping that the illiterate looking *tongawallah* may know little about newspapers or other literary pursuits.

'You are reporters?' asked the *tonga* man casually.

'No, no! We have to go to a place next to this newspaper office,' replied Garry.

'You work there?' persisted the cabbie.

'No, we are going for an interview.' Garry wondered if this was a safe line.

'Interview on a Sunday?' A very pertinent question. Dilip was about to intervene but thought it better to leave the conversation to Garry whose mother tongue was Punjabi.

'Look, we have work there. But you are questioning me like the police. To satisfy your curiosity, we will see the place today and then roam about in this beautiful area for a couple of days and attend to our business the day after tomorrow. Anything else?' Garry tried a mildly offensive approach, and it worked. The driver did not ask any more questions. And in a few minutes they had arrived at the *Chowk*.

'You may get down,' he said bringing the *tonga* to a halt. Harry pulled out a fiver and extended it to him.

The Breakout

'No change,' said the driver in English.

'Keep the change,' replied Harry in safe Hindustani.

The *tongawallah* looked thoughtfully at the three poorly dressed young men apparently coming out to seek employment but agreeing to pay four rupees for a seven minute ride and even paying out a one-rupee tip. There was some anomaly somewhere but he was not able to put a finger on it. Perhaps a little more time with them and he'll solve the riddle.

'If you tell me the exact address I'll take you there. It'll be convenient for you. And no extra charge,' he offered.

'Thanks very much, but we have quite some time on our hands till the offices and shops open up. We'll just roam about a bit,' said Garry as he began to lead them quickly away.

They walked briskly along the Jamraud Road. After a while Harry turned back to look at the *tongawallah*. He was still standing by the side of the *tonga* peering steadily in their direction.

'Suspicious chap,' said Harry. 'Let's quickly turn into a side street and get lost.'

They quickly turned left in to a side lane, went some distance and took a right, then another right a little further up and returned to the main road. They walked for almost three miles looking for a place where they could get off the road and hide during the day. They were now about twenty-six miles from the Afghan border, which could be covered by marching through two nights. But they could not leave the road as there were houses and small shops along both sides. Leaving the road for any reason other than a call of nature would invite attention and almost instantaneous apprehension. They also felt conspicuous in their totally out of place clothes. Everyone here was dressed in a white long shirt and *salwar*, and everyone seemed to be turning around to stare at the strange men, two in ill-fitting western clothes and one in a green Pathan dress. Cyclists stopped, leaned on one leg and looked them over, others wheeled back and circled them to satisfy their curiosity. They began to get a bit nervous, thinking that their luck might be running out. Harry dropped back by about a hundred yards thinking that two persons or a single one would be less conspicuous than three walking shoulder to shoulder. Soon he was joined by a Pathan youth on a bicycle.

'What are you carrying in the bag?' asked the youth in Urdu.

'Oh, just some food and water,' replied Harry.

'Why are you carrying food?' he persisted.

'We are going sightseeing, here and there, and will sit down somewhere and eat together when we are hungry,' said Harry, wondering whether he should brush off this obtrusive fellow who continued to cross-question him. Perhaps it was safer to play along, he decided finally.

'Are you sure it is food you are carrying? Not *aata*?' asked the youth, meaning that Harry may possibly be carrying wheat flour.

He divined that wheat flour may be a coveted item in these parts, an item on the priority list of smugglers, and the youth may be looking around to purchase some.

'No, no. It's not *aata*, only our food,' assured Harry.

'It's a large bag. I can carry it on my bicycle for you. Even you can take a lift with me,' offered the youth.

'I am not alone, you see,' said Harry. 'You can't carry all of us.'

The youth looked up the road at Dilip and Garry. He possibly decided that he could not tackle three smugglers at one go, and pedalled away.

It was now getting warm. Bright, hot sunshine, loaded bags, the excitement and fatigue of the preceding night were beginning to take their toll and they began desperately to look for some secluded place to sit and rest. There was no respite in the houses-and-shops lined main road, so they took the first lane branching out to the left. About a thousand yards up this road they came to a railway line, possibly the one they were to follow towards the Khyber. But that railway line, as described by Murray, was a narrow, meter-gauge track, whereas this was a broad gauge line. So they turned back and resumed the journey along the main highway. After a while the road opened up, the houses and shops thinned out and there were larger spaces in between. Another five hundred yards further they saw a police check post ahead of them. Garry quickly led them off the road into the vast grounds of the Islamia University. Here they briefly discussed the situation.

'I doubt if we will find a place to hide during the day. There seem to be no wooded areas or fields with high crops,' observed Garry.

'We also can't keep walking in these clothes, with these bags. We are so conspicuous. Everyone turns around and stares at us. Soon someone in authority will stop us and ask questions,' added Harry.

Dilip thought over the problem and seemed to come to a decision. 'What if we again chance it by bus?'

This seemed to be the best option to get as far away, as quickly, as possible. They backtracked along the road and soon saw a bus coming towards them. On seeing three possible fares the driver stopped the vehicle and signalled to them to climb aboard. The bus was jam-packed, a mosquito could not have got inside. So, like some others, they climbed on to the roof and sat down among a score of people who were already ensconced there. The bus moved up the road and halted at five or six check posts. At every stop the frontier militiamen climbed up to the roof and peered at the bags, sometimes lifting some of them and putting them down again. They seemed to be looking for some particular items and not finding them in the bags allowed the bus to proceed. No questions were asked. The three Indians held their breath each time the bus stopped at a checkpost and heaved a sigh of relief as it again moved forward. And thus they arrived at Jamraud Fort at about 09:00 hours, exactly nine hours since they had left the prison camp.

Their first impression in this frontier area was that the arms race between man and man had reached its zenith here. There was not one man who did not carry a gun and wear a cross-belt full of bullets. Only boys whose upper lips were still bereft of a shadow of a moustache roamed around with bare, unarmed hands. As they started walking up the road they could see mountains in the distance. Between the road and the mountains there spread a vast plain totally arid and without a blade of grass anywhere.

Death Wasn't Painful

All over this plain they could see fortress-like structures scattered at distances of five hundred to a thousand yards. Possibly these were the dwellings of the local tribesmen, situated carefully within rifle range of each other. The three Indians were tempted to get off the road immediately and head cross-country for the hills to the north. But large signboards in blue with white lettering hit their eyes:

WARNING
VISITORS ARE WARNED
NOT TO LEAVE THE ROAD

Next,

YOU ARE NOW ENTERING TRIBAL TERRITORY

Another,

VISITORS ARE WARNED NOT TO PHOTOGRAPH TRIBAL WOMEN

Yet another,

VISITORS MUST CROSS THIS PASS DURING
DAYLIGHT HOURS ONLY

Finally,

KHYBER WELCOMES YOU

After reading these signboards they felt that perhaps one more could have been added, 'YOU ARE NOW IN ALLAH'S HANDS'. They gingerly walked through the Khyber Gate while the tribals stared at them. A young boy rolling a tyre on the road with one hand and holding a toy pistol in the other walked up to Harry and aimed it at his head, calling out 'Bang'. Harry turned around, pointed his forefinger at the boy and said, 'Bang, Bang'. The boy grinned and got into step with him, still rolling the tyre along.

'*Angrez hai?*' the boy asked, wanting to know if Harry was an Englishman.

'No. Not *Angrez*. I am Pakistani,' corrected Harry.

The boy grinned again and blurted out, 'No. You are not Pakistani. You look like Hindustani!'

This hit the three like a bolt from the blue. If they could rouse such unnerving suspicion in a child, the grown-ups may indeed discover their true identities in a jiffy. Flustered, Harry said, 'You naughty boy, you should be ashamed of yourself for calling me a Hindustani. Now go away from here.'

The boy simply speeded up the tyre that he was rolling along the road, went ahead of them but kept zig-zagging the tyre and looking back for the next two miles that they walked.

It was plain to them that the road was the only safe area. Any deviation from it or any attempt at a cross-country walk would immediately invite a burst of rifle fire. The plains suddenly seemed sinister and hostile; recourse to bus travel appeared to be the only alternative. In the meantime a young lad came strolling up and Dilip exchanged the *Salaam Aleikum* greetings with him. He invited Dilip and his companions to sit on a culvert and then began asking questions. Dilip laughed and talked about Lahore and Karachi, even about his trips, as a Pakistani airman, to America and the Middle East. The boy had perhaps wanted some company, some diversion and here he was getting thrilling accounts of big cities and foreign lands, and being invited to travel with them in these parts. He may have happily joined them if asked to go to Lahore, but he had probably had enough of the bare wilderness of the frontier area to entertain any such thought. So, when asked about a bus to Landi Kotal he told them that it will come right where they were sitting. And as it came the lad stood up in the middle of the road, stopped the bus and helped the three to climb to the roof.

They passed over dry river beds and watched the small, barren hills, their steep slopes covered with loose gravel. Every other hilltop had a small, manned fortress. Together they served as a primitive but very thorough radar network. A man walking across the hills was bound to be seen by people manning one or the other fortress. As their eyes scanned the less steep slopes they saw holes dug into the hillsides and the tribals dwelling there with families and dogs. So even by night the area would be impregnable. Progress towards Afghanistan could therefore be made only by day and only along the road. Sitting on top of the bus the three Indians felt relieved that they were covering the miles in safety and comfort. Perhaps someone up there liked them!

Again the bus stopped at several check-posts and everyone's baggage was checked by the militia. At one post a policeman picked up two bags of rice and threw them down on the ground. A burly Pathan leapt after the bags and confronted the lawman. A loud and raucous argument followed, at the end of which the tribal was allowed to take away his bags of rice. Rice and wheat seemed to be high on the smugglers' priority list in this area.

Soon they were in Landi Kotal. Afghanistan was just five miles away! The transportation had been so quick, so easy that they had not quite mentally arrived at Landi Kotal. They felt a little bewildered, a little unsure about the next and final stage of the escape. So they walked into a side street and sat down at a tea stall. While sipping the beverage Dilip casually asked the waiter, a youth, how far Landi Khana was. The fellow looked around as if he had been asked where Transylvania was. But another customer occupying the seat next to them said, 'Landi Khana is about four miles from here.'

'Is it a beautiful place? Is it worth a sightseeing visit?' asked Dilip.

The man shrugged his shoulders as if to ask whether there was any place, anything, attractive in these parts.

'How does one go there?' persisted Dilip.

'You can walk along this road, or get a taxi. There are no buses in that direction,' said the man, partly in Urdu and partly in Pushto, but nevertheless conveyed the information adequately.

'What will be the fare for a taxi?'

The Breakout

'It'll cost one rupee per head, if 30 of you get together. Otherwise, it will cost full 30 rupees.'

Dilip worked out in his mind that the fare would be thirty rupees. 'That's too much,' he said. The tribal shrugged.

Outside on the street they saw several tourists, hitchhikers from the western countries. Then they spotted a Sikh of the frontier area, dressed in white turban, white shirt and *salwar*, the *Kara* on his right wrist clearly visible.

'Garry, look, there goes your caste brother,' whispered Harry. The Sikh was carrying baskets of vegetables suspended from a pole on his shoulder.

'Should you ask him for help?' nudged Harry.

'No,' admonished Dilip. 'He may give us in.'

Garry's pride in his religious community came to the fore as he said, 'No. He will never give me up. Even if he decides not to help.'

They didn't have to test Garry's assertion as the Sikh soon turned a corner and disappeared from view.

Dilip turned to the waiter and pointing at his cap asked, 'Where do you get these Peshawari caps?'

The boy pointed at a hole in the wall about fifty yards away, and said, 'There.'

Dilip got up from the bench and headed in that direction. Harry paid for the tea and he too followed along with Garry. Harry wondered if they should backtrack and get out of that street where they had already exposed themselves long enough. But he only told Dilip that being an Anglo-Pakistani, he didn't want the typically Muslim cap. Dilip went inside the market which was in fact the underground storehouse for all kinds of goods smuggled from all corners of the world. Dilip bought two round caps and came out. The one bought for Garry did not fit him. Dilip went down again to exchange it. One could have thought that their exposure at this crucial stage was unnecessarily long, that safety in this situation lay in movement. But such lucidity of thoughts is for the hindsight, not for those who, placed in a totally hostile environment, need time to decide on the next step, the next move, and, in the meantime, have to quell the bewilderment, the restlessness, the turmoil, the fear and the uncertainty raging within themselves. Perhaps it was all these factors and a host of other feelings and fears that drove Dilip to while away some more time by visiting the souk twice.

During his second trip to the underground market, the young waiter from the tea stall ran up to Garry and announced in a loud voice, 'You want to go to Landi Khana? The taxi fare has come down. You pay only twenty five rupees.'

The young waiter waited for the bargain to be struck, but Garry waved him off by saying, 'No, that's still too much.'

Harry quietly whispered, 'We might as well take it and get away from here. I am getting a funny feeling in my belly.'

Dilip had just joined them and they had just started moving out towards the main road for the taxi when an oldish man, bearded, bespectacled, benumbed them by asking, 'You wish to go to Landi Khana?'

'Yes,' replied Dilip.

'Ah!' said the man. 'Landi Khana is where you want to go? I see. But why?'

'You see, we are out touring. Sightseeing. Visiting different places, including this frontier area.' The defensive note in Dilip's reply was conspicuous, and it wasn't lost on the interrogator.

'You are not locals, you don't seem to belong to these parts. Then where did you hear of Landi Khana?'

'Yes, of course, we are not from this area. We have come from Lahore. But we know of Landi Kotal and Landi Khana. These places are on the maps too,' argued Dilip.

'Nonsense!' proclaimed the interrogator. 'Landi Khana is not on any map or atlas.'

Dilip felt like scratching his head, but desisted. Certainly Murray had written about Landi Khana and that English traveller—God bless his soul—had been there himself.

'I don't know about that, but several people I know in Lahore, in Karachi, who have been there,' was all Dilip could say.

The Breakout

'In Lahore? In Karachi?' asked the old man. The cadence of his voice changed and he asked authoritatively, 'Who are you, all three of you?'

Garry quickly intervened to put his Punjabi language to effective use. 'We are airmen of the Pakistan Air Force. But why are you asking? And, may we know, please, who are you?'

'Don't worry about who I am,' said the old man loudly as a crowd began to gather around them. 'Please show me your Air Force identity cards.'

'We are not allowed to carry identity cards when we are on leave, for security reasons,' said Garry.

'Then show me your leave authorisation slip,' demanded the old man.

'Look, we are just travelling around a bit in our own country. We don't carry all kinds of documents when we are on leave. I don't know why you are questioning us like this,' protested Garry.

'I'll tell you why I am asking these questions,' continued the old man. 'You see, there is no Landi Khana anymore. Half the local people do not know if ever there was a place called Landi Khana. It disappeared after the British left and all that remains of that outpost is a disused railway platform and a dilapidated hut. And here you come asking for Landi Khana twenty-five years after the British went away!'

They suddenly realised that their knowledge of local geography was hopelessly out of date. Murray had not misled them, his book had been published one year after India and Pakistan gained independence. And soon thereafter Landi Khana had been abandoned to reptiles and insects, the elements and time, and the railhead withdrawn to Landi Kotal. Local children played on the railway platform, goatherds rested in the broken down hut, but none ever asked the name of the place.

The crowd around them was swelling and so were their uncertainties and fears. Whispered comments were being made about the three of them, some implying that they were big time smugglers striking deals at the souk. But none had so far guessed that they might be Indians. Dilip and his companions knew that being discovered as Indians and worse, as Hindus, would be the biggest calamity, leading to public lynching and possibly a horrible death. Safety lay in getting away from this crowd and into the protective custody of some government authority.

'Please come with me,' ordered the old man. They followed him eagerly but he only took them to an empty stall a few metres away where he and a few others started inspecting their bags and pulling things out.

'Why are you delaying us thus? What, after all, is your doubt?' asked Harry sharply, in Urdu which he had been rehearsing in his mind all this while.

'I'll tell you, *janab*, what my doubt is,' said the old man. 'I think you are Bengalis, trying to run away to Dacca by way of Afghanistan.' The Pakistanis as yet referred to the former East Pakistan only as Dacca, its capital city. They were loathe to call it Bangladesh, an independent country carved out of their own empire.

'Bengalis?' sneered Garry. 'We look like Bengalis? Have you ever laid your eyes on a Bengali? *Allah kasam* we are not Bengalis!'

'I have lived all my life in this area and I've never seen such strange combinations in attire as yours. Kurta and canvas shoes, woollen pants in summer and canvas shoes, cotton pants and canvas shoes!'

'And then, these Peshawari caps!' he continued. 'You have come through Peshawar but you decide to buy Peshawari caps in Landi Kotal! Why? Because you see almost everyone here wearing these caps. Well, take it from me, every Bengali who was caught here had made the same mistake!'

He pulled out the two woollen jerseys from the bags and exclaimed, 'Ah! These warm clothes! Every Bengali was caught carrying woollen clothes, because, you see, while it is warm here, it is cold in Kabul!'

And then he pulled out a bag made with parachute cloth and looked in consternation at the blood stains on it. He looked at all three in turn, intently, suspiciously and turned back to again inspect

The Breakout

the blood-stained cloth. Then he personally pushed all the items back into the bags, picked three men from the crowd and handed over the bags to them.

'Follow me,' he said sternly. He stepped out on to the road, the three Indians and the three bag-carriers following closely behind, the crowd a few steps further behind. These were bigger fish than he had thought.

They came to a small government building which they learnt was the office of the Tehsildar, the local revenue official having magisterial powers. After a short wait the dignitary arrived. He invited them to sit on a string cot in the open compound of the building and himself took a chair. Fat, balding, wearing a brown coat over white shirt and *salwar*, the official sent for paper and pen and began the interrogation.

'Your names, please?'

'LAC John Masih, PAF Base Lahore, son of Mr. Andrew Masih, Christian,' said Dilip.

Garry gave his particulars next, 'LAC Ali Ameer, PAF Base, Lahore, son of Mr. Thomas Ameer, Christian.'

Harry spoke next, 'Harold Jacob, son of Mathew Jacob, employee at Hotel La-Bella, Karachi, Christian.'

'How long have you known each other?' asked the official.

'We work together in the same place,' said Garry pointing at Dilip. 'And we had met with Harry, I mean Harold Jacob, at Karachi when we had both gone there on duty. You see, we are, all three of us, Christians.'

'Why have you come here?' was the next question.

'You see, we often take holidays together and visit some new place. We had not roamed around in this area, and so we decided to come here this time,' exclaimed Dilip.

'You two ...,' he pointed at Dilip and Garry. 'Have you got any identity papers, any leave authorisation?'

'No. We don't carry official papers around when travelling on leave, lest they be lost,' said Garry.

Death Wasn't Painful

The Tehsildar pondered over these answers, searched their faces for clues as to their real identities, but apparently failed to come to a definite conclusion. So, in block capitals he wrote on a sheet of paper the word 'SUSPECTS' and showed it to them.

After a pause he told them, 'You wanted to go to Landi Khana, when nobody goes there. You are carrying woollen clothes, so obviously you are wanting to run away to a colder place. You can't establish your identities. And you have in your possession blood-stained clothes.'

Another pregnant pause, a little longer this time, the captives as well as the crowd holding their breath for the verdict that was sure to come.

'I am putting you under arrest and having you locked up while further enquiry into your antecedents proceeds,' he announced.

The game was up, realised Dilip. A way had to be found to quickly escape from the clutches of these civilians who, on discovering the truth, will become rabidly vindictive. The safest place would again be the protective custody of the armed forces, that of the Pakistan Air Force being the most desirable.

'I want to make a telephone call,' Dilip told the official.

'No. Nothing, until we know everything about you chaps,' said the Tehsildar.

'You have detained us for no rhyme or reason,' protested Dilip. 'And now you are even going to put us behind bars, again for no reason. Yet you will not allow me to make one telephone call that I may establish my identity and that of my friends!'

The official just sat stone-faced. After a few seconds Harry asked Dilip loudly, 'Whom do you wish to speak with?'

The Tehsildar leaned forward a bit to hear Dilip's answer. 'Naturally, I shall speak to the Provost Marshal at the Headquarters in Peshawar. He is the head of the Air Force police and he'll deal with these people.'

The official appeared to be in two minds. This fellow could not possibly hope to bluff and deceive the head of the Pakistan Air Force

The Breakout

police. He relented and said, 'Do you have the telephone number of your officer?'

'No. But I can get the Air Force Headquarters in Peshawar and they will connect me with the Provost Marshal.' Dilip spoke confidently and clearly, which carried conviction with the official. The Tehsildar picked up the phone and asked the local exchange to connect him with Air Headquarters in Peshwar. In a few seconds he was through.

'Air Headquarters exchange. Number Please?' asked the operator.

'One minute,' said the official looking inquiringly at Dilip.

In a swift movement Dilip grabbed the phone and spoke, 'I am LAC Masih. Please connect me with the office of the Provost Marshal. This is an urgent matter.'

'Wait, please,' said the operator. He came back on the line after about a minute. 'The Provost Marshal is not in his office. Any other number?'

Dilip's mind was racing on the other possibilities and suddenly it clicked. In an emergency, go as high as you can, even to the top.

'Please connect me to the office of the Air Chief. I ... I want to speak with the ADC to the Chief ... with Squadron Leader Osman' It all came out like an emergency drill, in a kind of perfection expected in fighter pilots, the ability to pull out from the unconscious the correct responses in a dangerous situation. Osman was the Camp Commandant at Rawalpindi when the Indian prisoners were first interned there and soon thereafter he had been picked up for the coveted post of ADC to the Chief of the Pakistan Air Force at Headquarters at Peshawar.

'Please hold on. He is coming on the line,' advised the operator.

Dilip felt relieved. Osman was a gentleman, affable and considerate while managing to maintain strict discipline. If compassion and fair play were to be found among the enemy, Osman was the man to manage it. In different hands, where anger at losing the war, and rabid vindictiveness against everything Indian predominated, they might have found themselves pushing up daisies along the Kabul river.

Death Wasn't Painful

As Osman came on the line Dilip said, 'Good morning, Sir. I'm Dilip here.'

'Dilip ...?' asked Osman in utter surprise. 'How did you get to a telephone, Dilip?'

'I don't know if you have already heard, Sir, but there are three of us here at Landi Kotal at this moment, being taken into custody by the local Tehsildar.'

'What! ...?' gasped Osman. He took a whole minute to digest the information. He then asked for the official to be put on the line. The Tehsildar introduced himself as Shahjehan and gave out graphic details of the capture of the three suspects. What he suspected them of, he did not say. After that he listened attentively for a long while, as Osman spoke from the other end. Finally, he beamed with delight as he put the receiver down.

'See, I knew all along that there was something wrong. Of course, you are Pakistani airmen. Osman *Saheb* told me so. Even I was thinking that you were not lying when you had said so yourself. But he has told me that you three are very dangerous fellows and I have to keep you locked up in a cell until further instructions. I knew there was something fishy, right from the start.'

The three Indians stood there quietly, putting on a great show of dejection and helplessness, while their hearts rejoiced at having been saved at the brink of discovery by the wrong kind of people. It was also obvious to them that their escape from Rawalpindi had remained undetected until now, that is up to 10:30 hours in the morning, a gap of over ten hours. For, the Chief's office would have been notified within minutes of such an occurrence coming to light.

'Beautiful cover-up job by Chati and others,' whispered Harry, and they all marvelled at the support managed by their fellow prisoners back in Rawalpindi.

Meanwhile, the three were searched and shoved roughly into a nauseating cell. They had seen so many jails and so many cells since their arrival in Pakistan, but in filth and grime this one took not only the cake, but the whole bakery. The search party found on their persons the POWs identity cards, small pink things on thick

The Breakout

paper and these were handed over to Mr. Shahjehan who peered at them intently.

'What did you say, your names were?' he asked grimly.

They gave their correct names. Shahjehan went red in the face, breathed faster and began asking more questions, grimly and menacingly.

'You all are prisoners of war? Indians?'

'All Hindus?'

'You ran away? From where? How? When? How many more?'

'Why did you lie to me? Why?'

For a moment it looked that he might order a bit of violence, a bit of chastisement for the deception they had practised on him and deprived him of the chance to personally carry forward the war against India. But their luck held. A messenger rushed up to the Tehsildar just at that moment and told him that Burki *Saheb*, the political agent, wanted him to produce the prisoners at his office immediately. So the small dignitary ordered the prisoners to be brought out and handcuffed. He returned to his original wheatish complexion and led the march back through the town and to the office of the political agent at the other end of the city.

As they were brought before the officer, they all wished him in the correct military manner and stood quietly.

'Remove their handcuffs.' This was Burki's first order.

'These persons are to be treated just as you would treat Pakistani officers,' was his second instruction to an astonished Shahjehan, and the even more astonished Indian prisoners.

Burki then took them to the window of his office and pointed out the hills in the distance.

'Bad luck, gentlemen. Afghanistan ... just five miles away, and you'd have been free men. Well tried, though! A damned good attempt.'

That was a very sporting though surprising welcome, in the best traditions of the defence services. A vanquished enemy is not to be humiliated, he is only to be wished Better Luck Next Time.

'Army, Sir?' asked a curious Harry.

'Yes, about eight years. In this job about twelve,' he stated. 'By the way, my father began his career in the Indian Army, pre-independence.'

'General Burki?' exclaimed Dilip. 'Look at that! I don't remember the context, but I am familiar with this name.'

Burki talked pleasantly with them for about ten minutes. He told them all that he had learnt from Osman and only wanted to know how they managed to travel so far so quickly. They gleefully gave him the details of the bus journeys and regretted vociferously that they got caught through mistaken identity, under suspicion of being Bengalis, a possibility that had not occurred to them at all.

'I'll now have to take leave, as I have to attend to some urgent work,' he said a little while later. 'My staff will look after you. So relax until the Air Force boys arrive to take charge of you.' He shook hands and left.

A sumptuous meal was laid out for them, the best in chicken, mutton, rice and other *tandoori* food that Landi Kotal could provide. It was served by tall tribals dressed in black shirts and *salwar*s with a gun on everyone's shoulder. They were courteous and correct. Shahjehan sent for the old man who was responsible for their capture and he too joined in the lunch. Harry congratulated him for his surveillance but he only muttered one word, 'Allah!'

Around 4 p.m. the Air Force police arrived, in the shape of Squadron Leader Syed and half a dozen corporals dragging chains behind them. Harry wished the officer with a cheery, 'Good Afternoon'. He only gave them a very dirty look. A bad sport, surly and mean, thought Harry. He could have been improved with more games in his childhood, observed Dilip.

He called out to his men to fix up the three. They immediately took out the handcuffs and chains, and began putting them on the Indians. Dilip requested if this could be done inside the transport after they had taken leave of their captors who had indeed treated them like POWs, and not like ordinary criminals.

'I told you to fix them up. So fix them up,' he shouted at his men in response.

The Breakout

Dilip and Garry were handcuffed together. The device had a long chain attached to it which was in the grip of a hefty policeman. Harry was handcuffed by himself and similarly kept on leash. The first two were led to a jeep and shoved in at the back and then blindfolded. Harry was placed in the officer's car.

As the car had travelled a short distance on the road to Peshwar, Harry tried to make polite conversation with the officer.

'Just shut up, and keep shut,' hissed the new jailer.

17

The Aftermath

Chati was maintaining vigil at the door of Cell No. 5. He heard the soft crunch of plaster as it fell away and knew that his three cellmates would be out and gone in a matter of seconds. Then he heard Harry's voice declaiming 'Freedom! Here I come!' and knew that they were gone. Chati lay on his bed, benumbed, in a kind of vacuum and an indescribable loneliness. The storm raged outside and soon it began to rain. No guard came that way. It was only when the rain stopped that he heard the thump of boots outside and came out of his reverie. Shamsuddin was on duty that night. He walked up to the cell door and peered inside. Chati stole a glance at Harry's dummy lying by his side and himself turned on to his side to show some evidence of life in the room. As the guard moved away, Chati slithered to the hole in the wall, piled back the bricks, rearranged the boxes, the shoes and all other items and finally pushed the bed back against the wall. He quickly returned to his bed and lay down again.

At about three in the morning Shamusuddin came again and stood at the door. Chati shifted his legs and coughed a bit and again the guard went away. Chati's mind was in turmoil. He was not thinking then about the imminent discovery and the rough handling and punishment that certainly awaited him, he was simply unable to cope with the burden of knowledge and desperately wanted to share it with someone. But it was too early to ask to be taken to the toilet and, on the way, whisper the information to someone lying awake in his cell. He had to endure it for a few hours more. He quietly lit a cigarette and the smoke soothed his nerves.

At five in the morning the day broke and the room began to light up. Chati swiftly patted the three dummies into shape and switched off the fan, lest the breeze should blow away the covering sheets. Then he called the guard and asked him to let him out for the toilet. He was taken out of the cell and the lock was put back on the door to safeguard the other three.

As Chati stepped into the veranda outside the toilet, Jafa leapt off his bunk and rushed to the iron door. Chati whispered, 'Gone, midnight.'

Chati went to the toilet and as he came out Jafa asked the guard to let him out urgently for the same purpose. On emerging from his cell he looked at Chati and exclaimed in Urdu, 'You don't look well! What's wrong? Are you all right?'

Chati took the hint and said, 'I feel queasy in the stomach. Maybe something in the food last night. I may have to rush to the toilet.'

Jafa turned towards the guard and addressed him. 'You heard. He is very unwell. He seems to be having loose motions. Let him remain in my cell, this is close to the toilet.'

Before the guard could reply, Chati hurried into Jafa's cell and lay down on the bunk. Jafa finished with the toilet and returned to his cell. The guard put the lock on the door, Jafa lay down alongside Chati.

'Well done, Chati,' said Jafa. 'I am proud of you. You have handled it very well.'

'Sir, I don't feel like going back to that room,' said Chati.

'You just lie here,' Jafa comforted him. 'We'll work something out.'

After that everyone started arriving at the toilet, one by one. Seeing Jafa and Chati together in the cell they all guessed that the escape plan had gone through. All the same, everyone found an excuse to come up to the iron-grill of the cell to quickly seek confirmation. It was clear that none of them had slept a wink during the preceding night. The knowledge of the escape and the possibility of discovery now weighed heavily on them. They had to remind each other to make conversation in order to maintain an air of normalcy.

As it was the morning of a holiday, breakfast was served lazily at about 8:30 a.m. The cells were thrown open and the prisoners allowed to head for the meals room. Corporal Mehfoos Khan stood in the courtyard to keep an eye on the prisoners. After a while Mehfoos Khan came into the meals room, counted the bodies and said, 'Where are the others? Why haven't they come?'

Before he could decide on a personal visit to Cell No. 5, Jafa loudly called out to Kuru, 'Kuru, go and call these chaps for breakfast. Why do they keep awake until late in the night and then not wake up on time? Tell them not to delay everyone like this.'

Kuru returned after a couple of minutes and said, 'I've told them to hurry up.'

Mehfoos Khan went away. They resumed eating desultorily and took time over everything. After allowing half-an-hour for the meal Mehfoos returned to the room. Finding the food portions of the three missing prisoners still lying there, he told Jafa, 'These three officers of yours delay everyone every day. It's a Sunday, the staff would like to clean up quickly and go home.'

'Kuru, go again quickly and see if they have got up,' Jafa ordered.

Kuru returned and said smilingly, 'They seem to be sound asleep, Sir.'

'I'll tell you what, Corporal Mehfoos. Let them go without breakfast. They can't hold up everybody. You have the table cleared. I am saying this to you. They must go without breakfast today. *Soney do saalon ko!*' thundered Jafa in mock anger, the mildly abusive words spoken in disgust conveying the meaning—let the idiots sleep.

The Aftermath

Mehfoos was happy with this decision. He was always looking for ways to deny some small thing, some comfort, some food to the prisoners. Depriving them of a full meal was a pleasure he was not going to miss. He asked the menial staff to clear the table quickly. The prisoners began leaving the room. But this day they could not head for Cell No. 5 as they had done every other day. Jafa went back to his cell, Chati went away with Kamy, and so did others return to their cells. No one among the guards noticed this strange dispersal. It was a hot and humid Sunday and all systems were lax. And that was the situation at 10:30 a.m. when the telephone in the Guard Room, fifteen feet from Jafa's cell, began to ring. Mehfoos Khan heard it in the courtyard and sauntered over lazily to receive the call. Jafa moved up to the door to catch the conversation from this end.

'What? ... Who? ... Chief? ...' Jafa heard Mehfoos utter the words in bewilderment. 'Yes, Sir! Yes, Sir.' He began to get a grip on himself.

'No, Sir,' Mehfoos said after listening to the voice at the other end.

'All are here, Sir,' he repeated, but continued to listen.

'Yes, Sir. Right, Sir,' he blurted out as the line went dead.

Mehfoos stood rooted to the ground, the telephone receiver still in his hand. It took him a few seconds to grasp the information he had received and then he sprang into action. He ran across the courtyard, called out to another police corporal, whispered something urgently to him and charged into Cell No. 5. The two policemen shoved at the dummies, the pillows and the sheets rolled away. They looked at the window and the ventilator, both were boarded and sealed and showed no signs of tampering. They pushed aside the beds, the cardboard boxes, shoes etc. and stood gaping at the pile of bricks in the lower corner of the wall. Mehfoos removed the bricks and peered through the hole at the world outside. His private world began to collapse.

In a matter of minutes another policeman, Choudhary, had joined them outside the guard room.

'The Chief knows. We are in trouble. We'll be court-martialled,' Mehfoos was voicing their common fears.

Jafa heard Choudhary say, 'Is that all you told him? Try to recollect properly.'

'Yes. That's all I said. I said 'Yes, Sir,' when he told me to go and look,' Mehfoos reiterated.

'Then they will not know what we two were doing while you were speaking on the telephone,' spoke Choudhary in a measured tone. 'We can say that four fellows tried to escape, three got away but we stopped the fourth.'

'Who? Who is the fourth?' asked Mehfoos eagerly, leaping at a possible chance to save himself and the others on duty.

The third Corporal suggested, 'Put this Jafa there. He is the *haraamzada*, the bastard who has managed all this. Put him in the hole and shoot him. We will say that we got one.'

'Get the key to his cell, quick,' ordered Choudhary. 'And give me your revolver.'

Mehfoos went rapidly to the other end of the courtyard where the guard on duty stood with the keys of the cells in his pocket. It hadn't occurred to them that their act of shooting Jafa would put the time of escape at about 11 a.m., the time when the three runaways were already seated comfortably in the political agent's office in Landi Kotal.

Jafa stood near the door in his cell, unable to believe what he had just heard. Then, rapidly, their words made sense and it struck him that the three policemen may indeed shoot him in their desperation to mitigate their own negligence. He will be overpowered, dragged to Cell No. 5, shoved into the hole and shot in the back. Just then his eyes went to the pillow on his bunk on which lay his copy of the Gita. He leapt forward and picked up the book.

'You saved me on the battlefield, you didn't let me die honourably there,' he hissed, holding the book in his hands and peering intently into the face of Krishna on the cover.

'And now you will have me killed like this, like a damned dog,' he continued hissing. 'Don't let me die like a dog, is all I beg.'

The Aftermath

And the telephone began to ring again, the loudest ring Jafa had ever heard, raucous, urgent, insistent. Someone moved towards the guard room. It was Choudhary's voice from this end.

'Yes, Sir. They are all here. Locked in their cells, Sir.'

'Yes, Sir ... seven of them, Sir.' Choudhary said again after listening to someone in authority at the other hand. 'Right, Sir. We won't touch anything, Sir.'

All activity in the camp came to a halt. Jafa wiped the perspiration on his forehead with his shirt sleeve and his breathing slowed down, though the turmoil in his head still raged. Krishna had saved him. From the frenzy of desperate men. He'll thank Krishna profusely and adequately when he was calmer.

A jeep started up somewhere in the camp and shortly went out of the gate. It returned with MWO Rizvi, who immediately began to take stock of the situation and heard whatever the policemen had to say. Later, much later, it was learnt from the grapevine that Rizvi had gathered the policemen and the guards around him and his talk had gone something like this, 'I've thought ... ah ... it ... all ... out. I was ... ah ... thinking ... ah ... on ... my way ah ... here. There is.... ah ... no need ... ah ... to ... panic ... I've ... ah ... been thinking ... ah ... where ... ah ... they could have ... ah ... gone ... and ... ah ... it ... hit me ... ah ... that they ... ah ... have nowhere ... to go.'

He paused for the weight of his words to sink into soft heads. 'They ... ah ... will be ... ah ... caught wherever they go ... so ... ah ... I am sure ... that ... ah ... they ... will ... come back ... ah ... latest ... ah ... by dinner time.'

It was learnt on good authority that, like drowning men, the policemen clung to the hopeful words of their chief and indeed sat down to await the return of the lost sheep, and took absolutely no steps on their own to ferret out information on the escape. After a while the Station Commander of the nearby Chaklala airfield arrived and panic began again. The prisoners were locked up separately, individually. Chati was pulled out of Kamy's cell and put in a dark, damp room where hordes of mosquitoes descended upon him. The punishment had begun, he thought. After a while Mehfoos Khan opened the lock and led Chati to the office building where a Wing Commander and a couple of junior officers awaited him.

'You were in Cell No. 5 last night?' the senior officer asked.

'Yes, Sir.'

'What time did the other three in that cell escape?'

'I don't know.'

'What do you mean you don't know? Didn't you see them go?' In a stern voice this time.

'No, Sir,' replied Chati, briefly, calmly.

'You mean that being in the same cell, you did not see when your roommates escaped?'

'That's what I am saying,' said Chati. 'I was asleep. I don't know what happened last night while I was sleeping. This morning I got up and went to the toilet. I wasn't feeling well and so I went to lie down in Jafa *Saheb*'s cell because that is close to the toilet.'

The Pakistani officers stared at him in frustration, in anger, and then exchanged glances with each other.

'All right. We are sending you back to your cell for now,' said the Wing Commander. 'You will be called again and you better come out with the truth, with full details. We'll have people who will know how to take out information if you do not cooperate.'

Wahid-ud-din arrived in the camp late in the afternoon. It was learnt that he had taken the long weekend off and was that morning enjoying a cool beer, en famille, in the sylvan surroundings of the hill station at Murree. The previous night's storm had uprooted many a telephone pole and so it was midday that Wahid received the devastating news that three prisoners in his charge had run away. He shoved his wife into the Volkswagen and drove like a man possessed. In less than half-an-hour he had skidded off the hilly road and found himself and his wife hanging upside down inside the overturned vehicle. Both scrambled out, unscathed and unscratched, climbed back to the road and hitch-hiked all the way to Rawalpindi. On reaching the camp, he spent a few minutes with his staff, inspected Cell No. 5 and then went straight to Chati's cell.

The Aftermath

'Tell me, you bastard smarty, what happened last night,' he shouted.

Chati had always been very allergic to any domineering or unnecessarily rude behaviour from the Pakistanis. Abusive language he could not stand from anyone.

'I told that Wing Commander of yours that I know nothing,' Chati shouted back. 'I am telling you also that I know nothing.'

'I'll break your bloody legs if you don't talk,' threatened Wahid.

Chati stood defiantly facing the enraged, frothing-at-the-mouth Wahid. The confrontation ended for the time being with Wahid walking away. Wahid visited all other cells in turn. Everywhere he ordered his minions to carry out a search and had all pieces of paper, books etc. picked up. On the pretext of body searches which he personally carried out, he pushed and shoved the prisoners around the cell. He was particularly vicious with Jafa whom he pushed onto the bunk and roughed him up badly. He continued to froth at the mouth and mumbling to himself but said nothing to anyone.

The next day Chati was brought into the presence of an Air Commodore and again questioned about the escape. He continued to deny any knowledge of how and when the escape occurred. He maintained, despite all kinds of threats and abuses, that he always slept very soundly at night and so he did not know when a hole had been dug in the wall or when they had escaped. He learnt of the escape only from what others had told him. Chati would later tell his friends that he had decided to stick to a simple denial of any knowledge and, if and when he was subjected to third degree, as they threatened, he would think of what to do about it if he could not bear the torture. However, better sense seemed to have prevailed among the Pakistanis. They had the three runaways in captivity once again, the entire evidence was before them, as also the negligence and lack of alertness of the guards and the supervisory staff when a wall was being broken through. There was no further interrogation. All prisoners remained locked up singly, fed individually and separately in their cells, not allowed to meet each other, nor given any books or newspapers to read to while away the time. Most of them took to singing loudly in their cells, the loudest, most raucous, out-of-tune song being Chati's *Chhor Gaye Balam, Haye Akela Chhor Gaye*, from a Raj Kapoor film. The guards and the policemen found this very annoying and admonished Chati again and again to stop. But Chati sang on.

The next morning Chati was woken up at 3 a.m. and told to quickly get dressed and to pick up his spare set of clothes, as he was being taken somewhere else. He wondered if he alone was being taken away, possibly as a follow-up of, and punishment for, the escape. But then he saw others too heading for the toilets one by one and felt assured that this was something that involved them all. An hour later, they were handcuffed and brought out into the courtyard. Wahid stood there shouting orders in foul mood and fouler language. He kicked pieces of furniture around, even took out his revolver and shot two rounds at something or nothing in the distance. Holding the smoking gun in his hand he advanced upon the group of prisoners.

'You are all being taken to some other place. You will remain handcuffed and blindfolded during the journey. Any indiscipline, any deviation from instructions shall be dealt with strictly.' He paused and fired off two more rounds before announcing, 'Which means, you will be shot!' The prisoners exchanged glances with each other. Chati smirked unashamedly. Wahid noticed it and frothed at the mouth a bit.

'You chaps are bloody ungrateful!' he said. 'You've had a very good time here. You have been treated decently. Now you will see what a real POW camp is like. You'll regret it all your damned lives.'

The prisoners were herded into several cars and jeeps with two armed escorts and a driver in each. They drove for over two hours and then halted in a mango grove where their blindfolds were removed and they were given *paratha*s and tea. Back into the vehicles, another drive of about three hours brought them to the high-security prison at Lyallpur (now Faisalabad), in the heart of Punjab where they were formally given into the charge of Colonel Lateef.

* * * * *

The Aftermath

Dilip, Garry and Harry were at this moment lodged in separate cells at some Air Force unit in Peshawar. It was around dusk time the previous evening when they had arrived. It was miserably hot inside the cells. The mosquitoes were large, innumerable and daring, attacking them from all sides. There was no fan in Harry's cell. He sat on the bare floor, trying to kill the mosquitoes by clapping his hands together. After a while he became aware of Garry's voice humming a Sehgal song somewhere. Harry let off a few whistles and loud whispers but got no response. Then he knocked an agreed code upon the walls one by one until he got an answering knock.

At normal conversational pitch he said, 'Garry?'

'Yah,' came the answer.

'Where's Dilip?'

'I don't know.'

'Do you have a bed there?'

'No,' said Garry. 'No fan either. The mosquitoes are killing me.'

'Same here.' They both resumed swatting at the mosquitoes with bare hands. Both wondered where Dilip could be.

Dilip, being the senior among them, had made this fact known to his jailors in a tone that demanded a modicum of respect and better treatment. He was accordingly placed in the third room which had a fan, a table and a chair. Soon after the policemen left him, he began to look around the room for some weak spot. He first prised an iron rod loose from the fire place in a corner of the room, placed the chair on top of the table and climbed atop to examine if the ceiling had any loose tiles which could be removed to make an exit hole. As he was probing the roof with the iron rod the door suddenly flew open and in walked the Flight Sergeant who was in charge of security there.

'What are you up to?' enquired the astonished official.

'Oh, I was wondering how to slow this fan down,' Dilip fumbled with the answer.

'We have electric regulators, you know?' said the Flight Sergeant calmly, sarcastically.

'Yes. Yes, of course!' Dilip was at a loss for words.

Death Wasn't Painful

'Then?' asked the official.

Dilip climbed down from the chair to the table to the ground and stood facing the Flight Sergeant. 'You know, Chiefy,' he said using the air force term for addressing an official of that rank. 'You have looked very angry since you took us in your charge at Landi Kotal. But you must understand that we haven't committed any crime by escaping from the camp at Rawalpindi. It was our duty.'

The Chiefy gave Dilip a hard long look and asked, 'Are you challenging me?'

Dilip returned the stare. 'I am only saying that it is my duty to escape. I'm also saying that if I get another chance, I'll run away again.'

Dilip was immediately handcuffed, blindfolded, and taken out of the room to a jeep waiting outside. He was driven around for a few minutes and eventually brought to Garry's cell which had an iron-grill door and barred ventilators. Garry in the meantime was taken to Dilip's room and was overjoyed to sit under a fan in relief from the heat and the mosquitoes. That night Dilip was handcuffed to the iron door of the cell.

A canvas ground sheet, and a pillow had been provided to each of them. Around ten in the night Harry was asked if he wanted to come out for a bit of fresh air. He jumped at the chance, but instead of a walk in the open he was taken to a room with a fan and asked to sit in a chair. Two men in civilian clothes sat facing him across a table. They questioned him at length on the escape. Now that the whole thing was over and, but for being mistaken for the damned Bangladeshis they might indeed have been far away, there was nothing to hide any more. So Harry broke into a friendly grin and began to talk of their escape of just the previous night. Actually, the main reason for his exceedingly cooperative attitude was the 20-pack of Players' cigarettes lying between him and his interlocutors. At the first suitable and interesting turn in the narrative he shamelessly reached for the pack and the box of matches and, with total sang froid, lit one up.

'You don't mind,' was all he said and carried on smoking and speaking.

The conversation and Harry's non-stop smoking proceeded side by side. All the salacious and juicy bits involving the bluffing and fooling of Pakistani servicemen and civilians as well as all the faux pas committed by him and his companions flowed out in an absorbing narration. Finally the dialogues, the monologues, began to peter out in keeping with Harry's growing satiation with tobacco smoking. As he finished the last cigarette in the pack he just shut up and informed the interrogators that he was too tired and needed rest, as also that he would look forward to seeing them again on the morrow. The Pakistanis too had had their fill and were poorer by about fifteen king-size cigarettes. Next day, Harry waited for another round of good smoking but he was not called.

Dilip spent the night in misery. His right hand was handcuffed to the iron door. In the absence of a fan, the mosquitoes launched an unchecked, unhindered attack upon him. All through the night his left hand waved and hit out and swatted over the empty spaces in a vain attempt to ward off the blood-suckers. He emerged into the next dawn tense, drawn, unrested. After a visit to the toilet, *paratha*s and tea were served to him in the cell. He quickly pondered whether he should eat right away, hungry that he was, or refuse to eat until his living conditions were ameliorated. He decided on the latter.

'I want to see the Assistant Provost Marshal (APM), please,' he told the police corporal who stood outside the door.

'Why?' asked the corporal.

'I'll only speak with the APM. You please call him at once,' demanded Dilip.

'He's not available,' answered the corporal.

'In that case,' announced Dilip,' I shall not eat until I am able to speak with the APM. I am on hunger strike, Corporal. You may inform your superiors that I shall remain on hunger strike until the APM comes to meet me, or I am taken to meet him.'

The APM, of course, was informed of the hunger strike within a few minutes. He pondered over this development. In his knowledge people had resorted to hunger strike as a weapon against the highhandedness of the British, particularly the man called Gandhi who did it for a variety of other reasons as well. He was curious to know what this Indian prisoner was up to, and so he went to Dilip's cell.

'Yes?' enquired the APM.

'Why am I being tortured by the men under your command?' Dilip demanded.

'Nonsense. No one has tortured you. Tell me plainly whatever complaint you have.'

'I was chained to the door last night. I was not provided with a fan. Hordes of mosquitoes were let loose on me to suck my blood and give me a fatal dose of malaria. And you say that I was not tortured?'

'That's because you were still trying to run away. We may have to secure you even more firmly,' said the APM.

'Look, you can try me for the attempted escape. You can give me 30 days' solitary confinement or stoppage of 15 days' pay, that too by a proper court-martial. The Geneva Convention is very clear on this. But you cannot treat me the way you did last night. You can put any number of armed guards around my cell, but inside the cell, I live as in a single officers' quarters,' Dilip rattled off.

The Pakistani officer smiled, the first time that he had allowed a bit of human softness to escape the hard exterior he had been at pains to project since he had taken charge of the prisoners at Landi Kotal.

'I like your spirit,' he said, still smiling and shaking his head in approval. He conveyed with these few words that Dilip and his companions were Okay chaps, good soldiers, good sports, upright and daring, the stuff that officers should be made of, anywhere, in any country.

'But I won't let you get away from here,' he announced as he walked away, still with a smile on his face.

Within minutes an additional armed guard was placed inside the building. Dilip and Harry were also provided with table fans and a bed each. They were all made very comfortable.

The Aftermath

'What a man!' said Dilip loudly, admiring the Pakistani officer. 'What a sport! When he could have made our lives miserable!'

Then Dilip spotted the corporal and called out to him, 'Incidentally, Corporal, remember the breakfast I sent back? Can I have it now, please?'

They spent a whole week at Peshawar, locked up separately but well looked after, Harry even managing to wheedle a tube of mosquito repellent out of the staff. Corporal Lal Khan was in charge of messing and he took pains to provide them with excellent meals, tasty and filling. The discipline was tight, there was no deviation in the laid down daily routine, no let up in the rigid security measures, and yet they found here, among the staff, the real and genuine face of the people of Pakistan, total devotion to duty tinged with generosity, humanity, care and concern. Elsewhere, they had mostly encountered rigidity, pettiness, and an element of vindictiveness.

A week later they were readied for a journey, which, they guessed, had to be for Rawalpindi. Blindfolded and handcuffed, as the regulations demanded, they were brought out and placed in two vehicles. Dilip and Harry found themselves in a Volkswagen minibus while Garry sat comfortably in the APM's car. From the voices they could make out that the escort party consisted of the same police corporals who had looked after them at this camp. And as they crossed the city of Peshawar and emerged on to the highway, the APM ordered their blindfolds removed. A pleasant, comfortable drive of two-and-a-half hours brought them back to the No. 3 Provost and Security Flight of the Pakistan Air Force at Rawalpindi. A very distraught, red-faced Wahid-ud-din received them and had them immediately locked up in Cell Nos. 1, 2 and 3. They regretted not being given a chance to say thanks and goodbye to Squadron Leader Syed and his staff from Peshawar, they regretted even more the surly, hostile, cheated looks that were given to them by the Rawalpindi personnel.

Much later, in the quiet of the afternoon, Wahid came by Harry's cell looking like Caesar just after Brutus had added a stab or two in his back.

Death Wasn't Painful

'You did not pay me, like I paid you,' he said sadly.

Harry took a while to comprehend. 'Please don't think, Sir, that we did it just to get you into trouble,' he tried to pacify Wahid. 'It was just that we were fed up with this kind of life and decided to do something about it.'

'But why wait for eight months to do it?' asked Wahid uncomprehendingly. 'Why not in the beginning when we expected Dilip and Garry to attempt an escape? Why now when we thought that you would await repatriation?'

The next day they were produced before a military court assembled in Wahid's office. They made brief statements on the escape. But from the questions put to them it was apparent that the Court had already persuaded itself to believe that the camp was a place where the prisoners were the masters, Wahid a private secretary and the guards just menial servants. The trial was over within an hour. Then they were again taken to the same office one by one where Wahid-ud-din now sat formally at his desk, and briskly announced the sentence.

'You have been found guilty of an unsuccessful attempt at escape, in that, on 13 Aug, 72 at about 00:30 hours you broke out of the camp at Rawalpindi and were apprehended at Landi Kotal at 10:30 hours on the same day. I am, under the Geneva Convention, paragraph ... awarding you 30 days solitary confinement as punishment. However, due to various factors, the period from your recapture till today will also be counted towards this punishment.'

'Do you have anything to say?'

'No, Sir.'

'Please carry on.'

Just before midnight the same day they were all taken out of the cells, handcuffed and blindfolded. They were driven to the Rawalpindi Railway Station and placed separately in three air-conditioned compartments, handcuffed to the upper berths and guarded by six armed men each. Whenever they desired, they were taken to the toilet, but on a long leash, an iron chain attached to the

The Aftermath

handcuff for the purpose, and they felt like very pampered Spaniels or Labradors.

Around midday they were handed over to Colonel Lateef at the Lyallpur high-security prison and put into solitary cells. There was a water closet, a water tap and an empty can in each cell. Meals were served inside the cells. They occupied themselves with the cleaning of the cells, washing them twice or even thrice every day, changing the arrangement of toiletries a couple of times a day, exercising with push-ups and sit-ups, killing flies and mosquitoes, watching spiders on the ceiling trapping soldier ants and devouring them systematically, and singing sad songs. They were conducting their waking hours exactly in the same manner as their fellow prisoners were doing in an adjoining barrack in the same prison.

18
Wages of Sin

Colonel Lateef was a soft-spoken, past-middle-age soldier of the old school. As Commandant of the high-security prison housing the Indian POWs, he left the bullying and the harsh meannesses to his subordinates. He seemed more interested in drawing out the Indian prisoners. With gentle, seemingly innocuous questions he was able to open the floodgates of monologues, of all the pent up thoughts about families back home, of individual war experiences, perceptions of tactical gains and failures of the two armed forces, even the regional, communal, casteist diversities and resentments in the two countries. Jafa would often warn his fellow prisoners against venting too freely their personal prejudices. An enemy ought to know only so much about your weaknesses, and no more, he thought. And so Jafa would be on the look-out whenever the heavy iron gate creaked open between 11 and 12 in the morning for it was usually then that the Colonel visited the Indian prisoners.

In the beginning Lateef came escorted by a JCO and a couple of stengun-toting guards. Gradually he did away with the armed guards and finally came only with an unarmed JCO. Occasionally, he would bring with him persons in civilian clothes, from the manner of whose dress and conversation it was apparent that they were what they looked, pure civilians. Jafa suspected them to be intelligence agents and cautioned everyone to exercise care in conversations with them. But sooner or later they would home on to Jafa himself as he was fluent in Urdu or Hindustani and could talk with some facility of contemporary writing in the sub-continent, the democratic and dictatorial politics of the two countries and the inevitable Hindu–Muslim question and the sore issues like Hyderabad, Junagadh, Kashmir and now Bangladesh.

As the iron gate opened one morning, Jafa was astonished to see the Colonel walking in his direction with a young girl in tow. Well ... well! A young girl in a prison camp! Bringing men from different walks of life who wished to meet the prisoners out of curiosity was one thing, but getting a woman inside what was, technically, a single officers' living area was something quite extraordinary. What was the Colonel up to? Either the people in this part of Pakistan were very liberated, or the Colonel was one of those privileged ones who made their own rules wherever they happened to be.

Then suddenly he realised that he was standing there with just a towel wrapped around his middle. He had that morning washed the only trouser issued to him in the prison and had put it out to dry. Something had to be done about his indecent exposure before the female company got any closer. Telling the Colonel to wait he lunged for the still wet trouser and disappeared inside his cell. In the next minute he emerged with a dry shirt and a wet trouser upon his slim frame.

'Oh, I am sorry. I should really come some other time,' said Lateef, trying to turn away.

'No, Sir,' said Jafa. 'Now that we are prim and proper ...'

'But these wet clothes, really ...'

'May be the same next time too. So come and sit.' He gestured towards the two chairs in the veranda and himself sat on a bench.

Typically, Colonel Lateef did not introduce his companion. As he talked about the weather, the food and the books that he procured for the prisoners, the other Indian officers, sensing and smelling a young woman in the vicinity wasted no time in gathering

Death Wasn't Painful

around. Staring unabashedly, they tried every trick in the book to draw her into conversation. But the little girl sat demurely, eyes downcast, fingers a bit fidgety, a little crimson spreading on her countenance every now and then.

It was finally left to Jafa to draw her out. 'Colonel *Saheb*,' he began, 'I believe there is not one family in your part of the country which has not provided at least one male member to the armed forces.' Then turning to the girl directly he said, 'Tell me, little lady, who all from your family are in the forces?'

Instead of receiving a reply Jafa saw that the fingers on her lap suddenly tightened, the lips quivered, the beautiful dark lashes lifted as she looked at him, and the eyes welled up with tears. A small sob, the face quickly hidden behind the veil, more convulsive sobbing. Gradually the grief ebbed, the eyes were wiped with a corner of the veil, the face relaxed into sublime sadness. Jafa, distressed and unable to summon words, looked at the Colonel.

'She lost her only brother in the war,' said Lateef simply. Jafa felt a strange empathy with the unknown, alien girl. He could not now let her go away with so much sadness inside her, he must make her unburden some.

'I am sorry, very sorry to hear it. May God give you the courage to bear this loss. Such is the tragedy of our lives ... innumerable families on both sides ... sisters left without brothers, parents without sons, and little children without their fathers. But do tell me, your brother was in the Army or the Air Force?'

'In the Army,' she said softly, and the ice was broken.

'Which front was he on?'

'He was in your Ferozepur area, in a jeep with other men, trying to go across a field to his post, when one of your planes ...'. And the words came pouring out, her account of the battle, gleaned together from countless recountings by her brother's erstwhile colleagues, the daring dash of a young subaltern to his fighting post to take on the attacking enemy aeroplanes, and an explosive end!

* * * * *

Wages of Sin

Jafa was that morning summoned by the Base Commander to undertake an urgent mission. One of our infantry battalions had been cornered by the Pakistani Army on the western bank of river Sutlej in the Ferozepur sector. In fact, the Indian territory on that side of the river was just a few kilometres deep. It could serve as a jump-off point for our troops in the event of an advance into Pakistan but, if faced with a superior force, withdrawal across the river was the only alternative.

That morning the Pakistani tanks in considerable numbers advanced upon this battalion and began to squeeze our troops from three sides. Their snipers got busy to prevent the men from crossing the river back to safety. The battle raged and desperate demands were made on the Air Force to stop the tanks. Three attempts were made by our aircraft but the foggy weather and good camouflage by the Pakistanis made it impossible for our pilots to locate the tanks.

Explaining the position to Jafa the Commander said, 'Here is an SOS from our army. Unless we can stop the tanks they will all be finished, a thousand men. They can hold out for about one hour, but no more. You think you could try?'

The Commander's suggestion, as usual, was an order. Jafa called for Jaggu and took him along to the two aircraft loaded with rockets and cannons, ready for the mission. In about fifteen minutes they were in the target area. Jafa began a wide circle at low height to scan the ground for signs of tanks. One circle, two circles, they reversed the direction, raised the flying height a bit, again came down to tree top level, but there were no tanks to be seen.

'Tanks are hiding under the trees, Red One,' cried the ground liaison officer on the radio. 'They halted as you came in. They are giving us hell. Look under the trees and let them have it, Red One. We are in trouble.'

Jafa looked hard in the shadow of the trees, Jaggu looked harder. Just then Jafa saw a jeep, out in the open, trying to dash across to a clump of trees on the other side of the clearing. In desperation and anger at not being able to find the tanks, Jafa pulled up slightly, turned his aircraft and began a shallow dive in the direction of the

Death Wasn't Painful

jeep. At the right height and angle he squeezed the trigger and two rockets headed out towards the hapless jeep. He saw the rockets speeding towards the jeep, he saw men huddled in the jeep, he even imagined their consternation, fright and final oblivion as the rockets hit and splintered metal and men into a thousand pieces.

* * * * *

Jafa sat before the sad girl, his thoughts far away, his own sadness equally heavy. So many had lost their near and dear ones, brothers, husbands, friends dearer than relations, he thought. Fighting the enemy? And who was the enemy? Did I know him, did I exchange hot words with him ... did he harm me in anyway? He sat quietly for a while, all sat quietly, busy with their private thoughts.

'Are you my enemy, little lady?' he asked of the girl suddenly. 'Or am I yours?' All eyes turned towards him. Some understood, some did not.

With tears in her eyes, she stood up. Withdrawing a hand from the folds of her veil she brought out a small box of sweets and proffered it to him.

'I could bring only this,' she said softly. Even with the enemy she had honoured the social convention of carrying fruits or flowers or sweets to persons in hospitals or jails.

And then they were both gone. Jafa and others stood looking after them. Dilip coughed to break the spell. Jafa held out the box of sweets to him.

'The wages of sin, Sir?' said Dilip, putting his arm around Jafa.

An Air Force pilot dealt death indirectly; he squeezed a trigger in the distance, in space, with just an electronic display guiding his actions. He never smelt the acrid smoke of guns and rockets, he did not hear the explosion of bombs. He never saw pain, anguish, fright and hopelessness on the countenances of those arrayed against him. To him a battle was merely a tally of objects destroyed or lost— aircraft, tanks, vehicles. He did not know those who died as a result of his actions, and if he were to die himself, he would also never know who had dealt death to him. After two wars and countless operational missions Jafa had suddenly come close to the human face of a battle adversary. And it was profoundly unsettling.

'I don't know, Dilip ...,' he said. 'I don't understand ... this matter of foes and friends. This girl ... she came to see the kind of people who killed her brother ... perhaps ... perhaps ... she is just as confused.'

'But you also keep saying that the whys and wherefores are not for us. For us ... only blind duty,' said Dilip as he tightened his arm around Jafa.

19
Ayesha

On a Sunday in the month of April as the sun rose higher in the sky and the time for the mid-day meal neared a strange kind of lull settled in Cell No. 5 where the Indian prisoners were gathered. Their eyes were riveted on the approach road from the main gate of the camp. They were perking up at the faintest sound of a moving vehicle in the expectation that the Volkswagen they were waiting for would soon pass in front of their cell and come to a stop outside the administrative block. Wahid would keep his word, they were sure.

Despite the bluster and the carefully contrived tough exterior Wahid was a soft, sensitive person. Unlike many others, he was usually ready to help with things that could alleviate the isolation and boredom of life in the prison. Of course, food was one item he could do little about either in respect of quality or quantity. That appeared to be in the control of some remote persons who took delight in deciding what the Indian prisoners shall eat and how much. A rumour had gone around Pakistan that their men in Indian custody were being kept on half rations and so some faceless officials at some level had decided to similarly curtail the rations for the Indians. Some months later when both the quality and the quantity of food suddenly improved, Garry was quick to remark to the Pakistanis, 'My God! It took you all these months to discover that your chaps in India were being well and fully fed!'

Ayesha

'Look, these are political matters,' said a Pakistani officer. 'So don't blame us.'

In the meantime Kuruvilla's arrangements with Aurangzeb, the man Friday in the camp, were working out well. With Rizvi's munificence and Wahid deciding to look the other way all the spare funds from their allowances were getting diverted for the clandestine procurement of the delicious *chappal kebabs* and, occasionally, even the delectable rice pudding, *phirni*. These were the high points of delight in the culinary field. But this also whetted their craving for more food and other delicacies. Even their conversations with the Pakistanis of all shades and standings now mainly dwelt on food and the modes of cooking in the different regions of the country. In the same vein Wahid one day described with relish the great feasts he had partaken of in the Middle East where they barbecued young camels stuffed with lambs stuffed with pheasants stuffed with chickens stuffed with partridges stuffed with quails stuffed with eggs and ate them with *rotis* of a dozen varieties and rice *pulaos* giving off the fragrances of Arabia.

'Please stop it,' shouted Garry suddenly. 'I can't take it any more! As it is I am half-starved here. Having to hear about such food is unbearable. Either get us some good things to eat or don't talk about them. I can't take it any more.'

'Yes, that's an idea,' said Harry to Wahid. 'You are our boss here. You can't let the single officers down. You better tell Mrs. Wahid that, like a good CO's wife, she has to give us a good feed once in a while!'

'How can we do that?' commiserated Brother. 'That would be unfair. We are not exactly visiting guests in this country.'

'Don't worry about that,' said Wahid with typical Punjabi large-heartedness. 'I think I shall give you chaps a treat. Let me see ... I'll get *kebabs* and *roomali rotis* from a place that's the best in Pindi, and *korma* and rice from another joint that few people know about. Then *tandoori chicken* that you'll like, with some ...'

'Are you serious?' wondered Garry, smacking his lips.

'Thanks!' said Dilip. 'But, no! Definitely, No!'

As everyone turned towards him, Dilip continued,' We want home-cooked food. Just one dish. But, cooked at home!' There was an instant chorus of vehement agreement.

'Okay, Okay,' capitulated Wahid with a smile, cheerfully accepting his role as the notional head of that group of officers, everyone forgetting for the time being that they were actually supposed to be enemies. 'We'll do something about it this coming Sunday.'

Such had always been the bonhomie between the Indians and the Pakistanis, between the Hindus and the Muslims, thought Jafa, when the *mullah*s and the *pundit*s, the politicians and the diplomats were not within earshot!

And Wahid kept his word. Precisely at 1 p.m. he drove up in his Volkswagen. But what was that? The car was packed with many bodies, with women and children. Perhaps Wahid would unload the food and then drive away with his family for a Sunday outing.

'Ah! They are taking out the *degchi*s,' exclaimed Garry in happy anticipation at the sight of the large containers of food being taken out of the car's boot.

'Look, the ladies and the children are coming out too,' said Brother excitedly.

'They are all coming this way,' reported Kuru even more excitedly.

'How should we greet the ladies?' asked Harry, always correct in courtesies. 'Good afternoon ...? Or, should we say ... *adaab* ...?'

No one replied. Each one was occupied with his very personal thoughts and reactions.

'Oh, look at the children,' cried Bunny as the kids came running forward ahead of the adults.

The door of the cell was open. Bunny stepped out and stood before the children as they came up to the cell. The children stopped suddenly and looked up at the tall, dark, strongly built Indian. Undoubtedly they had been told that they were going to meet different kind of people, and Indians to boot. The kids now curiously scanned each face, different in complexion, features and general appearance from their kind of people.

Bunny bent down and touched a child's hair. Brother patted a cheek. Dilip lunged forward and picked up the third. Harry cuddled the fourth. And then the children were touched, felt, patted, fondled, kissed, hugged and passed from hand to hand, from one embrace to another. The children too felt the deep human warmth flowing out to them. They did not squirm, flinch or draw back. They revelled in the liberties the unknown strangers were taking with them. Human warmth has no barriers, least of all with children.

And then a tear dropped. No one was able to recall later who began it, whose eyes were the first to moisten up, who was moved the quickest at the sight, the touch, the feel of children, at the sight of women, at the presence of a family, at the remembrance of human bonds.

The women were now walking towards the Indians with Wahid a few discreet paces behind them. Youthful, well-groomed, well-dressed, well-endowed, fair, lovely women, boldly erect, demurely confident of their attractiveness. They quickened their paces as they saw their offspring being lifted, hugged and passed from one embrace to another as a kind of tussle began among the Indians to grab them, hold them, ruffle their hair and kiss their glowing cheeks. The young mothers hurried forward not for any worry on account of their children but rather for the warmth emanating from the congregation of ten Indians and four Pakistani toddlers that drew them like a powerful magnet. And as they came closer and saw the tears coursing down the faces of the Indian officers they stopped in their tracks and watched with astonishment their offspring in the affectionate arms of their enemies. A strange kind of empathy rose up in their breasts and reached deep into their hearts, touching every nerve of their intuitive feminity that instinctively, sensitively sensed the isolation, the abject loneliness of the Indian men in their forced separation from their families. The tender susceptibilities of the Pakistani women began pouring out in tears of their own, in sobs and sighs for the plight of the deprived men arrayed before them.

Their reactions also probably reflected their sadness and anguish at the similar fate of their men—brothers, cousins, husbands, uncles—who were at that very moment incarcerated in India. There is that underground of the bereaved, the hopeless, the deprived, the lonely, the unhappy, who recognise their kind with unfailing accuracy and seek consolation from each other. And so no words were necessary, no explanations were needed. The enemies had found commonality in grief.

Harry hadn't said Good Afternoon, nor Dilip an ... *adaab*. Warmth and an unspoken sharing had already enveloped them all. And as the tears ebbed the women wiped their eyes with dainty handkerchiefs, the men with shirt-sleeves. The quivering nostrils and tremulous lips of the two women returned to a state of repose and then their faces began breaking out into smiles, beatific, beautiful, captivating, devastating. They laughed, gently, softly, like the tinkling of small bells. The Indian men laughed too, even Kamy whom an enemy, man, woman or child could seldom move to any emotion other than aloofness and antagonism.

'Thank you ... for coming ...,' began Dilip haltingly.

'More than that,' interjected Harry,' thank you for caring.'

'.... and crying ...,' added Brother. He looked like he might break into sobs all over again.

Kuru flashed a smile, perfect white teeth gleaming in the black countenance,' You know ma'am, we haven't set eyes on a child, a family in all these months! Thanks for reminding us that there still are tender things in this world.'

Wahid stood behind his family bewildered and dumbfounded. The soldier in him was unable to cope with such moving sentimentality. When he found the words he muttered,' My wife, her sister ... my sister-in-law ... our children.'

'Ladies,' said Bunny Coelho. 'Don't ask for our names, you won't remember them in any case. We are your husband's prisoners. He looks after us very, very well, and today by bringing you here he has done the greatest kindness of all. Thank you, Wahid *Saheb*.'

Ayesha

'We have brought some food, cooked at home as you wanted,' said the leading lady softly, shyly.

'*Aapa* and I were wondering about what to cook. And now we are wondering whether you'll like it at all,' said her sister with roses in her dimpled cheeks and rapidly fluttering lids over eyes that were blue and green and brown and a thousand other shades.

The Indian men made no replies. They stood transfixed, staring at the women, grinning from ear to ear, touched to the core of their beings with this gesture from the Wahid family.

Wahid coughed to draw attention and said,' Well, the food shall be served to you soon. I hope you'll like it. And now if you excuse us we shall move on.'

'*Insha Allah*, you will go back to your families soon,' said the leading lady.

'We will pray for you, just as we pray for our men who are on the other side. *Khuda Hafiz* ...,' said the beautiful one.

And then they were gone. The Indians stood rooted to their places, staring in the direction in which they had gone. Again, an all-pervasive silence, the silence of expectation having given way to the silence of a vacuum. The food when served was eaten desultorily. The dishes were painstakingly prepared and they were certainly not spared, rather polished off to the last scraps, but somehow, somewhere, the relish had gone out. The sight and closeness of women, the feel and smell of children, the tenderness of human contact had all triggered an emotional upheaval, an insatiable longing for homes and families. Everyone there was just not there, he was far away in a private retreat of human affections, of clambering children and hugging bodies, of simmering emotions straining to burst in an oblivion of bliss at the first touch of the loved ones.

The aura of the Wahid women pervaded the camp. Wherever one looked they were there, now smiling, now knitting their brows and empathising with the lonely men, then breaking into sobs and finally looking up shyly as smiles began to erupt on their youthful faces, the smile that recognises a sharing of pain, of understanding,

Death Wasn't Painful

of faith in human goodness, the smile that shines through coursing tears as the eyes sparkle from behind wet limpidness, the lips quiver and draw back over sensuous mouths revealing gleaming, even teeth, the most tantalising, devastating aspect of the seesaw of female emotions.

Like one never can really relive the fond moments of one's childhood and youth, never really return to the favourite lanes and haunts of yore, never really experience again the heartfelt stirrings of particularly moving moments except as enshrined in memory and recalled from time to time, Dilip and Harry, Teja and Kuru, Jafa and Bunny, they all knew that the tenderness of the moments just gone by shall now only remain imprinted upon their hearts, like a passing fragrance, like an ethereal experience. It could never be recaptured. And so even though the allure was strong they never requested for a repeat of that visit, but they remembered the women and the children everyday, several times a day, as perhaps they would do till the end of their days.

* * * * *

Some months later as the Indian prisoners sat listlessly whiling away time on a hot summer day, a guard arrived to announce the arrival of a visitor.

'An officer, Mack *Saheb*, is coming to meet your Jafa,' said the guard in gruff Punjabi, even as the officer appeared in the distance being escorted by a police corporal. Jafa stood up and peered through the iron-grill door, his features broadening into a grin as he recognised an old acquaintance.

'Mike,' shouted Jafa. 'My God! What a surprise, what pleasure! Come along, man! Long time no see.'

The door was unlocked and Mike ushered in. They shook hands warmly and embraced. Jafa introduced his colleagues who, infected with Jafa's enthusiasm, welcomed the guest with equal warmth.

'Ena should be joining me in a few moments,' said Mike as he settled into a chair.

'You and Ena ...,' squealed Jafa with delight. 'After all these months in Pakistan! Frankly, I was giving up hope of meeting up with you. I was beginning to think that you too might be locked up somewhere on our side.'

'No. No such luck,' replied Mike banteringly. 'I was safe and sound doing my bit in this part of the country. I did get to know that you were here, sojourning with us, but I am at a place quite a distance from here and one waits for an opportunity to visit the capital.'

And then Ena arrived, a tall, erect, tough, Pathan Christian girl bearing a large hamper from which peeped bottles of pickles and jams, biscuits and dried fruits, nuts, chocolates and cheeses and many more titbits that do not fill the stomach but vastly soothe the soul.

'*Salaam Aleikum*,' said Ena to one and all, raising her hand to her forehead as all the men stood up to welcome her with bows and pleasant inanities.

'Welcome to our castle, Ena, I mean ... our cell,' said Jafa as he moved forward and took Ena's hands in his own.

'Thank you, Ena,' said Jafa again. 'Very touched by this. My stay here would have been a waste of time if I had gone back without seeing you. Now sit down and tell us what we can get you to drink?'

'Well, well,' said Ena. 'Jafa the gentleman, always, everywhere, even here in this jail. But thank you ever so much. I won't have anything. Nothing at all, other than your company.' She kept up the pretence of social grace and etiquette.

'I am tempted to believe that you landed up in Pakistan just to meet me ... and Mike,' she said laughingly. 'I will have to tell my friends about this honour.'

That was what Jafa had remembered about her, the direct, confident manner of speaking. Even her *Salaam Aleikum* was spoken with a kind of boldness, albeit a bit laboured, a bit thrusting, as if asserting an identity that was not quite natural to her. In England too where Jafa had first met her and where Good Mornings and Good Afternoons were the usual forms of salutation, her *Salaam Aleikum*s had stood out as constant declarations of her Pakistani

Death Wasn't Painful

identity. She wore *salwaar kameez* and covered her head with a veil even as other women from Asia and the Middle East quickly changed over to casual western attire for convenience, for style, for merging into the colonial ambience of the British war college. Jafa had often marvelled at the uniformity of dress and etiquette that Pakistan had imposed on all its citizens, unlike India where everyone beat his own drum and where the Christians brought up in densely Hindi-speaking areas still persisted with the typically Anglo-Indian type of language of *dawl* (for *daal*, lentils) and *mangta hai* (I demand, as from minions).

'You know, Mike's brother was in the Indian Air Force?' Jafa stated with a question mark for the information of his compatriots.

'What!' exclaimed the Indians in unison.

'Yes,' said Jafa. 'He was a Tempest pilot. He died fighting for us during the 1948 Kashmir operations.'

The Indians looked at Mike with greater affinity. 'How come you came away to this side?' asked Garry.

'No, I didn't come away. Rather my brother chose to stay behind in India. He was too fond of his squadron mates and didn't want to part,' replied Mike. 'You see, my people belong to this part of the sub-continent and while my brother continued with the Royal Indian Air Force, of course the Royal had gone out by then, we simply stayed put where we were.'

'But how did your parents allow you to join the PAF, I mean, after losing one son to this damned bug of fighter flying?' asked Brother.

'Well, as children we do get stubborn sometimes,' said Mike simply.

'Wasn't that strange, splitting the family like that?' wondered Bunny. 'Or did your people think that Partition merely meant a new system of administrative control, that comings and goings from one side to another would remain free and easy as of old?'

'I really wouldn't know,' said Mike. 'I was only a kid at the time.'

And that was Mike, thought Jafa, studiously avoiding any comments, any discussion on matters pertaining to the two countries.

While a Muslim officer would have readily countered Bunny's opinion with his own and entered into a lively debate on the perceptions of the Partition days, a Christian officer had to tread very, very cautiously in such matters and avoid giving the slightest impression that he may even remotely be in agreement with a viewpoint that might have originated in India. Suspicion of softness towards India could spell doom on the members of the religious minorities.

'Well, well,' said Jafa rubbing his hands together in mock glee in an attempt to avoid contentious issues. 'I suppose we are the only peoples in the world who can sit together so soon after fighting a vicious war and exchange memories, recall funny things and laugh! It is amazing how officers of your Air Force keep visiting us, arguing and laughing with us.'

'But you remember how in that college in UK the Brits had segregated us?' asked Mike. 'They expected to see us shooting at each other the moment we came face to face.'

'Yeah, they even lodged us at two extreme ends of the campus and were perhaps disappointed that we actually shook hands and smiled at each other rather than exchange blows,' added Jafa.

'Incidentally,' said Mike, 'your group leader, Wing Commander Peter Wright had made very anxious enquiries about you and we had it conveyed to him that you were OK, though with some injuries.'

'Awfully nice of him,' said Jafa, touched at the concern shown by an Englishman of just a few months' acquaintance, wondering at the same time if Peter Wright would have made the effort to inform his wife in India. Of course, Jafa had thought later, Peter Wright was the kind of man who would overcome all barriers if the cause was right. A couple of centuries earlier he would have been a foremost empire builder for the greater glory of his King and Country.

Jafa quickly brought himself back to the present. 'Any news of the other officers who were at that college with us? The Kuwaiti Major, the handsome Lebanese, Farivar of Iran?'

'Ah, yes,' effused Mike. 'I ran into Ghorbanzadeh. He asked me to convey his regards to you and to thank you for your help with the English language.'

Death Wasn't Painful

'Is he here?' asked Jafa excitedly, without a pause.

'No. He went back,' said Mike, and then he clammed up. Perhaps he realised that he had unwittingly let out that an Iranian F-104 pilot had been in Pakistan some months earlier. The rumour that Iran had provided a squadron of F-104s for the defence of Karachi during the war now stood confirmed.

After a small but noticeable lull in conversation Kuru interjected, 'By the way, we helped to find for your Flight Lieutenant Parvez, the F-86 pilot, his stolen motorbike.'

'How was that?' bantered Ena. 'Don't tell me it had reached India.'

After the laughter subsided Kuru said, 'You see he had come to meet us one day with a couple of other Air Force buddies and it was then that he told us that his bike had been stolen from outside a shopping complex in 'Pindi. But our in-house astrologer, Tejwant, assured him that he would get it back, and he did!'

Teja, behind his bushy beard was all smiles at this reference to his predictions and forecasts which had never come true except this once. For most of the time Teja sat away from others with the *Gutka*, the small prayer book, in his hands, reciting the *Gurbani* softly, incessantly. Once in a while a small snatch of a conversation sneaked through the *Gurbani* and entered the spiritual recesses of his brain. At such occasions something was always thrown back at the audience as a resolved fact. The loss of Parvez's bike was one such matter. Teja had suddenly suspended the reading of the *Gutka*, returned to the mundane world and pronounced, 'You will find your motorbike!' The following Sunday Parvez had returned to the camp bearing a big carton that contained a 2-kg cake.

'I found my bike!' he announced joyously as he entered the Indian prisoners' cell. 'It was lying abandoned off the Peshawar highway. The bike had run out of petrol. I don't think it was a particularly hardworking thief because he just walked away rather than push the bike to a filling station.'

Teja, with the thumb and forefinger of his right hand smoothed out the moustache on his upper lip but stopped short of actually twirling it. He then proceeded to first stroke his flowing beard (the uncooperative Pakistanis had not yet provided the 'Fixo' for his beard) and then lifted the *Gutka* to his forehead and mumbled '*Wah Guruji da Khalsa* ...' He finally stood vindicated and fortified in his faith.

'Madam,' said Dilip, addressing Ena.' Meet again and specially our soothsayer, the great Tejwant, the unfailing master of astrology and mumbo-jumbo! We intend to announce to all the people in Pakistan with misplaced pens, missing motorbikes, failed examinations, jilted in love, neglected by spouses, oppressed by phlegmatic uncles and constipated cousins to come, one and all, to avail the services of our spiritual advisor and in-house astrologer, the incomparable, Teja! No money, no cash! Just some cakes and *kebabs*, pickles and jams.'

'Hold it!' said Ena, laughing. 'You better count all the items in my hamper and tell me how many questions I am entitled to ask. I'll come someday for the answers.'

And on this note, with laughter on all sides, she got up and moved out of the cell and stood facing them. Her husband shook hands with each Indian officer and went out to join her. They stood silently together looking at the Indians. Myriad emotions seemed to flit across their countenances, including perhaps one of regret that such fine people on both sides were condemned to be foes for no purpose!

'Good to have known you, Jafa, 'said Mike with a kind of finality, a last good-bye. 'And all you gentlemen, God Bless.'

'God Bless. And God Speed,' said Ena. Whatever she meant, she said it from the heart!

Yes, God Preserve You, Mike and Ena, thought the Indians.

* * * * *

Mumtaz loved to project a kind of mystique about himself which Jafa first found pretentious, later boring, and finally laughable and unnecessary. For their first meeting he had literally come in from the cold, walking in furtively from out of a dense fog on a winter morning. He had stood peering down at Jafa who was still wrapped in blankets. Drawing his eyebrows together and looking over the rims of his glasses he had said, 'I know all about you ...,' and said it something like an accusation. He had then announced that he was an intelligence officer in the Pakistan Air Force. Whether it was to overawe and frighten him or it was just plain fraud, Jafa was unable to decide. Possibly, the latter because as things unfolded he perhaps gave away more than he took.

'Oh ...', was all that Jafa said when he repeated the statement, wondering in which sphere of his life and deeds Mumtaz's knowledge lay.

After eyeing him for some more time, scanning him from left to right, top to bottom, leaning forward to take a closer look, tilting back in the chair for a longer shot as if placing the man before him in the correct perspective, Mumtaz shook his head and said, 'Mistake! Yes, a definite mistake!'

'I beg your pardon,' said Jafa, not knowing what else to say.

'Not yours,' he pronounced in a resigned kind of voice. 'Ours.'

Then he thrust his neck out at a bewildered Jafa and hissed, 'Why did you come here? You were sent here, weren't you?'

'I beg your pardon,' repeated Jafa, totally perplexed about the man and his mission.

'Why did you leave the job at your headquarters and re-join the squadron a few days before the war? Tell me. Answer this,' he shouted. 'People do it the other way, they get out of a fighting unit and slip into a desk job. I knew all along there was something fishy about you. So tell me why.'

Jafa thought hard and fast but was unable to fathom this line of questioning. Perhaps the sleuth in Mumtaz was trying to smell a rat that wasn't there.

'Well, one goes where one is sent. During a war it is usually to a frontline unit. '

'No, friend!' countered Mumtaz, 'at that time we didn't know what job you were holding there. Our chaps were in too much hurry to proclaim to the world that we had shot you down and captured you alive. By the time I could advise against it they had even released your photograph to the press.'

'I don't understand,' said Jafa. 'You would announce the names of the prisoners you take, wouldn't you? Particularly, the pilots. News about them looks good in the papers.'

'If we hadn't announced your name you would be singing, answering our questions even before we asked them. You wouldn't be talking your way out smartly and leading us up the gum tree as my colleagues tell me. You know you are safe now and we can do little to you.'

'My God!' exclaimed Jafa as the true import of these words dawned upon him. 'Besides the fact that people like me know precious little about anything beyond the immediate tactical situation and our weapons and about which you know everything in any case, do you mean to say that if the outside world did not know about my incarceration here you would have kept me under constant threat and possibly made me do or say what you liked?'

Mumtaz narrowed his eyes and looked at him over the rim of his glasses and nodded his head a few times. Abruptly he got up and walked out of the room. Outside he said something to the guard that Jafa was unable to hear.

He remained lost in unsettling thoughts. His belief and faith in the values held sacred among the armed forces of all the peoples were shaken to their foundations. Yes, there were instances of prisoners being slaughtered immediately on capture or surrender but that usually happened in the heat of battle. To deliberately hold prisoners secretly and to plan on using them for some undefined, inglorious purpose in later times may be justified in the world of spies and secret agents, but could not be explained or condoned in the honourable profession of arms. There was no honour of any kind in any activity or profession any more, pondered an agitated Jafa, only some kind of malice sinewing the thoughts and actions of peoples and nations!

After a gap of a few days Mumtaz again arrived one early morning when the winter mists still hung over the courtyard outside.

Death Wasn't Painful

Without a Good Morning, without a smile, without even an acknowledgement of the presence of another body in the room, Mumtaz dragged the chair, lowered himself into it and peered at Jafa over the rim of his glasses.

Jafa could not contain the questions raging in his mind since Mumtaz's last visit and he blurted out, 'Tell me, please tell me, how many of us are in your custody whose names have not been announced?'

Mumtaz said nothing. He continued to peer at Jafa with an enigmatic smile on his face. Jafa continued, 'Our chaps in this camp, those who landed up here towards the end of the war, those who knew which pilots on our side were missing in action ... well ... they expected to see certain other colleagues here. But they aren't here!'

'So? Anything could have happened to them,' countered Mumtaz.

'But others had seen them bailing out, seen their parachutes opening, even seen them landing on the ground. What happened to them? Where are they?' asked Jafa in distress.

'Who can say? It was war. Not some child's play,' said Mumtaz with that all-knowing, supercilious smile of his which Jafa was beginning to dislike.

'Your radio announced the shooting down of their planes giving the exact time and place of occurrence, but said nothing about the pilots dying with the aircraft which is usually mentioned in war bulletins. So what happened to the pilots? They have to be in your custody,' persisted a distraught Jafa.

'Any names in this connection?' asked Mumtaz with a show of concern.

'Yes,' said Jafa, a hope rising in his breast. 'Dandass, Tambay, Mistry ...'

'Never heard of them,' said Mumtaz with a touch of scorn and walked out of the room.

A sad Jafa lay upon his cot morosely imagining the worst about the many Indian pilots who were believed to be alive in enemy custody but over whose fates a big question mark now hung. When he reported this conversation to his colleagues Bunny asked, 'But what will they do with them? I mean, after all the questions have been asked and the answers extracted? Of what use would they be to the Pakistanis?'

'These are early months yet,' said Brother simplistically. 'I feel they will be brought out and quietly placed in some camp soon.'

'Suppose they have already made a declaration of the prisoners in their custody. Do you think they will come out with a supplementary list and say, 'Sorry, we forgot these.' and risk arousing all kinds of suspicions?' added Garry.

'You think they will keep quiet even in the case of Dandass about whom our wireless people are in possession of intercepted messages that were exchanged between Pakistani police outposts clearly stating that he was taken into custody alive and uninjured?' asked Teja agitatedly.

'Well there are instances of people remaining locked up and languishing in jails and nobody knowing anything about them or their sins ...,' Harry pondered aloud.

'That may be true about petty criminals, perhaps nobody came looking for them,' observed Bunny. 'It can't happen in the case of the soldiers, that too pilots.'

'Don't underestimate the sadistic streak among these people,' said Kamy. 'You heard what that fellow told Jafa, that they had made a mistake by announcing his name to the world. They may not have made that mistake in the case of some others. And now they will just keep denying their existence, like telling a thousand lies to cover the first.'

Mumtaz had disappeared, as suddenly and inexplicably as he had arrived. Surprisingly, he had not visited, talked to or questioned any other prisoner for Jafa had in detail described his appearance and mannerisms to his colleagues and they were sure that they had not set eyes upon any such person. Jafa was even more baffled about the purpose of Mumtaz's visits, the deliberate allusion to the possibility of undeclared Indian prisoners languishing in Pakistani jails, clearly an attempt to alarm and frighten him, to torment him. But to what purpose? And why single him out?

A few months later very early on a warm summer morning the iron grill door of Jafa's cell was opened by the guard on duty. That was unusual as the door was normally unlocked on the request of the inmate to be allowed to go to the toilet. Jafa willed himself into alertness and soon saw an apparition entering the cell in the still light of dawn.

It was Mumtaz.

'What the bloody hell!' said he to himself at the sight of the man who had so far only taken delight in tormenting him. But aloud he said, 'Good Morning,' which went unacknowledged.

After gazing into his eyes for a whole minute Mumtaz said, 'I know all about you.'

'Yes, you said so the last time too ...,' said Jafa feebly.

'Yes, our authorities may not, but I and my people know all about you,' he repeated in an accusatory tone. 'Your people ... they opposed us ... they went about lecturing and hectoring against the formation of Pakistan ... your people defied us when the Quaid gave the call for Direct Action ... they gathered our enemies and challenged us to fight ... those enemies of the *millat* who advised everyone not to deal with us, not to buy our lands? But were you able to stop us? See here ... we are hale and hearty ... we extracted the best prices for our houses and lands and came here to our own *millat* and *mulk* ... you could do nothing to us ... and we shall yet teach you a lesson ... *Insha Allah!*'

Jafa's mind was instantly awhirr with many possibilities. Most of the upper class Muslims from his hometown had migrated to Pakistan. And only someone from that class could know so much about his people. These clever ones had led the movement for Partition in their cities and feudal fiefdoms, they had guided from safe distances the poverty-stricken mobs to plunder, loot and kill when Jinnah called for Direct Action, in other words for violence against the Hindus to show to the world that the two communities could not live together in harmony. These were the people who

Ayesha

planned and contrived to sell their properties for handsome amounts, pocketed the money and quietly slipped away into the new country to again live in style and comfort while those that had made it possible for them remained in their ghettos and faced the opprobrium and wrath of the Hindus around them. Mumtaz had to be from some such family. He searched his mind desperately for some clue, some commonality that could help him to place Mumtaz in his original *avatar* and be able to say to him, 'I too know all about you.'

Like water finding its level, men too gravitate towards their equals. And so it was among the Hindus and Muslims of all classes and characteristics, *zamindar*s unto *zamindar*s, intellectuals unto each others' poets and writers, the dilettantes among the Hindus seeking out the kite-flying whore-hunting decadents of Muslim aristocracy, the poor of both communities sharing their *bidi*s, *hooch* and miseries, the farmers the inclemencies of weather and the heartlessness of money lenders, the *pundit*s and the *mulla*s the vagaries and faithlessness of their respective flocks. Besides fulfilling cultural and social urges at all levels such interaction provided the vital safety valves in the sense that irritants of a communal nature could be discussed and misunderstandings removed. But as the idea of Pakistan gained ground it was these channels of communication that snapped and people withdrew among their own kind behind veils of distrust and mutual suspicion.

In childhood and early adolescence Jafa had mingled with Muslim children and exchanged visits with their families. He had also witnessed the snapping of ties and regretted terribly that he was not welcome any more in their houses, nor they in his. Particularly galling was the denial of visits to the Masood household on all kinds of pretexts but just one purpose—even a fleeting and distant glimpse of the girl in the *gharara*. And then the stunning news that the Masood family had left town in the dead of night, quietly driving away in a car. Some said that they had gone to Aligarh, others that they had made it directly to Pakistan. Letters received by their poorer relations talked of the Masoods settling down in Karachi. Jafa eagerly lapped up every scrap of information about them though there was little about the one person he was so desperate to find out. Years later came the information that their eldest daughter had got married to an officer in the Pakistan Air Force. Jafa had not enquired about them after that.

Now it was his turn to narrow his eyes and look intently upon Mumtaz and say ... 'Ayesha? ...'

Mumtaz did not flinch at the mention of this name. He merely moved his head from side to side a couple of times, less in affirmation, more in confirmation that the pieces had fallen in place. And then he walked away.

Ayesha ... the girl in the *gharara*, thick tresses of black hair in loose plaits, the cream-and-peach of the face shining against the background of brown and black girls of the Mission School, adolescence bursting out and straining against the thin veil upon her chest, the roving dark eyes flitting from face to face, resting momentarily upon his as he liked to imagine, before being lowered and the head turning away, bashfully aware that a thousand eyes were focussed upon that lovely face, the fairest of all.

The girls of the Mission School and the boys of the Government School were gathered in the former's assembly hall for the annual debating competition, the most keenly awaited and looked-forward-to-event of the year. The contest had little to do with debating skills although the teachers on both sides made serious preparations by writing out sparkling speeches and bullying their wards into committing them to memory. In the days when girls went to school in veiled, covered horse-drawn *gharries*, this event's excitement lay in bringing the senior boys and girls face to face albeit in very controlled conditions. Here they were separated by a five-feet aisle, outside it was two separate worlds. Here the girls stole furtive glances at the boys to their right while pretending to be attentive to the speakers and the speeches; the boys made no pretences at all as open-mouthed, wide-eyed they ogled the girls, unashamedly soaking in the tender glow of youthful innocence.

Among the many skits, poetry recitations and patriotic songs presented by children of all ages and kinds the attraction of the evening was always the last item, the debate between the grown up boys and girls, two from each side. The subject also always touched gently upon the sexes and, in the days of reticence and restrained behaviour the innuendos and digs at the opposite sexes that liberally laced the speeches were hugely enjoyed by the audience. The topic for this day—'Woman's Place Is in the House'—promised much in this line.

By a strange custom the girls stood together on one side of the dais and the boys on the other. They would remain in full view of the audience until all four had made their speeches and collected their prizes. The first to be called on this day was a girl who spoke softly, haltingly, and the audience in the rear grew restive for not being able to hear her clearly. The boy who followed her was better and drew a round of applause. And then it was Ayesha.

She moved up to the front and stood in the full glare of lights. A hush fell on the gathering in the hall as everyone strained to take a good look at her. A fairer girl had not ascended that stage in living memory. She did an elaborate *adaab* to the audience, her hand rising from the knees to the forehead, a thick plait falling over the shoulder upon a small breast, the eyes downcast, the body leaning gracefully forward. And when she spoke it was in a ringing voice, each word floating over the gathering and reaching to the ends of the hall, the large kohl-covered eyes flitting from one group to another and returning to the front row where sat the judges. She spoke the lines with abandon as if she was rehearsing in the privacy of her bedroom, even consulted her notes unashamedly when she got stuck and returned to the declamation as if there had been no pause at all. Every other sentence drew an applause, the ovation and the clapping at the end of the speech were deafening. The star had already wrapped up the evening, only the formalities of winding up remained.

Jafa had not taken his eyes off her. He had stood in a trance, mesmerised. When called upon to speak he did move up to the dais and even began, 'Honourable Judges, Respected Parents, Brothers and Sisters ...' Then he stole a glance to the right and froze.

No further words came out. There was noise in the hall and he began again, 'Honourable Judges ...' and again lost track of his prepared speech. He was still looking to his right when the audience began to hoot. Flustered and ashamed he looked at a teacher standing close by and stammered, 'I ... I can't remember ...' The teacher gave him a withering look and in utter confusion he ran down the steps and through a side door outside the hall. There he stood behind a pillar in the dark, shamed and unhappy, yet he did not leave the place. After a short while she passed by, the *verandah* lights full upon her face, a large shining cup in her hands. She was beautiful, the cup looked good in her hand!

After that Jafa was a boy possessed. He befriended her brother and hung around her house on all kinds of pretexts. The festivals of Holi and Eid were now awaited with greater eagerness as they involved visits among the families. These were occasions when boys and girls could come face to face though conversation of any kind was taboo. The most exciting time was during the Teej festival when girls, Hindu and Muslim, got together to ride the swings in the mango arbours of each others' gardens and where the boys came in handy to tie the ropes and push the swings. And then the demand for Pakistan and Partition, the jolting of an ambience, a culture, a way of life, an amalgam of social graces, the fusion of civilisations, the bonds of generations, the dehumanising of humans in the flaunting of religious fervour by the faithfuls and the departure of the Masoods.

When Mumtaz came after a gap of a few days he was in a state of agitation. After the customary peering down at Jafa he launched into a monologue, 'We ran things in undivided India, did you know that? Even under the British it was we who were the effective rulers as we manoeuvred the administration. We created Pakistan because we could not remain masters in our own lands after the departure of the British. And we have to rule here too ... the thinkers, the people with brains and imagination ... those from Patna and Lucknow, Allahabad and Aligarh, Bareilly and Bhopal ... It is we who have to finally deal with you, because we understand you, we know how you conspire and contrive.'

'Why do you speak like this?' asked Jafa sadly. 'Why do you think like this? You made your choice. You took your share of the country, of everything. So what's the problem now? Why not live and let live? Why this nagging hostility?'

'You won't understand,' said Mumtaz and got up to go. But Jafa stopped him in his tracks by saying, 'How is Ayesha?'

Mumtaz held up his hand to stop him from saying anything further, shrugged his shoulders and walked out.

On his next visit he surprised Jafa by asking, 'Is Mr Amir Chand still there? And that Judge *Saheb*, Braj Narain?'

Jafa understood now. The hostility was at least in part contrived, it was the product of deliberate thought, the decision of a conditioned mind, not an occlusion of the heart. It was his childhood, his adolescence, the tender, soul-satisfying memories of that period that were drawing him irresistibly to Jafa in a kind of love-hate relationship. But Mumtaz quickly checked himself, pulled a bit of sternness over his countenance, and declaimed, 'Mistakes have been made. Follies committed again and again. Some people think that they can simply march down armies as in the olden days and conquer everything in their path. They don't realise how vastly everything has changed. It is brain power that will get us anywhere ... our time is bound to come ... it is coming.'

Jafa's mind was on other things. He had no wish to enter a futile, endless debate. So he said what he had been wanting to say all these days, 'Can I meet Ayesha? Can I see her just once?'

Mumtaz stared at him. He stood thinking for a whole minute, then turned and walked away. Jafa's mind was in a turmoil. Was Mumtaz offended? Would he take the request in the right spirit, in the spirit of harking back to times gone by, to happy, wholesome times? Possibly, yes. possibly, no.

Mumtaz broke his own routine when he next arrived during an afternoon. More than that, Jafa was called out of his cell and taken to a room in the administrative block where he faced Mumtaz who was already seated behind a desk and who now signalled to him to take a chair on the opposite side. Mumtaz was about to begin speaking when a police corporal came rushing into the room. He whispered something in Mumtaz's ear and Mumtaz immediately stood up as if to leave.

'A senior officer is coming to take a look at the arrangements in this camp,' he said. 'It won't do for me to be hanging around.'

Mumtaz walked out and away. The policeman signalled to Jafa to follow him back to his cell. As he stepped out of the room a car started up on the side of the building, turned a corner and came into view. As it drove by, he glimpsed in the window ... a cream-and-peach face ... thick dark tresses falling over her shoulders ... kohl-smeared eyes looking at him ... perplexedly, confusedly, nostalgically.

Open-mouthed, wide-eyed, Jafa raised a hand to stop her, to tell her to wait. The car sped away. He had missed her again.

⓴
The Great Homecoming

27 November 1972

In the high-security prison at Lyallpur, part of which housed the Indian POWs, it was time for the evening exercise. Whether fit or ill, this was the time everyone looked forward to. The Air Force officers were allowed to come out of their block of cells and join their Army colleagues for an hour at the volleyball court. It was here that they laughed and discussed their encounters with the rude and bloody-minded Pakistani officers and guards; it was here that they aired their frustrations and suspicions.

'Did you notice the cleanliness drive that's been going on since this morning?' asked an army captain.

'Yes, lots of chaps cutting grass and clearing the area,' observed Bunny.

'We've been here almost an year now but never seen this kind of effort,' said the Captain.

For the next few days there was no let up in the drive for sprucing up the camp. Finally, on 30th November as the Air Force officers came out of their block they noticed the roads being marked with limestone powder, a sure sign of an impending visit by someone important. Brother Bhargava could not contain his curiosity about what was up, who was coming. He confronted the first responsible Pakistani he saw on the road, the Subedar-Major in charge of administration in the prison camp.

'The General *Saheb* coming tomorrow?' Brother shot an innocuous enquiry at the official, in the manner of saying hello to a passing acquaintance on the street.

The Subedar-Major was about to say something but checked himself. Smugly, he said, 'Let's see who comes!'

'It's bigger than a General, I feel,' said Brother to his colleagues.

'Yeah, no one needs to keep a General's visit under shrouds,' commented Kuruvilla.

As they proceeded further towards the army officers' block, Dilip stopped near a civilian who was sweeping the road.

'So? Preparing for Bhutto *Saheb*'s visit tomorrow?' asked Dilip with an innocent smile.

'Yes, *saheb*,' said the simple sweeper. The riddle was solved.

No one played that evening. Bhutto's visit on the morrow was upper-most in their minds. Having formed definite impressions of the Pakistani leader's personality and style they understood instinctively that he was coming to address the Indian POWs and gain some kind of political mileage. He was certainly not coming to study the general living conditions in the jail teeming with life-termers in irons and chains.

'I think we are going home,' said Brother suddenly. All others turned to look at him as one would look at the Oracle.

'Yes,' said Garry softly, firmly. 'There is no other reason for Bhutto to come here. He will set us free and score a point against India.'

The Indian prisoners had weathered all seasons in Pakistan. They had arrived in December, seen the severe winter of the north-west change to balmy spring, the summer interspersed with frequent storms, the rains sparse and pleasant, and once again the onset of winter. The woollen jerseys emblazoned with the letters, POW, which they had dumped in the hope of never seeing them again, had to be pulled out for use once more. Just this act, simple

The Great Homecoming

and protective in itself, but representing the continuing state of incarceration and hopelessness, depressed them no end, and triggered a debate on the justification for remaining in enemy custody for so long.

'Looks like our countries have decided to play poker with the prisoners of war,' said Harry to no one in particular.

The Indian prisoners had avidly followed reports in the Pakistani press on the exchange of prisoners. They had also watched on the TV innumerable discussions on the subject. It seemed that some kind of diplomatic game was being played out between India, Pakistan and Bangladesh over the Pakistani troops that had surrendered to the Indian Army in the erstwhile East Pakistan.

'Everyone is talking only about the 93,000 Pakistanis captured in the east. No one talks of us, of the prisoners taken on the western front,' Chati had said regretfully when the debate had just begun.

'Should there be a distinction between prisoners taken on the eastern front and those taken on the western front?' asked Brother, and himself answered, 'After all, it was one war.'

'No,' Kuru had disagreed. 'Technically, legally, we and Bangladesh jointly fought Pakistan in the east and so there would have to be a distinction from the west where we alone fought Pakistan.'

'All the more reason that there should have been a clean swap of prisoners of the western front immediately after the ceasefire. If what Kuru says is true then we shouldn't have got mixed up with the POWs on the other side,' observed Garry.

'No, Garry boy, it's not so simple,' said Dilip. 'With 93,000 prisoners in the east, we have these chaps by their bloody balls. Mrs. Gandhi knows this and she wants a final settlement on Kashmir. That's basically what we have fought for on this side. Mistakes were made in 1948, again in 1965, when nothing got resolved. The Lady is not going to repeat those mistakes. And that's why there is no mention of us, she can't show any weakness while negotiating. Of course, we may get stuck here, but if Kashmir is getting settled it'll be worthwhile.'

Death Wasn't Painful

And so the prisoners kept up a brave front in the thought that if their country had not taken any pains to get them back it was for a higher purpose, for the final resolution of a problem that had defied solution for twenty-five years and landed them in three destructive wars. They had faith in the Iron Lady, the architect of the massive victory in the recent war, and felt elated that they were, in howsoever an indirect and obscure manner, a part of her grand design to secure a lasting peace on the sub-continent.

Then came the Murree talks in March 1972, the first between India and Pakistan after the ceasefire. It was expected that issues such as the repatriation of POWs of the western front and the civilian internees would get resolved right away, if only to create an atmosphere of goodwill while the ground was being prepared for the more substantive issues of Kashmir and Bangladesh to be taken up later and at a higher level. But the reports emanating from Murree were perplexing in that they gave rise to a new debate on whether the normalisation of relations such as exchange of prisoners and territories should begin on 'cessation of hostilities,' or on the 'conclusion of peace'! And, what was the difference? Does peace begin when you stop shooting at each other or does it begin when you have finally identified and eradicated the cause of the fight itself, and signed a document to say so?

'Can the causes of conflicts among nations be discussed, debated and deleted from the collective psyches, just like that, around a conference table?' asked one Indian prisoner.

'Howsoever that may be,' intervened Garry, 'but the basic cause of the conflict does not appear to have even been touched at Murree.'

'How's that?' asked Brother. 'Surely they are discussing Bangladesh and the prisoners taken there.'

'Exactly,' said Garry. 'Bangladesh is their problem and they are discussing it. Our problem is Kashmir and that is not getting discussed at all.'

'Amazing!' commented Kamy. 'Our great diplomat and policy-maker, the ace advisor of the prime minister, backed by all the whiz-kids from our foreign office is harping only on the recognition of Bangladesh by Pakistan, not on the settlement of Kashmir. Bangladesh is Pakistan's problem, let them sort it out. Ours should be a single-point agenda—Kashmir.'

'But, what have such intellectual semantics got to do with us?' asked another officer. 'We did our duty on the field of battle. There is no need for us to be played on the fields of politics and diplomacy.'

'Let them play politics with whatever they want, but not with us, not with the soldiers whose job ends when the war is over,' said they all.

Just like the Pakistanis, whose sons were locked up in India, and who said the same things and asked the same questions.

It was bad for morale, thought Jafa, this kind of negation of expectations from own countrymen, for, if the soldier was expected to think of the country first, he too expected the country to worry about him a bit and do the utmost to bail him out of unnecessary, avoidable hardship and harassment. The prisoners were aware, they had read, of the pains taken by the Americans to trace each one of their missing soldiers after the Korean war and their insistence upon instant release of all those alive in enemy custody, even going so far as exhuming the bodies of their dead colleagues and shipping them back home to the kith and kin. Even as recently as the last conflict in the Middle East, Israel had insisted on the exchange of prisoners before starting peace negotiations. Perhaps military manpower was regarded as a great asset in these countries, a body of men that had to be nurtured and taken care of painstakingly, if only because so much sacrifice was demanded of them for the safety of the rest, irrespective of what material benefits might be allowed to them during peace. And in our country perhaps manpower, trained, specialised or otherwise, was in such abundant surplus that a few thousands, even a few lakhs, languishing or dying here and there did not really matter to the nation at large!

Alternating between anger and despondency on one side and, on the other, the need to keep up a brave front in enemy country,

Death Wasn't Painful

the Indian prisoners awaited the much-awaited meeting between Bhutto and Indira Gandhi at Simla. For two days there was no agreement and apprehensions were there that the talks might break down. Then, on the third day, the two leaders, dressed in pseudo-military manly brocade and gracefully feminine womanly brocade, took a long walk in the wooded dales of Simla. When they returned and beamed at the cameramen, there was really no need to announce that an agreement had been reached.

'What sort of a blessed agreement is this?' cried Kamy when the details of the Simla Agreement came out. 'It's all wishy-washy. There is nothing concrete except that we are giving back the 5000 square kilometres that we had taken during the war. What are we getting in return? And there is no mention of us, not a word about our repatriation.'

Kamy shook with anger. Bhutto had walked away with everything that was at stake for Pakistan, with everything that India held as bargaining chips. With smart talk and vague, off the record, promises on Kashmir, he succeeded in freeing his territory and returning to the status-quo-ante on Kashmir, nullifying in three days all that India had gained during a whole year at such enormous human and financial cost.

'What the hell,' shouted Dilip. 'There is no blooming agreement on Kashmir, just a vague assurance that there won't be violence there and matters would be sorted out through talks! Talk, Talk, Talk! All that we ever achieve, at ever-greater cost, is TALK! We TALK in Delhi, we TALK in Islamabad, and we TALK in New York and in Geneva. TALK! TALK! TALK! Fight every few years all over, fight everyday in some areas. Beat them back, then give back all that is taken. And again, TALK, TALK. Stop halfway in '48, let them keep half Kashmir and go all the way to New York, to UN, to TALK. That spindly man from Kerala, he TALKED. For nine hours! In '65, beat them again, take the vital mountain passes and go all the way to Tashkent, to TALK, and to give back all that had been taken, with promise to further TALK, TALK, TALK! And now this time. TALK at Murree, TALK at Simla, and agree to give back all that

The Great Homecoming

could have put a damned end to all this TALK! And, lauded by all, resolve solemnly to keep up with TALK! TALK! TALK!'

So said Dilip. So, said all the Indian officers. And so said the *jawans* and *sardars* when they met together for Sunday morning prayers.

'Is it true, *saheb*, that we are giving back Shakargarh?' asked a *jawan* innocently, one who had fought to gain control of that area. 'And without making them vacate Kashmir?' he asked further.

'There is nothing in the Simla agreement about us?' asked another *jawan*, unable to believe that he, the spearhead of Indian victory, had been quite forgotten and sidelined in a grand strategy which, he knew instinctively, would take him, as before, towards another war, another disaster.

The discussions and debates went on. Soldiers, brought up traditionally to function under clear-cut policies and directions, with the aims of battles and wars and the dispensations for peace palpable and well defined, with the perspicacity and probity of the civilian masters unquestioned and their tenacity of purpose in the execution of State policy undeviating and ruthless as the war itself, were now in their long, tedious, forced leisure in enemy prison, beginning to notice political dithering and military mismanagement which seemed to get worse with each successive crisis.

'What have we resolved by fighting three wars with Pakistan and the one with China?' asked one.

'We had a whole year to formulate policy and assemble the resources to execute it. And if Kashmir wasn't central to our policy and its final settlement the main objective, I shall never understand what I have fought two wars for!' said another.

'If we are the dominating power this side of the Himalayas, the little fellows must be made to respect this fact. Shouldn't be unjust or shabby or ungenerous but they can't be allowed to defy us and become pin-pricks in our sides,' said a third.

'And Pakistan, one-fifth our size, one-fiftieth of our potential! And the sole damn focus of our foreign policy! A damned millstone around our necks! A shame that we haven't cast it aside in twenty-five

Death Wasn't Painful

years. Some funny kind of mental, emotional fetters and shackles that we don't break,' said a fourth after some deliberation.

Yes, thought Jafa, there was a strange kind of dichotomy in the Indian, rather, the Hindu, psyche. Harping on one people and one country for half-a-century, then allowing ten percent of the population to get away with two nations and two countries. Gandhi doing little to keep Jinnah in the Congress fold, then begging Jinnah to head the government of a free but united India. Gandhi tacitly surrendering to the idea of partition and the creation of two countries, two armed forces, two systems, two enemies, then fasting to compel India to give away crores without a settlement on assets and liabilities. Nehru ordering a ceasefire in Kashmir in 1948 when we could have cleared the whole state of Paki infiltrators and then running to the UN on high moral principles, follies that were to cause so much political and military embarrassment later. The gains of 1965 frittered away at Tashkent, the gains of 1971 at Simla. A country unaccustomed to gains on the battlefield, the last being perhaps two thousand years in the past, suddenly presented with a grand victory by its armed forces did not seem to know what to do with it. Like an unexpected bounty inducing euphoria and intemperate generosity the country's leaders thought of everything and everyone except their own fundamental interests.

'A very funny mind set, really,' said Kamy. 'They break up the mother country, they belligerate, they maim and kill. But we simply box their ears and send them off with a warning. Instead of tightening the noose around them militarily, subversively, clandestinely; politically, diplomatically, economically; Islamically, Ecumenically; Afghanically, Israelically; Slavically, Uncle-Sam-ically, and All-other-cally, after each war, each confrontation, our Vinobas and our Jai Prakashes begin to sing songs of oneness, of brotherhood, of non-violence, of moral sublimities, of big brotherliness, of *vasudhaiva kutumbukam*, of lighting candles at the borders, without ever noticing the contemptuous silence on the other side.'

Yes, thought Jafa, there was no substitute for national strength, the ability to give two hooks for each finger raised against you.

The Great Homecoming

The dichotomy lay in treating Pakistan not simply as another country but as a Muslim country. The dichotomy lay in our own inability to dissociate politics from religion. The dichotomy lay in substituting military strength with pretensions of moral superiority. The dichotomy lay in our confusion about the nature of our adversaries, so adorable in their individuality and so unsparing and so uncompromising in their species.

The long, purposeless incarceration in enemy jail. Feelings of abandonment and neglect by own countrymen. Long hours to think and debate. Monologues, discussions and arguments.

Anger and frustration at having to fight over the same issue again and again. Then seeing the gains frittered away, again and again. At such cost, at such sacrifice of life and limb. Nothing to show in the end. No lasting gain for the country. No lasting honour for the fighting man. All this interspersed with peace. Peace worse than war. More tensions, more problems. More uncertainties and deprivations. Constantly disturbed family lives, constantly corroded children's careers. Move to north-east, move to J&K, move, move, move. Earthquakes, floods, avalanches, riots. Move, Move. But, ALL ACCEPTABLE. In the National Interest.

Neglect and disdain at the hands of the wielders of power. Low wages, lower esteem. Minor concessions, major resentments. Men in uniform, intellectually inferior, culturally pretentious, strutting about as in the Imperial days! Guards of the borders entertaining delusions of the colonial past, of participation in policy and the pursuit of national aims, of parity with the new inheritors of the empire, the stalwarts of the so-called steel frame now busy gaily, malleably, manipulatively propitiating political gods for pelf and personal aggrandisement, wielding total power, disclaiming total responsibility and pushing the country into total chaos. NOT ACCEPTABLE! But, Lump it!

And now the arrival of Bhutto on the morrow. 9:00 a.m., 1 December 1972.

All Indian POWs herded into a special enclosure cordoned off with colourful marquee panels. *Jawan*s on durries, behind them, officers on chairs. Facing them, a large raised platform with tables, chairs and lots of mikes. Empty spaces on the sides.

A whirr of helicopters. Two, three, four, more. Landing, cutting off engines, silence. The starting up of car engines a short distance away, the caravan coming closer and closer.

'You will all stand up to welcome the Honoured Guest,' a command in military voice, from behind.

No need for advice, thought the Indians. Bhutto, a Head of State. Will get courtesies due to him.

A flurry of cameramen, TV men, a lot of them fair, foreign media men, shuffling backwards looking into their lenses, clicking, whirring gadgets, then quickly grabbing places on two sides of the dais. As the shuffling and the clicking and the whirring subsided, there was Bhutto on centre stage. No introductions, no preliminary speeches. No introduction needed or necessary.

'I see before me these Indian prisoners of war,' he spoke into the microphone immediately on ascending the dais. 'I see before me these brave soldiers who have been forgotten by their own country, who have been away from their families for so long, for so many months, without their country taking any steps to sort out the pending matters so that they could go to their homes, to their mothers and fathers, wives and children.'

Cameras panning from Bhutto to the Indian prisoners. Pakistani officials whispering to Indian officers and men, 'He is going to send you home. Immediately. Today. Clap when he finishes. Clap and shout thanks. Okay?'

Jafa heard the whispering and whispered back to the officers, 'There will be no clapping and no shouting of thanks. Get down on your knees and pass the word to all our soldiers. There will be no clapping, no smiling.'

They will not have a contrived jubilation exhibited all over the world. Bhutto had the power to throw this titbit at them, but they must not be seen lapping it up.

'I regret that our neighbouring country has no regard for human values, no regard for old mothers who long to see their sons,

The Great Homecoming

no regard for the longings of innocent children to be in the arms of their fathers, no consideration for fathers, sisters, friends whose dear ones are locked up by India unnecessarily, unjustly, inhumanly.'

'But we Pakistanis, we Muslims, who have been imbued by the Great Prophet, Peace Be Upon His Soul, with compassion, with kindness, for fellow human beings, cannot do such a thing, shall not do such awful deeds.'

'And so, I, Zulfiqar Ali Bhutto, on behalf of this country, and on behalf of the compassionate people of Pakistan, set you free. Arrangements have been made to immediately despatch you to your country. Whatever Indian leaders and Indian Government may do or not do, we want you to be in the bosom of your families, with your fathers and mothers, brothers and sisters, wives and children. Go home and tell your Government to similarly return our soldiers who are in prisons in your country.'

All this and more words to this effect, this meaning, this generosity in the face of Indian perfidy.

The filming and recording over, the speech concluded, Bhutto waits for the applause. It doesn't come. A Pakistani official on his knees at the front row frantically urges the Indian *jawan*s, '*tali bajao, tali bajao, shukriya bolo*.' Clap, say Thanks! Two *jawan*s begin to clap, tepidly. Not joined by others, they stop quickly. A couple of Sikh *jawan*s softly meow, '*shukriya, janab*.' Bhutto waits a couple of seconds, turns towards foreign media men and walks away saying things to them.

As the cars drive away the Pakistani officials, military and civil, turn to look at the Indian officers and *sardar*s with faces that barely hide their thought—Ungrateful bastard Indians, as always!

'Some way, somehow, setting us free was Bhutto's compulsion,' Kuruvilla thought aloud. 'Clapping and thanking won't take us home faster.'

'Yes, we shall go home, but rather shamefully,' lamented Dilip.

'We should have been going home at the behest of Indira Gandhi, not as Bhutto's charity', regretted Kamy.

'Yes, this repatriation, like a damned charity from Bhutto,' said Teja disgustedly.

'This doesn't make me happy,' said Bunny sadly.

'We should have been spared this humiliation after winning the war,' said Garry dejectedly.

'We shall be leaving at their mercy. Not at the behest of our Government,' said Harry disappointedly.

'Can't walk out of here with our heads up,' said Brother discontentedly.

And in that mood they returned to their enclosures and sat around quietly, absorbed in private thoughts. What might have caused jubilation and hilarity had it come out of the Murree or the Simla talks, as a result of a conscious, deliberate effort by their own country's leaders, was now like a damp squib in their hands, a kind of anti-climax.

After a while Dilip bestirred himself and addressed Jafa, 'A penny for your thoughts!'

Jafa merely smiled. Then Dilip said, in general, to nobody, 'Back home, a spot of leave, meet family, friends, feel like a hero for a while. Then what?'

'Then what?' asked Kamy in surprise, and himself answered, 'Then start preparing for the next round!'

'Yes. The next round is bound to come. Sooner or later it will come,' said Brother.

'Bhutto has bitten dust twice. Both times he was behind the wars. He would like to even out the score, if he can,' said Kuru.

'But do you think they can fight us?' asked Bunny. 'With the threat in the east gone, the Chinese holding back and standing aloof, do you think they can stand up to us?'

'Yes, that's a thought!', said Harry gleefully. 'In that case we can relax during the rest of our service and have a ball!'

'No, you can't. You won't,' admonished Kamy. 'Haven't you seen in the faces of their officers the frustration, the rage, the seething anger at having lost the war? Haven't you noticed a deadly kind of determination to somehow bring India to her knees? It's

The Great Homecoming

only a matter of time, but they will come back at us, in some form or the other.'

'Alright,' said Garry. 'That is one side of it. But haven't you also noticed among the smaller people here, the menial class, the *jawan*s, the airmen, even the civilians and some women whom we have met in our limited contacts, that there is also a fairly strong desire for good relations with India, for the need to call off the tensions and the fights?'

'I too feel that the common people do not want wars between India and Pakistan,' said Brother who was always striking up conversations with any and all Pakistanis in the mood for it.

'Ha!' sneered Kamy, 'Who is bothered about the common people? Certainly not the dictatorships in this country! The common people have no mind of their own and even lesser meaning.'

'But,' said Dilip in a solemn voice. 'Everything is always done in the name of the common man, for his safety and well-being, even though it leads to his own ruin ultimately. It looks that here in Pakistan the common man is of even less consequence. He is driven by Islamic rhetoric to perceive Hindu India as the ogre poised to deprive him of his religion, defile him and send him into the fires of purgatory. His masters understand that they had used Islam to found a new political entity, and every time that its foundations get shaken Islam has to be stirred up more vigorously, more virulently. Every time a Pak ruler feels threatened he takes the only recourse for survival, falling back upon a harder, harsher version of Islam. And therefore, so long as Pakistan continues to think of itself as a crusader for Islam in Asia, so long as Islam continues to be used as the surest road to political power, and so long as the vested interests of the landed gentry and the army brass continue to be served in this kind of dictatorial democracy, there can be no adjustments, no lasting peace with India.'

The steel door to the enclosure opened in the late afternoon and the Subedar-Major came in. 'There will be early dinner. Please be ready to move soon after that,' he announced.

Death Wasn't Painful

Early dinner, as ordered. Then, dressed in the POW clothes they trooped out to the waiting transports, clutching personal toiletry items. A brief drive, then into the compartments of a waiting train on a cordoned-off platform. Locked from outside, left to themselves.

Lying on bunks, minds tossing between visions of homes, families, wives, sweethearts, children, and, the injustice of it all—release from prison by kindness and mercy of the enemy.

Initiative—Bhutto!

Coup of sorts—Bhutto!

Late start, early arrival next morning. An interminable halt, perhaps the destination, Wagah. Then, out of the train, a short walk to a non-descript army barrack. The three Ss—shit, shave, shampoo. Spruced up, each in his best mode, for the final walk—to freedom, to motherland.

But, in the meantime, sitting in the sun on standard army easy chairs, waiting. Waiting and thinking. Thinking of the year gone by, of the years since Partition, of the great divide, the wars, the uncertainties of the future, democracy and dictatorship, personal ambitions and public posturings, receding public morality and creeping corruption. Nothing got changed; nothing got resolved. Old wine in old bottles, served by ever newer hands. What will it be like when they got back? ... A few perfunctory welcoming speeches ... a round of applause ... a half-hearted chorus of 'Well Done, Chaps!'... a cup of tepid tea?

The arrival of a Pakistani officer broke the reverie. 'Please follow me,' he said.

They rose and walked behind him in a single file, all the way to the border. Then through the two gates—from the gate of captivity to the gate of freedom.

Motherland! India! Indians!

Throngs of people just beyond the gate of freedom, pushing and shoving in their eagerness to reach the returning soldiers. Being held and pushed back by Indian militiamen. A great roar from them, indistinguishable words but unmistakably welcoming sounds. The first into the crowd, Bunny, swallowed up in embraces, lifted and passed on. Each one smothered with kind words and bear hugs, pulled deeper into the bosom of the sea of humanity.

India! Indians!

Showers of flowers, garlands of marigold. Kisses from the elderly, handshakes from the young.

Our People. Our Brothers.

The ones we fought for. They know it. They show it.

Old women placing hands upon shoulders of returning men, gazing into their eyes, their eyes brimming with tears, blessing others' children in place of their own who did not return.

Yes, they had waited. Waited for a whole year, for the unknown soldier to return. The unknown soldier who had stopped the enemy beyond their homes and hearths, who had safeguarded their fields, the lives of their men, and the honour of their women. But they had remembered him; they had waited for him.

The hardships of high mountains, the travails of the north-east, humiliation and hardship in enemy prison, death and decimation in battle— that was for these men and these women, the ones who remembered and who waited, waited with affection, with gratitude.

A posse of school girls, singing a patriotic song, showering flower petals, welcoming shyly with kohl-covered eyes.

The Young India! The Mother India!

Whether the quest for money and the arrogance of civilian power had overshadowed the grace and dignity of military service or not, whether the gains of war obtained through blood and sweat got squandered or not, whether the abandonment and neglect suffered in enemy prison was a matter of supreme indifference at the hands of the political masters or not—it was for these people, these countrymen, this land of Bharat, for which life and limb had been put out on the sacrificial altar.

It was the people who had called. It will again be the same when they call, when the country calls. Once again the Harrys and the Dilips, the Tejwants and the Kuruvillas, the Jafas and the Coelhos, the Vikrams and the Mullas, the Bhargavas and the Garrys, the Kamats and the Chatis shall sally forth, when the country calls....

Annexure:
Pen Portraits

Wing Commander B.A. Coelho

An officer of Mangalorean descent brought up in the North, Bunny Coelho was a gentleman to the core, with a very strong moral streak in his personality. Once his mind was made up on the rightness of an attitude, no external pressure could change it. He led a very disciplined and uncomplaining life even in the prison camp. If he had a grouse with anyone in life it was with the butcher who would slip bony portions instead of the *golboti* into his purchase.

Bunny was born in 1932 in New Delhi. His father was a senior engineer in the Telegraph Department. On the Viceroy's request he installed the first fully automatic telephone exchange at Connaught Place, Delhi, and a similar device in the British summer capital in Simla. When offered a reward, the senior Coelho requested the viceroy for admission of his son in St. Edward's School, Simla, an exclusive institution for the education of European children only. Being the only native boy, Bunny suffered enormous racist indignities at the hands of the white boys. He later completed Senior Cambridge from St. Columba's, Delhi, and then moved to DAV College, Kanpur, where Atal Behari Vajpayee, the future prime minister was among his seniors. But, here he suffered discrimination of a different kind. As a Christian, he was not allowed to enter

Annexure

the dining hall and all his meals were poured into his *thali* from a distance inside his room.

Bunny wanted to be a doctor, but, under the domicile rules prevailing in those days, he could only get admission to a college in Delhi, and Delhi in those days had a medical college only for women. He finally joined the Air Force in 1951 and was commissioned as a fighter pilot in 1953. He flew different fighters, served in Iraq as an instructor, and was commanding No. 7 Squadron on Hunters at Bagdogra when the 1971 War broke out, the unit launching itself into operations in Bangladesh. The squadron was then relocated to Bikaner, in the western sector. It was from here that, on 9th December, while attacking Suleimanke bridge that his aircraft was hit by ground fire and he had to eject. On the ground he was fired upon by the enemy, but, fortunately, he was not hit. Then a Pak Army Major, whose seven men had been killed in Bunny's attacks, put a gun to his chest and was about to squeeze the trigger when another Pak officer pushed the gun away, telling the Major that the Indian pilot was wanted for interrogation, and, in any case, the Major, having shot down an Indian plane was now in line for a *Sitara-e-Jurrat* decoration. The idea of the award so enthused the Major that he began dancing the 'bhangra' on the spot. Later, Bunny was transported to the camp at Rawalpindi.

He rose to be an Air Vice Marshal in the Air Force. He now lives in NOIDA with his wife, his three children work and live in the USA and Australia.

Squadron Leader Dhirendra Singh Jafa

Born into a *zamindar* family in 1935 in Uttar Pradesh, he was commissioned into the Air Force in 1954. He flew the Spitfire XVIII, the Vampire, the Toofani (Ouragon, French), the Hunter, the Gnat, the Mig-21 and the SU-7 aircraft. He trained with the United States and the USSR Air Forces and graduated from the Royal Air Force Staff College, Bracknell, U.K. He served in the Policy and

Plans division of Air Headquarters, and as an ADC to Air Chief Marshal P.C. Lal.

He flew 23 operational missions on Gnat aircraft into West Pakistan during the 1965 War. In 1971, he flew the SU-7 in No. 26 Squadron based at Adampur. During attack on enemy artillery concentration on 5th December, he was shot by ground fire, ejected and was taken prisoner in Pakistan.

He was decorated with the Vayu Sena Medal and the Vir Chakra. On account of spinal injuries sustained during ejection in Pakistan, he had to retire early from the Air Force.

In civilian life, he was awarded the Samaj Ratna by the Vice-President of India for leading efforts to maintain communal harmony and avoidance of bloodshed in Faizabad-Ayodhya during the disturbances of 1989.

Squadron Leader A.V. Kamat

A very mature officer with a strong sense of right and wrong, never shy of articulating differences in viewpoints, but loyally following the line laid down by superiors. Also, to him, an enemy was an enemy and he would give him no quarter ever. At the same time he would go to any length, any risk, to help out his own.

Born in a family of engineers and businessmen in 1940 in Mumbai, he was educated at St. Xavier's School and Siddharta College. He chose the Air Force for a career and was commissioned as a fighter pilot in 1960. After going through the mill he stood posted to No. 10 Squadron on HF-24 Marut Aircraft at Uttarlai in Rajasthan when the war broke out. On 9 December 1971 he was attacking Pak Army positions at Kotri near Hyderabad (Sind) when his aircraft was hit by ground fire and he had to eject. His ejection height was low and the rate of fall rather high, with the result that both his knees and ankles got fractured on impact with the ground. For three months both his legs were in plaster cast from the knee to toe. Kamy expected no softness, no concern from the Pakis; he bore his travails stoically.

Annexure

Kamy contributed greatly towards the success of the escape attempt by three of the Indian prisoners. It was his imagination and skill with hands that gave them a rudimentary compass, a tube for carrying water, and cloth bags made from stolen curtains and parachute cloth. After repatriation he returned to fighter flying, commanded a fighter squadron and was awarded the Vayu Sena Medal for his effort in the war. He took early retirement. Unfortunately, soon after, he passed away. His wife and children live and work in Mumbai and Dubai.

Flight Lieutenant Dilip Parulkar

A bundle of energy, a compulsive doer, ebullient and outgoing, a natural leader of men who attracted trust and loyalty, life to Dilip Parulkar was an unending joy and a sport. He was constantly on the move—flying aeroplanes or playing tennis, boxing or riding horses. In the Pakistani prison camp the only possible and exciting activity for him seemed to be to break out of the jail, and as a compulsive calling he went for it.

He was born in 1942 at Kolhapur, Maharashtra, in the family of an eminent teacher of English. At a young age he had witnessed a light aeroplane performing aerobatics; his life's aim was set there and then—to be a pilot. So, immediately on completing studies at a Jesuit School in Nagpur in 1959 he applied for and succeeded in entering National Defence Academy as an Air Force cadet. He was commissioned in 1963 as a fighter pilot and in the same year he was sent to England for training on Hunter aircraft.

During the 1965 War he was on an attack mission against Pakistani tanks when a bullet from the anti-aircraft artillery pierced the right side of the cockpit, cut through his upper shoulder, went through the headrest and exited after shattering the canopy. Dilip was bleeding heavily and the shattered canopy was blurring his vision, yet he bravely managed to bring the aircraft back to the base. Just as well, because the exiting bullet had already cut through the ejection mechanism that was housed in the pilot's seat headrest and, if he had tried to eject, the parachute wouldn't have worked.

Dilip was later trained on the SU-7 in the USSR and after getting the fully operational category on this aircraft he opted to become a Flying Instructor. He was training young pilots when the call came to rejoin his squadron just as the war clouds were thickening in 1971. As a senior pilot he led several attacks against the Pak Army in the western sector. It was during the eighth mission on 10 December 1971 against a radar unit east of Lahore that his aircraft was badly hit by ground fire and he had to bail out over enemy territory. As he was gently swinging down with the parachute he could see scores of people from all sides rushing towards his possible landing site. Sure enough, on touch-down he was surrounded by villagers who showered the choicest abuses upon him and began beating him up systematically with fists, kicks, sticks and whatever came to hand. Fortunately, a police inspector in uniform arrived on the scene and restrained the villagers saying, 'You fools, he is more valuable to us alive as we will get vital information out of him.' The crowd moved back. Soon the Pak Air Force personnel arrived to take charge. They blindfolded and handcuffed him, placed him in the back of a truck and sent him off to Rawalpindi. Later he led a breakout from the Pakistani jail and almost made it to Afghanistan before being apprehended under suspicion of being a Bangladeshi fleeing to his country.

For his outstanding work in the IAF, Dilip was awarded the Vayu Sena Medal and the Vishisht Seva Medal. He took early retirement, and now lives in Pune with his family and is a known name in the town's social circles.

Flight Lieutenant Jawahar Lal Bhargava

A genial extrovert who felt comfortable only in company—his family or his colleagues and friends. Being alone was anathema to his nature. That always led him to take interest in others' affairs and he always went out of the way to be helpful to any one in need.

Annexure

He was everybody's friend and appropriately earned the sobriquet, 'Brother', which rhymed well with his surname and he was always referred to as Brother Bhargava and addressed fondly as Brother.

Born in 1942 at Pataudi, he graduated in Arts from Mahendra College, Patiala. At age 17 he played for Punjab in the Ranji Trophy cricket tournaments. (After capture in Pakistan he met an elderly Pakistan army officer who had earlier lived in Patiala, and they exchanged memories of their coach, Baba Ram Kishan). In 1961, he joined the Air Force as a trainee pilot, and was commissioned in 1963. He flew the Vampire jet fighter, the Mystere and also the Sabre in the United States.

When the 1971 War began, Brother was among the leading pilots of No. 220 Squadron flying HF-24 Marut aircraft, designed and produced in India. On 5th December, Brother was No. 2 in a two-aircraft formation attacking Pakistani army positions in Naya Chor area of Sind. Towards the end of a successful mission, Brother's aircraft was hit by ground fire. His left engine flamed out, the right engine too was losing power, all the systems were failing one after the other. He was losing both height and speed and decided to eject. He bailed out at a very low height, but successfully. By coincidence, another Marut pilot, Flying Officer H. Mulla-Feroze, was on duty in the same area as a controller for aircraft attacking enemy positions. He saw Brother's aircraft crashing into a sand dune and bursting into a ball of fire just 500 metres from his position. But he missed seeing the pilot bail out by parachute. Brother was lost to him behind a sand dune. Brother's companion pilot came over and circled the scene of the crash; he too missed seeing Brother on the ground. If anyone of the two had spotted him, he may well have been picked up by an IAF helicopter and saved himself the hardship of being a prisoner for a whole year.

After landing on the ground Brother quickly buried the parachute in the sand and hid the flying suit in some shrubbery in order not to leave a trace. In civilian clothes now, he walked and ran across the desert in an easterly direction in the hope of crossing the border into India, which he estimated to be 10–12 kilometres away.

After covering some distance he was exhausted, and lay down in a depression in the sand to rest. Suddenly he was challenged by three persons who wanted to know who he was. He told them that he was Mansoor Ali, a PAF pilot, his aircraft was shot down by the Indian Army, and he was now trying to walk towards Pakistani territory. The men had already suspected that he was actually trying to run towards India and so they forced him to accompany them to their village. On arrival there he was surrounded by the local people and all sorts of questions were put to him to ascertain his true identity. Brother thought that by his clever answers he had succeeded in maintaining his Pakistani and Muslim identity, but the sudden arrival of four Rangers (Pak militia) in the evening changed the situation.

Eventually, the leader of the Rangers, one Awaz Ali, asked Brother to recite the 'Kalma' which of course he could not. Brother confessed his real identity, gave them his real name and told them that they could now do with him whatever they wanted, even kill him. In one voice the villagers assured him that now he was a guest in Pakistan and no harm would come to him. He was given a chicken dinner and then the Rangers took over. All items on his person like wallet etc. were taken away, he was handcuffed, blindfolded and placed on a camel to begin the captive's journey. The caravan consisted of three camels, he on the middle one with one Ranger sitting ahead of him as a guard. This was the first camel ride in Brother's young life, and all the bobbing and pitching was breaking his back. They rode through two nights and two days in the desert. Brother was miserable, particularly when they stopped for tea and made the camel sit down in order to dismount. Brother hated that camel, and for that matter hated all camels ever since.

During the journey one Ranger asked him why he was in civilian clothes. On replying that the flying suit was too heavy to walk in, the Ranger said that he was a spy and called out to the leader—*Goli Maar de Dalle noo*, meaning, shoot the pimp. Brother requested Awaz Ali to remove his blindfold and handcuffs before shooting him. But Awaz Ali stood firm and declared that no such thing would be done so long as he was around. The crisis had passed.

Annexure

On the morning of 8th December he was handed over to Captain Murtaza of Pak Army somewhere in the desert. From here onwards he was driven in a jeep, arriving at Pak Air Force base at Drigh Road, Karachi two days later. On the 12th December he was placed in a piston-engine aircraft along with two other Indian pilots—Squadron Leader A.V. Kamat and Flying Officer Mulla-Feroze, flown to Rawalpindi and incarcerated at the POW camp.

After repatriation Brother served in the Air Force with distinction, rising to the rank of Air Commodore. He now lives in Gurgaon with his wife, Anu, but his love for the uniform is apparent in the lives of his children—his son, a Wing Commander in the Air Force, is a test pilot, and his daughter is married to a Colonel in the Army.

Flight Lieutenant Tejwant Singh

A simple, straightforward Sikh officer with a serious mien, Teja (as he was known to friends) had two devotions in his life, both equally strong and all-consuming—the Air Force and his religion, Sikhism. At all times, he would either be involved in professional matters or be seen sitting with the 'gutka' (prayer book) in his hands.

Tejwant was born in 1942 in Lyallpur (now Faisalabad) in pre-partition Western Punjab. His father and grandfather had both served in the army, and the desire to serve the country was perhaps so strong in the family that later both he and his brother unerringly found their way into the Indian Air Force.

In 1947, at age 5, Tejwant had migrated to India with his family, having lost many relatives in the riots at partition time. They settled in Hissar district of Haryana and the family took to farming. In 1954, Tejwant was admitted to King George's School in Bangalore, an institution that prepared boys to become gentlemen cadets in the armed forces. He joined the Air Force in 1961 and was commissioned as a fighter pilot in 1963. He flew various aircraft from the Vampire to the Gnat and finally the Mig-21. He had also trained with the US Air Force on the Sabre aircraft.

Death Wasn't Painful

During the 1971 War his Squadron No. 29, operated from Amritsar. Tejwant himself flew 21 operational missions into Pakistan, mostly escorting ground attack formations and air defence missions. It was on the 17th December, just a few hours before the ceasefire, during an attack on Pakistan's Pasrur air base, that he was shot down by a Sabre in air combat. He suffered spinal injury and was under treatment in Pakistan for over three months.

In jail Tejwant passed his time with sobriety and dignity, making good use of his talent for drawing and sketching. The Pakistani guards and other staff were always requesting him to draw their portraits, and to benefit from his other gift—palm reading.

After repatriation, Tejwant served the Air Force with distinction, rising to the rank of Group Captain. He was awarded the Shaurya Chakra for bravery in 1973. He now lives in Gurgaon, studies the religious scriptures and writes on the history of the Sikhs and the Gurus.

Flight Lieutenant Melvinder Singh Grewal

This well-built, handsome Sikh officer, unleashing a sense of physical power in every movement, yet so controlled and balanced in his actions, laughing and joking at every hardship, taking calamities in his stride, an excellent team member who never flinched from assuming responsibility, Garry, as he was known in the Air Force, added lustre to any group in which he found himself. He never brought up any personal problems, did not ever mention the injuries he had received at the hands of the villagers on landing up in Pakistan. He was the first to join hands with Dilip Parulkar when he first broached the idea of escaping from the Pakistani prison.

Born in Sheffield, England, in 1942, to a Sikh father and a British mother, he grew up in Britain along with two siblings. In 1947, the family moved back to India and settled in their ancestral residence at 9, Temple Road, Lahore. Soon the partition of the country was upon them; they had to abandon their home and move to India, finally settling down at Patiala. Young Garry received his early education there and was studying at the Khalsa College when he successfully took the entrance examination for the Air Force. After commissioning in October 1963 he flew the Vampires, then the Mysteres and finally graduated to the SU-7 fighter bomber.

He was with No. 32 Squadron stationed at Raja Sansi Airfield, Amritsar, when the war began. On 4 December 1971, during his second mission of the day into Pakistan he was No. 4 in a four aircraft formation attacking Rafiqui airbase at Shorkot. During this successful attack Garry's aircraft was hit by anti-aircraft artillery. As the aeroplane went out of control, he ejected and reached the ground by parachute. Immediately he was surrounded by villagers who pounced upon him savagely, taking away all valuables like the watch etc., and then began beating him with sticks. He received cuts and bruises on the neck and all over the body. But soon an army detachment from Rafiqui came to his rescue. They took charge of him, blindfolded him and tied his hands behind his back and took him to the air base. Later in the night he was hogtied, placed in an open jeep and driven all the way to Rawalpindi. He was lodged in a filthy cell somewhere in the city, with a pitcher of water in one corner and a pitcher for defecation in another. The next morning he was made to appear at a press conference where BBC, CNN and a few Pakistani correspondents asked him only personal questions. After this he was taken to the Pak POW camp in Rawalpindi and locked up in a solitary cell.

Garry was awarded the Vir Chakra for gallantry. He took early retirement in the rank of Wing Commander and now lives at the sprawling family farm at Village Alinagar in district Rampur in Terai and enjoys the open-air life with his wife Mandeep. His two sons work and live in the United States.

Flight Lieutenant Harish Sinhji

A diminutive figure, a slight build, a smile on the lips, a lighted cigarette between the fingers, the demeanour and mannerisms of a casual traveller on a brief stop-over at a wayside station, that was

Death Wasn't Painful

Harry (Harish Sinhji) in the Pakistani Air Force POW camp at Rawalpindi.

A Rajput from Kathiawar, he took his hereditary valour for granted and expected everyone else to do likewise. In a way he exemplified the dictum that courage resides in the mind, not in the muscles of the body. He treated the restrictions of the camp and the occasional rude behaviour of the Pakistani jailors with aristocratic indifference and disdain.

Harry's family belonged to the Rajput tribe of Jhalas who ruled over a small principality in Gujarat. His grandaunt was married into the royal family of Mysore and, in time, the family moved to Bangalore. It was here that Harry was born in 1945 and schooled at St Joseph's European. In 1964 he joined the Air Force and after flying training he was commissioned in 1966. He flew the Vampire, the Hunter, the Gnat and was finally on the Mig-21 in No. 29 Squadron when the war broke out.

During an interdiction sortie (a sweeping mission in which you attack targets of opportunity like trains, vehicles etc. carrying equipment for the troops) in the Suleimanke area, his aircraft was hit by ground fire. He ejected and tried to run and hide from the villagers but was ultimately caught and given a good beating. The arrival of Pak Army personnel saved him and thereafter he was treated decently and handed over to the Pak Air Force as a prisoner. He was among the three spirited and courageous Indian fighter pilots who escaped from the Pakistani jail.

On return to India he remained in active flying, won the coveted 'Jam Sataji Sword of Honour' for being an outstanding fighter leader, and served with the Iraqi Air Force as a flying instructor. He rose to the rank of Group Captain, and took voluntary retirement in 1993. He settled in Bangalore with his family and resumed his old hobbies of playing 'ragas' on the Sitar and 'taals' on the tabla. He was always inclined towards spiritualism and now became more focussed in the search for the meaning of life. He practised pranic healing, reiki and meditation, and spent considerable time with like-minded people.

During a spiritual group holiday with his family in Europe he fell ill and was flown back to India. He died of an undiagnosed disease in 1999. He left behind his wife, Jyoti, a daughter, who is a known figure in the travel and fashion world, and a son who flies with civil airlines.

Flying Officer V. S. Chati

Young, lithe, quiet and imbued with remarkable personal courage, Chati could never tolerate rude behaviour even in the enemy's prison and always gave back as good as he got. He did not care for the consequences. He was chosen to give cover to the three IAF pilots by staying back in the cell from which they escaped—a very demanding and risky job which he handled to perfection.

Born in 1946 in Arvi (Wardha area), Maharashtra, in a medical doctor's family, Chati went to school in Nagpur. In 1964 he completed studies at the Institute of Science and entered the Air Force through the National Cadet Corps stream. After training at Allahabad, Jodhpur and Hakimpet he was commissioned in October 1966. He converted to Hunters at Pune and then joined his first unit, No. 27 Squadron at Halwara. For the war, the unit was positioned at Pathankot.

On 4th December Chati was on his second attack mission in Pakistan, this time the airfield at Mianwali. The two aircraft formation reached the target and, amid heavy firing from the ground, attacked the airfield. While firing the four cannons from his aircraft, Chati suddenly felt a loss of engine power. He levelled out at a low height and headed homewards. The engine's booster pump had failed and hence the loss of power. In that condition, while nursing the engine and somehow heading home his aircraft was hit by a Pakistani aircraft or by ground fire that is still uncertain, and Chati ejected.

As he touched the ground, someone fired at his chest with a small calibre rifle. Luckily, the bullet grazed his stomach, and while there was heavy bleeding, no permanent damage was suffered.

Death Wasn't Painful

Despite the bleeding he received the full share of beatings and looting. At night he was tied down to a cot and placed in a cowshed. The next day he was handed over to Pak Air Force personnel who drove him to the Rawalpindi camp.

Chati took early retirement from the Air Force and settled in Secunderabad but continued flying with civil companies. His wife, Jayshree, practices as a gynaecologist. His son is a highly placed IT engineer and his daughter a marketing executive.

Flying Officer Aditya Vikram Pethia

The lean, tall, young Vikram was a social being and mixed well with other Indian prisoners. He was an expert at contract bridge and soon taught this card game to all the other prisoners. This came in very handy for passing long hours in the jail throughout the year of incarceration. Of course, Vikram's keen mind could keep track of all the 52 cards and his mastery over the 'finesse' ensured that he remained the champion par excellence.

Born in 1943 in a family of civil servants at a village called Sainkheda in district Narsingpur in Madhya Pradesh, he was commissioned in the Indian Air Force as a fighter pilot in 1964. He flew the Vampire and then moved on to fly the Mystere aircraft. In October 1971, his unit was stationed at Nal airfield in Rajasthan.

On 5th December Vikram was attacking a freight train carrying tanks for the Pak Army in the Bahawalpur area when he was hit by ground fire. He ejected and on coming down to mother earth he was surrounded by villagers. One young man was about to shoot him with a gun when an old man intervened and saved him. After the usual beatings, he was tied down on a tractor and taken to a police station. Later he found himself in a large room with four other persons in civilian clothes. They tied his hands and hung him from a cross bar. While one beat him on the buttocks with a table tennis racket, another gave him a few blows on the chest and the stomach. Yet another fellow extinguished his burning cigarettes against Vikram's skin in several places. He was shifted to various places and had no idea of time or date. Eventually he was driven in a jeep and taken to Rawalpindi.

Vikram's ribs were damaged during the merciless beatings and quite often there was a trace of blood in his sputum. In May 1971, he was repatriated to India in an exchange of sick prisoners.

Vikram was awarded the Vir Chakra for gallantry in the war. He rose to the rank of Air Vice Marshal, filling many sensitive posts on the way. He now lives in Bhopal with his wife Geeta, who was an outstanding sportsperson, playing volleyball and basketball in national teams. They now play golf together. Their elder son is a fighter pilot in the Air Force and the younger son an engineer in the United States.

Flying Officer K.C. Kuruvilla

The youngest of Indian fighter pilots in the Pakistani jail, this handsome, well-built Syrian Christian from God's Own Country—Kerala—was always cheerful and smiling. Yet he was perspicacious beyond his years and interjected very sensible ideas in discussions on serious matters.

Born in Kayamkulam in 1945 to a family closely associated with teaching and with the Syrian Christian Church, Kuruvilla did his schooling at Shillong, Calcutta and finally at Salem, imbibing a national ethos. He joined NDA in 1962, went on to Captain the cricket team and win accolades in boxing. He was commissioned in 1967, standing 1st in order of Merit, winning the Sword of Honour, the Chief of Air Staff Medal for Best All-Round Jet Pilot, and the Ramchandani Trophy for being Best in Academics—an all-round champion with a most promising career ahead of him.

He flew the Vampire, the Hunter, and then graduated to the SU-7. During the war he operated from No. 222 Squadron based at Halwara. On 6 December 1971 he carried out a very successful attack on the Dera Baba Nanak Bridge and then used the remaining ammunition to attack Pak Army strategic reserves that were moving towards the Chhamb area. Unfortunately, he flew through a barrage of Pak anti-aircraft artillery, his aircraft caught fire with all the lethal hits it received. He ejected and landed near the forward-most Pak army picket. For four hours he evaded the enemy but was finally caught by them. He barely escaped being shot on the spot, but received a fair share of beatings and harassment. He was later taken to Gujaranwala where he spent the night in a filthy cell. The next day the Pak Air Force took charge of him and drove him to the Rawalpindi camp.

Kuruvilla was awarded the Vir Chakra for his courage and bravery during the attacks on Pakistan. He rose to the rank of Air Commodore and handled several sensitive appointments. He took early retirement and now lives in Bangalore with his wife, Grace. His two daughters command high executive posts in companies with global reach.

Flying Officer Hufrid N.D. Mulla—Feroze

This enthusiastic, pleasant, well-mannered, and always well-meaning young officer, through quirks of fate, usually landed up with a raw deal.

Born in Mumbai in 1944 in a Parsi family, he went to Christian missionary schools and joined the National Defence Academy in 1963 as an Air Force cadet. He was commissioned in 1967 and thereafter flew various aircraft, finally getting posted to No.10 Squadron on HF-24 Marut aircraft at Jodhpur. He was under operational training when the war broke out. Lacking sufficient proficiency on the aircraft, he was deputed with the army in Rajasthan sector as controller for aircraft attacking Pak army positions. His task was to guide our fighters onto their targets on the ground, a job which he handled very efficiently. He was thus moving all the time with our forward—most troops and usually remained in eye contact with the enemy troops.

During the rapid advance by our troops in the Naya Chor area of Sind, the irrepressible, enthusiastic Mulla moved forward even more rapidly. In the darkness of the night he spotted an army camp

Annexure

and approached a tent that he thought was in the officers' area. Flamboyantly, and with a 'Hi' on his lips he lifted the flap of the tent and swaggered inside. A revolver shot instantly rang out. Mulla gasped with pain as the bullet hit him in the upper left arm.

'What are you doing, you silly fool?' Mulla shouted at his assailant. As he held his left arm with the right one, the revelation came to him that he was facing a Pakistani officer. Fortunately, the Pakistani officer held further fire. Mulla was disarmed, given first aid and sent off to Karachi where he received further medical treatment. On 12th December he was sent to the Rawalpindi camp.

As a wounded prisoner, Mulla was repatriated to India in February 1972. He continued to serve in the IAF until 1992 when he took early retirement and settled in Secunderabad. He suffered a stroke and passed away on account of cardiac arrest in 2011. He left behind his wife Khursheed, a daughter and a granddaughter.

Acknowledgements

A deeply felt thank you to the eleven fellow POWs for helping in keeping the period of incarceration in Pakistani jails bearable and hopeful, and for providing many crucial details of their personal adventures that enriched these true stories in many ways.

Gratitude is owed to the Sage India team: Vivek Mehra who provided an inspiring confidence in the worthiness of this book; R. Chandra Sekhar and Shambhu Sahu for guiding the completion of this manuscript and despite my reservations persuading me to use the pronoun "I" in the interest of authenticity and towards establishing a more direct rapport with the reader; and to Neha Sharma for her painstaking editorial efforts at giving it the final shape.

A special mention for Colonel Vivek Chadha, young friend and outstanding strategic analyst, who was always ready with guidance and help on technical matters. As were Sanjeev Bhargava, Asim Sharma and Rahul Singh who saw merit in the narrative of these stories being of value to a general reading public.

I thank Anil Kumar Nigam, Mahinder Kumar Parashar, Sudeep Kumar, Sukh Ram, Rajeev Dang and Vinit Kumar for their uncomplaining labours in the collation of vital data and preparation of the manuscript and Raj Bilochan Prasad for his unstinted help for the sketch of the airfields and radar stations in 1971.

I remain grateful to Surgeon Captain (Dr) Subhash Ranjan for his constant concern and infusing me with buoyancy by always taking on the mantle of shielding me from multiple ailments.

Acknowledgements

Finally, it was the invaluable support of my daughter-in-law Sayantani, herself an author, and the enthusiastic persistence and encouragement of my son Sarit, who took upon himself all the onerous tasks, that really made this book possible.

Dhirendra S. Jafa

Glossary

Aapa	Elder sister.
Aata	Wheat flour.
Adaab	An Arabic word, meaning respect and politeness, is a hand gesture used as a secular greeting.
Allah kasam	I swear by *Allah*.
Arjun	A great archer, hero of the epic Mahabharata.
Avatar	Incarnation.
Baba	A respectful address for elderly people.
Bazaar	A market place.
Bhangra	An energetic dance form from Punjab.
Bhai	Brother.
Bhaiya	Term applied to migratory labour from Uttar Pradesh and Bihar.
Bidi	Rolled up tobacco leaf. A poor man's cigar.
Bindi	The round, vermilion dot that adorns the forehead of married Hindu women.
Chamaar	A low caste person dealing in animal skins.
Chamara Karigar	Skin worker, shoemaker.
Chapatti	Flat, round Indian bread.
Chappal Kebab	A flat, long, meat kebab.
Chaupal	A village get-together, usually in the evenings.
Chowkidar	A watchman or a gatekeeper.

Glossary

Chowk	An open market area in a city at the junction of roads.
Daal	Lentils.
Degchi	A cooking vessel.
Dhaba	A way-side, usually open air eating house.
Fixo	A glue-like substance the Sikhs use to dress their beards.
Gharara	A loose skirt type garment worn mostly by aristocratic Muslim women.
Gharries	Horse-drawn covered carts.
Golboti	A small morsel of boneless meat.
Gnat	British swept-wing, small, fast jet fighter.
Haraamzada	Illegal son (a curse).
Hunter	British second generation jet fighter.
Hindiwallah	One who speaks Hindi.
Insha Allah	If *Allah* wills it.
Janab	A respectful form of address for a man.
Janab-e-Ala	Grand Sire.
Jawan	An Indian or Pakistani soldier.
Kara	A loose, round metal wristband worn by Sikhs.
Kebabs	A dish of pieces of meat roasted or grilled on a skewer or spit.
Khuda Hafiz	God be with you.
Lungi	A broad cloth used by men to wrap around the lower half of the body.
Madrasi	One belonging to the southern state of Tamil Nadu.
Mangta Hai	I demand—an expression used with minions.
Mazar	The grave of a saint where people go to pray.
Mig-21	Russian Supersonic fighter.
Millat	The Islamic community.
Mohajir	A Muslim migrant to Pakistan.

Mulk	Country.
Mullah	A Muslim learned in Islamic theology and sacred law.
Mystere	French second generation jet fighter.
Pak	Short for Pakistan.
Paki	Of Pakistan.
Panchayati Raj	Local self-government by the village council.
Paratha	A fried chapatti.
Peshawari chappal	A slipper.
Phirni	A rice pudding.
Pulao	Indian dish of rice cooked with vegetables, spices and/or meat.
Pundit	An expert in a particular field or subject who is frequently called on to give opinions about it to the public (mostly Hindu priests are called pundits).
Purbiya	Inhabitant of eastern Uttar Pradesh & Bihar states of India.
Ram Rajya	An ideal system of governance, as by gods.
Sabre	F-86, US fighter of British Hunter class.
Saheb	A polite title or form of address for a man.
Salaam Aleikum	Salutation in Arabic.
Salwar Kameez	The long, loose shirt and trousers worn by most Muslim women.
Starfighter	F-104, US advanced fighter.
Shukriya	Thanks.
Sitara-e-Jurrat	Star of Courage, is the third highest military award of Pakistan
Spitfire	Piston-engined fighter aircraft of World War-II fame.
SU-7	Russian Supersonic fighter-bomber.
Talaaq	The Islamic divorce.

Glossary

Teej	A festival in the monsoon rainy season, especially celebrated by young women.
Thali	A metal plate for eating food.
Tonga	A horse-drawn carriage.
Toofani	French jet fighter (The Ouragon).
U.P. wallah	One hailing from the state of Uttar Pradesh.
Vaitarani	A mythical river to be crossed after death, before entering the realm of gods.
Vampire	British first generation jet fighter.
Vasudhaiva Kutumbakum	The entire world a family.
Vayu Sena Medal	Award for a job well done usually in peace time, also in war where it is one rung lower than Vir Chakra.
Vir Chakra	Award for gallantry in battle during war.
Wahe Guru	The supreme God.
Zamindari	The system of big land holdings by individual families.